A POINT OF VIEW

CLIVE JAMES is the author of more than forty books. As well as essays, he has published collections of literary and television criticism, travel writing, verse and novels, plus five volumes of autobiography, *Unreliable Memoirs*, *Falling Towards England*, *May Week Was In June*, *North Face of Soho* and *The Blaze of Obscurity*. As a television performer he appeared regularly for both the BBC and ITV, most notably as writer and presenter of the 'Postcard' series of travel documentaries. He helped to found the independent television production company Watchmaker and the multimedia personal website www.clivejames.com. His book *Cultural Amnesia* was widely noticed in all the English-speaking countries and is currently being translated into Chinese. In 1992 he was made a Member of the Order of Australia and in 2003 he was awarded the Philip Hodgins memorial medal for literature. He holds honorary doctorates from Sydney University and the University of East Anglia. In 2012 he was appointed CBE.

BY THE SAME AUTHOR

A POINT OF VIEW

CLIVE JAMES

PICADOR

First published 2011 by Picador

First published in paperback 2011 by Picador

This edition published 2012 by Picador
an imprint of Pan Macmillan, a division of Macmillan Publishers Limited
Pan Macmillan, 20 New Wharf Road, London N1 9RR
Basingstoke and Oxford
Associated companies throughout the world
www.panmacmillan.com

ISBN 978-0-330-53439-0

1 3 5 7 9 8 6 4 2

A CIP catalogue record for this book is available from
the British Library.

Typeset by SetSystems Limited, Saffron Walden, Essex
Printed and bound by CPI Group (UK) Ltd, Croydon, CR0 4YY

Visit **www.picador.com** to read more about all our books
and to buy them. You will also find features, author interviews and
news of any author events, and you can sign up for e-newsletters
so that you're always first to hear about our new releases.

To Peter Goldsworthy

Contents

2009 – SERIES TWO

Introduction

When I began broadcasting my share of the BBC Radio 4 *A Point of View* programmes early in 2007, it was the age of celebrity, fraud, religious fanaticism and global warming. By the time I finished, late in 2009, the global warming scare had passed its fashionable peak but celebrity, fraud and religious fanaticism were as prominent as ever. One was perversely grateful for these big, mad themes because the format of the programme – it was slightly less than ten minutes long – demanded a simple argument. On the other hand, the simple argument had to be nuanced in its expression, or there would be no reason for the listener to stay tuned. About three million of the brightest people in the country were within arm's reach of a button that could turn you off. I was only one of the small team of people who took turns doing a short season or two during each year, but I think my colleagues would agree with me that putting the weekly piece together was the devil of a writing job, if only because you couldn't afford for it to sound like that. It had to sound like speech.

Before I got as far as the first draft of my first show, I had already learned that the family honour was on the line. Now that I had taken it upon myself to climb into a pulpit and preach the same sermon twice in a weekend with the whole district in attendance, I needn't think that my opinions were going to be passed for publication on the nod. At a lunch table that usually consisted of at least five people not counting my little granddaughter and her blue plastic-handled spoon, I was obliged to make clear exactly what I meant by democracy, free speech, women's rights, the right to strike, the obligation of immigrants to adapt to their new country rather than requiring their new country to adapt to them, and the advisability of at least listening to a bunch of old climate scientists who said that the climate was not in crisis, even if there were thousands of younger ones who said it was. Always keen to pronounce myself left-wing in politics – in the sense that I thought nobody's idea of either conservatism or progress should penalize the worst off – I found myself grappling with the opinion, sometimes shared by everyone except myself, that my principles, when articulated, sounded pretty rigid, not to say fossilized. I tried to take this kind of obstructionism calmly but something about my face would make my granddaughter ask her mother and grandmother what was wrong with me. She pointed at me with her spoon.

But it worked. The whole agonizing process was a lesson in the validity of the scientific principle by which our theories should be thrown open to every possible objection. More often than not, my script for the following week would be less about my initial opinion on a subject than about the various other opinions that could rationally be had about it. This is not to say, however, that I abandoned my convictions. Far from it: though I might have acquired them early, they had cost me a lifetime to refine. But I did clarify them, and that proved crucial, because in a script only 1,600 or so words long you have to say exactly what you mean. At greater length you can waffle if you wish, and if you have no idea at all of what you mean, but a tremendous urge to be taken as someone who has, you can write a book. A large number of putatively serious books are written out of just that impulse, and in this great age of fraud they do quite well.

Even in this introduction I keep coming back to the subject of fraud because in these few years it was in the air like influenza. Nominally lawful activities were infected by it with daunting ease: management-speak, for example, was the linguistic equivalent of selling real estate in the Everglades. Even the legitimate financial system had all the trappings of a racket, including a wonderful mechanism by which the banks that lost your money were saved from ruin by being given more of your money so that they could award it as bonuses to the very people who lost your money in the first place. This was a Swiftian scenario vividly recognizable to anyone who had ever read *Gulliver's Travels*, a book which I kept near my desk for three years running while I tapped into its author's spirit without making the capital mistake of trying to copy his voice. It can't be copied, any more than Dr Johnson's can, but their joint example should be kept in mind when we ponder the sad truth that one of the effects of modern flim-flam is to make us forget how it had its noxious beginnings hundreds of years ago, at a time when tulips were traded like carbon futures and there were only a few clear heads to warn the public that their gullibility might cost them dear. First Swift and then Johnson had that rare voice of hard-headed sanity. It was a pity that Johnson did not speak more warmly in Swift's memory, but that's life.

Or it might have been the celebrity culture, making one of its early appearances. Perhaps Johnson found it hard to brook a predecessor in his role. We can be sure, however, that the mania for celebrity did not really get going until the twentieth century, when that hydra-headed monster the Media – eventually referred to in the anomalous singular – grew big enough to assume its historic task of trivializing even the greatest human lives. Yet more depressingly, it managed to trivialize everything else as well, reducing even science to the vocabulary of a computer game. By the twenty-first century – which, for all its absurdities, I am still grateful that I have lived to see – the language of mass delusion was more common than not. Words and phrases of objective description gave way to ideological bumper stickers. Mrs Thatcher never really meant it when she said that there was no such thing as society – she was simply trying, in her tone-deaf way, to say that individual responsibility should come first – but she might have been making an accurate statement about the immediate future. In the time we inhabit now, the word 'society' has almost disappeared from print, crowded out by the word 'community'. A big community consists of smaller communities, and you have to go a long way down before you get to actual people. Conflicts within society have given way to problems in community cohesion. For anyone sensitive to language, it was obvious from the start that talking about community cohesion was a device for glossing over the brutal fact that some poor kid had just been stabbed.

In the face of this universal temptation to overblown rhetoric, the *Point of View* format offered the welcome discipline of requiring the broadcaster to put his written language back in touch with the spoken language. Incipient bombast could be more readily detected, and thus more easily staved off. One conceived of a kind of bonsai sermon, with overtones of the eighteenth-century essay, in the rich period when essays entertained the educated classes from week to week, before the rise of the novel in the second half of the century. The Augustan essayists set the mark for the modern broadcaster by combining gravity and gaiety so that each was a vehicle for the other.

They also set the volume levels. At the start of the Augustan century, Swift gave an example for all his successors by confining his choler to his house, and always being cool on the page. As the great critic George Saintsbury later observed, Swift was quiet. That same rule carries double force in a radio studio. Let the sound engineer do the amplifying.

With that ideal measure in mind, I dialled down the exuberance by packing it tight into its own spaces. The aim was to treat the contemporary talking-point while covering the history of the globe in the volume of an orange: an exercise in miniaturization, like reinventing the transistor once a week. In pursuit of this aim, a few gags might help. (These could be tested at the lunch table, in scenes that became reminiscent of *Strictly Come Dancing* without the footwork.) I hope the centripetal pressure wasn't apparent, but I really did try to get as much said as possible. One of the secrets of paying your way in the popular arts is to provide value for money, which is achieved by the focusing of energy: and broadcasting is a popular art even in its highbrow form. In fact any highbrow broadcast that doesn't know how to be popular probably doesn't know how to be highbrow either. Leaving your listeners behind would be a damned silly thing to try, especially when so many of them are ahead of you.

Spurred by the requirement to get long arguments into a short space, one occasionally – and here I examine my buffed fingernails – came up with a usefully portable phrase, upon whose cogency one could preen oneself. In the course of several years, 'the rage for simplicity' was the neatest tag I could devise for evoking the sinister energy of the totalitarian dream, and I was to use it again in both essays and books. It's essential, though, not to get too puffed up when a snazzy formulation pops into your head. The chances are high of some well-informed listener reminding you that Hume or Burke said exactly the same thing.

Helping to protect me in advance from such embarrassments was my squad of BBC producers, with the excellent Sheila Cook at its head. Let me praise her here as a short-hand method for praising all the others, because they all shared her qualities to a great degree, although only she, when pointing out some *bêtise* looming in my first draft, could so exactly remind me of Joyce Grenfell's sketch about the teacher and the unspeakable small boy. An elegant woman, I would mutter to myself, but with a tendency to *fuss*. Being pecked at, however, was almost always what my first draft needed, and after writing it on Monday evening and taking the objections on board during Tuesday morning, I usually had a finished script by Wednesday, although if the subject was tricky I was sometimes still writing right up until studio time on Thursday morning, and in either Bush House or Broadcasting House – the venue alternated – I would be busy doing what broadcasters have done since the invention of the medium: fixing the script at the last minute. It might sound like an awful lot of effort for a little thing, but that's what makes a short broadcast more like a poem than like anything else: you have to keep at it until it clicks. My other producers, who took over *seriatim* from Sheila when she had to be away, were Adele Armstrong – who did a whole series – and Rosie Goldsmith, Sue Ellis, Maria Belinska, Leonida Krushelnycky, Bill Law and Paul Vickers. I mean it as a high praise when I say that they were all remorseless pedants worthy of her tutelage.

Today, with my stint done, I am very glad that nobody can see my first drafts. The final scripts of all sixty broadcasts, in the words that I read out on the air, can still be heard in the Audio section of my website clivejames.com: a provision that was made possible by Radio 4 controller Mark Damazer's far-sighted campaign to overcome the BBC's traditional retentiveness. The Beeb bigwigs would rather have kept my miniature achievements under their sole control for ever, which I suppose is a kind of compliment. Indeed I know it is, and I remain very grateful for having been asked to do the broadcasts in the first place.

People often kindly want to know whether I have been asked to do any more, and the answer is yes; and perhaps, one day, I will; but by the end of 2009 I rather got the impression that I had covered my major themes, and that the Committee of Public Safety at my Cambridge dining table was getting restive. On top of that, I fell ill early in 2010, and for a good long while I couldn't contemplate hitting a deadline of any kind. One of the blessings of being legally confined to bed is that you can stop trying to keep up. New books start looking very pale beside old ones. Among other things I read Milton's three big poems again, still determined to find merit in them somewhere. The politics of the present day, even at their most violent, looked pettifogging beside the tumult of the seventeenth century. In the light of what Dryden was saying about the Earl of Strafford, it was worth the effort of trying yet again to get a handle on Strafford's character. But there seemed no point at all in diverting any of my precious energy to the task of distinguishing one Miliband from another. Later in the year, I could tell I was getting better when I got interested in Australian politics again. It was time to set aside my studies of how Clarendon helped to develop the English language and turn my attention to what Julia Gillard was doing to destroy it. When she invented, perhaps through a peculiarity of her elocution, a new Middle Eastern threat called the Taliband, I knew I was back in touch with today's reality. Taliband, Miliband: I could have done something with that.

Would I like to do it again? You bet. But then, I would like to be a TV critic again. Once you have hit a groove in any genre, it always tempts you to return. But there are other things I want to write, and as of now I feel that I have done my share. Not that doing my share made the slightest difference to the world, except in tiny ways that I couldn't calculate. But those are the ways that matter. The business of the broadcaster isn't to correct abuses. It is merely to point them out, to those capable of seeing the implications. By definition, that audience is already ahead of the broadcaster, so it doesn't really need him, except for consolation. But consolation can be important at a time when it feels as if the world is going mad. Probably the world always feels like that. But today it raves in a multiform jargon that sounds all the more demented because of its approximation to common reason: the patois of a Bedlam that confers degrees. This peculiarly modern interlingua of unjustified omniscience, now that it is here, will probably never go away. It will always transfer itself to a new area, because there will always be people with an interest in inflating their own importance by distorting reality. But part of reality, a heartening part, is that there will also always be people who know sense when they hear it. To this valuable audience we must be careful what we say. Hence the importance of scrupulosity, which is not only as valuable as expressiveness, but is actually a large part of expressiveness in its best sense. The best writing is done, by those who care a lot about language, to be read and heard by those who care even more, because they think it must be a privilege to have that knack. Well, yes. It is.

2007 – SERIES ONE

ATTACK OF THE WHEELIE BINS

Dates of show: 2 and 4 February 2007

In my household, I'm the last man standing against the belief that global warming is caused by human beings. Three women with about a dozen university degrees between them have been treating me for years now as if I were personally responsible for the forthcoming death of the planet. They're probably right. They were right about the cod.

After it was impressed upon me by my daughters that the number of cod in the sea had declined to the point that there were twenty miles between any two cod, I stopped eating cod, and immediately the cod-stocks began to recover. I couldn't help noticing, however, that there were no complaints about the declining number of haddock. Since it was crumbed haddock fillets that I took to eating instead of crumbed cod, by rights there should have been a noticeable and worrying decline in the number of crumbed haddock being caught in the North Sea. There wasn't, but if there had been I would have listened to the evidence.

Hard, observable evidence should convince anybody sane. I know the sea is polluted because I can see plastic bottles on the beach. Whether the sea is indeed rising might be a matter for computer modelling, which is evidence only if it suits your prejudice, but you know what a couple of hundred plastic bottles are when they come in riding on a wave like a flock of dead seagulls. Where I used to go on holiday in the Bay of Biscay in the days when I could still swim over-arm, the empty plastic bottles on the beach were only a few centimetres apart all the way from France into Spain. I marvelled at the perversity of people on board ships who, after drinking the contents of the bottle, would carefully screw the cap back on so that the bottle would float for ever, unbiodegradably carrying its unwritten message of human imbecility until the ending of the world.

Some countries litter more than others. Sometimes the same country litters less than it used to. Australia was a litterbug's paradise when I first left it in 1961. Fifteen years later, when I first went back, the littering had largely vanished, because a government campaign had actually worked. At present, the same global coffee-bar chain has cleaner forecourts in the US than it does in the UK because, in the UK, dropping trash is a yob's right. But wherever you are, in Birmingham or in Birmingham, Alabama, biodegradable packaging in general is clearly a necessary and welcome step, well worth paying for if you've got the money.

The fact that only a very small proportion of the total human race has got the money we can leave aside for now, because this is really about us, the people who can afford to do the right thing after we've either agreed what it is or been prevailed upon to do it by a government which has proved its competence in other areas, such as finding a use for the Millennium Dome.

This week, for a packet of organic tomatoes still gamely clinging to their own little vine, I gladly paid extra because the packaging was almost as enticing as the contents. By means of a printed sticker, the packaging promised to disintegrate at some time in the future. It would have been a help if the exact time in the future had been specified – perhaps about the time when the last remnants of the human race left for the planet Tofu in the constellation of Organica – but at least the green promise had been made, and I would be able to put the empty tomato packet into our wheelie bin devoted to compostable matter.

In Cambridge we divide our garbage into two wheelie bins, marked compostable and non-compostable. The two classifications don't apply to the wheelie bins, both of which are made of heavy-duty, non-compostable plastic, but do apply to their contents. As the dolt of the household, a mere male and therefore little more than a brain-stem with a bank account, I myself am correctly regarded as too stupid to decide what goes into each bin. My job is to substitute one bin for another in the garden shed according to which week which bin is collected. Only women are clever enough to plan this schedule but only men can do the heavy labour involved, employing the brute force for which they have been famous since the cave, when everything was biodegradable.

A world nearer to a bone-strewn cave is one to which some in the green movement would like us to return. I can say at this point that the eco-wiseacre who has just been elected Australian of the Year foresees an ideal population for Australia of less than a third of the number of people it has now, but he doesn't say whether he includes himself and his family among the total of those to be subtracted.

Each time I change the bins I almost subtract myself from the present total of the inhabitants of East Anglia because for evolutionary reasons I am unable to lug one bin out and push the other bin in without impacting my forehead into the top frame of the shed door. After the first time I fell to the flagstones clutching my bisected skull, when I jokingly suggested to the three watching eco-Furies that if I croaked in mid-manoeuvre they could always recycle me, I was informed that this possibility was on the cards because just outside of town there is a cemetery where they will bury you in a cardboard box.

There is also a graveyard called All Souls which has two wheelie bins standing outside it, one marked 'All Souls Compostable' and the other marked 'All Souls Non-compostable'. One of the permanent lodgers in that graveyard is the great philosopher Wittgenstein, whose key principle was that we shouldn't be seduced by language. He wanted us to say things so clearly that our meaning couldn't be mistaken. But he could only dream of that, because in fact we *are* seduced by language. The world couldn't work if we didn't spend most of our time being open to persuasion on subjects that we will never personally investigate because we lack either the time or the talent, and usually both.

Everybody knows there are too many plastic shopping bags. You can see millions of them decorating the hedgerows. Everybody knows that it's a good sign when a supermarket puts a sign on the side of its plastic bags saying that its plastic bags are recycled from other plastic bags. But where most of our recycled non-compostable garbage gets sorted out, hardly anybody knows. I was recently told that most of it goes to China, but I can't believe that their economic boom depends on reprocessing our tin cans, and that they won't produce rubbish of their own, and lots more of it.

There are good reasons for cleaning up the mess we make, but finally it's what we make that makes us an advanced culture, and only a highly developed industry knows how to keep itself clean. At Bhopal in India a chemical plant once killed at least 3,800 people, but that was because it was badly regulated. Loose supervision made it lethal. Very few nuclear reactors even in the old Soviet Union have ever gone as wrong as the one at Chernobyl, or even the one at Three Mile Island in the US, but that's because they have regulations to meet, and the regulations themselves are the product of an industrial society. There was a time that Japan's burgeoning post-war industry was poisoning its own people with mercury. The industry that did the poisoning found the solution, because it was forced to. But a law to suppress that industry would have helped to produce a society less able to control its own pollution, not more.

As far I can tell with the time I've got to study the flood of information, which is less time than I would like, the green movement can do an advanced industrial society the world of good by persuading its industries to spread less poison. Whether or not carbon emissions really do melt the polar bears and kill the baby seals in the rain forest, the pressure on industry and even on government is already helping to persuade Hollywood stars that they should drive hybrid cars, and finally we'll do what Leonardo DiCaprio does, because we'll be seduced by language, not because we know very much about how carbon dioxide keeps in the planet's heat.

The other day I met a carbon-dioxide expert who said that his favourite gas has already reached the density where it can't keep in any more heat, but I did notice that he was sweating. It was probably when Sir David Attenborough noticed that the bottle-nosed dolphins were sweating that he finally gave his illustrious name to the campaign against global warming. That would be enough for me even if Prince Charles hadn't joined in as well, having already placed his order for a horse-drawn Aston Martin.

But I don't really know they're right. I'm just guessing. The only thing I do know is what won't work, because it shouldn't. We shouldn't expect the less fortunate nations to cut themselves off from industrial progress in the name of a green planet. It wouldn't be fair even if it was likely, and anyway, we aren't civilized by the extent to which we return to nature, only by the extent that we overcome it. I wish I'd said that. It was Sigmund Freud, actually, when they showed him the blueprints of the very first wheelie bin. When push comes to shove, he wrote in German, this thing could still save male pride, even if it can't save the planet.

Postscript

Disguised in a cloak of lightness, I took on, from the beginning, what seemed to me weighty themes. Pollution was the first of them, and I still take it to be a far more important theme than putatively catastrophic man-made global warming, which is only a conjecture, whereas pollution is a tangible fact. It also seemed clear to me – but worth making clear to the audience because in the current context it was a counterintuitive proposition – that it would take advanced technology to combat pollution's effects, and that the idea of unwinding Western industrial society was wrong-headed on that account alone.

Still working out my protocol and too keen to avoid the deadening effect of unknown proper names, I should have specified the name of the 'eco-warrior' who had been appointed to the position of Australian of the Year. It was Professor Tim Flannery. Though his concern for the future of what he always called 'the Planet' was no doubt genuine, he had the wherewithal to be a natural comic turn, because of his habit, fatal in a futurologist, of saying that dire things would happen tomorrow, rather than the day after tomorrow when they would be harder to check up on. Thus he would predict that Sydney would run out of water in two years, and then, two years later, he would be filmed in Sydney with heavy rain falling on his head. Even then, he would predict that Perth would run out of water a year later. A year later the weathermen of the Perth television stations would be wearing raincoats, but by then he would be in Adelaide, threatening the whole of the south coast of Australia with a thirty-foot rise in sea level by next Tuesday. In 2009 he kept announcing that the Copenhagen summit would be our 'last chance as a species' to save the Planet, as if there might be another species – the giraffes, perhaps – ready to take up the challenge. There was a certain charm to him, as there often is in the person you can rely on to be wrong. He was a constant reminder that Cassandra, had the technology permitted, would have been born holding a microphone.

THE MIND'S CONSTRUCTION IN THE FACE

Dates of show: 9 and 11 February 2007

According to all media, so it must be true, plastic surgery is a growth industry worldwide. People who've had face-lifts are having their face-lifts lifted. The Taiwanese are having New Year face-lifts to bring them luck. Often the resulting luck looks bad, but it's hard to sympathize when someone becomes a victim of failed plastic surgery that they never needed.

Usually that's a decision that we make for them: that they didn't need it. Knowing what they looked like before they did it, we decide they didn't need to do it. But they mightn't have felt like that. Anyone who undertakes major plastic surgery really doesn't like the way they look, even if we never saw much wrong with it.

There is a person called Pete Burns who went on Channel 4's *Big Brother* and got famous for being a forgotten rock singer. He got additionally famous for being a forgotten rock singer who'd had something unforgettable done to his mouth. He'd had that thing done that people who want new mouths do. They don't want new mouths in the sense of a mouth like the old mouth, only young again. They want a new mouth in the sense of a different mouth, a mouth that has been seen nowhere on earth except below sea level. Apparently the idea is that the top lip should be at least as big as the bottom lip, and the result, even done in moderation, always looks as if the original mouth has been removed, inflated like a small plastic paddling pool, and put back on upside down.

Pete Burns had the advanced version. I switched *Big Brother* on accidentally one night and there he was, so I switched it off immediately, but not before having my retinas seared with the image of one of those car-sized fish that lurk deep below the reef, waiting to ingest the brass boot of a deep-sea diver. After leaving the show, Pete mercifully sank out of sight, but recently he got famous all over again because he wanted to sue the surgeons who hadn't, in his view, put his mouth back the way it was, although he hasn't yet made clear how long ago he means by the way it was: he might only mean the way it was last year, when it was already uncommonly large but still more or less attached to him.

Apparently it now more or less isn't. It's easy to laugh until you see the pictures, and then you realize he's in real trouble, physical trouble to match the psychological trouble he must have been in in the first place. And there's the connection between plastic surgery that doesn't serve an obvious purpose and plastic surgery that does. The second kind started at East Grinstead Hospital, where a pioneering team of surgeons developed the techniques to help make continued life possible for Battle of Britain fighter pilots whose faces had been ruined by flame. The young men called themselves the Guinea Pig Club as a sign of the cheerfulness they needed to live with what they looked like, and it was a long time before anyone knew how to do the cosmetic surgery that went some way towards making the first necessary repairs look anything like normal. So the Guinea Pigs, booked up for years of operations, had to learn to accept each other's appearance, and the people of East Grinstead, who met the boys in the street, had to learn to live with visual shock. An awful lot gets learned in a war, and plastic surgery would certainly not have gone ahead so quickly if there hadn't been hundreds of young men who needed a new face: a real new face, meaning a face something like the old one.

After the war, the techniques of repairing damage graduated naturally to the techniques of improving looks. Again there's a connection, and the connection first showed up most powerfully in Brazil. In 1961 a disgruntled employee expressed his dissatisfaction with the management of a circus by setting it on fire. He killed at least 323 people, many of them children, and disfigured many others. The plastic surgeons gave a lot of faces their lives back. One of the surgeons was Ivo Pitanguy, who later taught a generation of students to do the two things that a plastic surgeon can do: correcting disfigurements in the unfortunate, and making not perhaps entirely necessary improvements to the rich.

I met him there once, and it was immediately obvious why every beautiful high-society woman in Rio looked at him in worship. He'd given all of them eternal youth. He'd done the same for himself, and although I found it sad how even his own face proved that you can't remove the signs of age without destroying the signs of life, I couldn't rebut his argument that if rich people were ready to go under the scalpel, they must have real griefs that they wanted to counteract.

Our difficulty is to see why such inner feelings should be catered to in the same way that we, or rather the surgeons, cater to obvious physical needs. At the moment, in Africa, there are units of plastic surgeons financed by charity to correct childhood disfigurements, some of them so hideous they make you wonder if the man upstairs really knows what's going on down here. Arising from malnutrition, there is a disease called noma, and its first results are a rapid degeneration of a child's facial tissue, with results you don't want even to imagine. But plastic surgeons can repair that damage.

Always, however, some of the know-how used in such an impeccable public service is developed in the private sector. There's an interchange, and you might say that the angel of mercy is financed by human folly, and that there'd be folly anyway, because nobody really knows how to fix the mind, especially when it has the means to get its way. That beautiful British television actress who wrecked her mouth: she didn't need to do that. But she thought she did. That beautiful American film star who did the same: why did she, of all people, think her face was ugly? Her face was a dream, but our dream was her nightmare. So she fixed it.

And so, reluctantly, we get to Michael Jackson, whose original nose shares the condition with Pete Burns's original mouth of being rejected by the face where it grew up. But the real pity about Michael Jackson is that the man who sings 'It doesn't matter if you're black or white' obviously thinks it does matter. While my daughters were growing up, Michael Jackson was a hero in our household, and even I tried to learn his 'Billy Jean' moon-walk. My version looked like Neil Armstrong's moon-walk, but I didn't blame Michael Jackson. But when I saw what the plastic surgeons were turning him into, then I blamed him. I thought he was undoing the work of a century of African-Americans who had put their lives on the line for equality. If he wanted to look like someone else, why didn't he want to look like Denzel Washington? I would have.

It took me a while to figure out that it was his business, not mine.

We who admired him never owned him, and perhaps he had no other way of telling us except making himself impossible to love by anyone except the kind of fan who would have gone on loving him if he had turned himself into a wheelie bin. He wants another identity, but so do all those rich women who try to stay young by having their faces lifted. Even if they know when to quit, before the Botox looks like latex, they must still be aware that the backs of their hands will tell the truth about that strange blankness underneath the eyes. The falsity is blatant, yet it's often the voluntary absurdity of the most subtle people alive. So it's got nothing to do with intelligence. It goes far deeper than that. It's the soul, believing that with the right kind of intervention a face can stop time.

In Hollywood I once got invited to a lunch party of women who had been stars fifty years ago. If they'd stayed unaltered I would have recognized every one of them. But in their bid for eternal life they had become nobodies. Yet how can you blame them? Their beauty had been their life. On that same visit to Hollywood I met a plastic surgeon who said there were no stars, even among the males, who didn't come in for a pit-stop. That same plastic surgeon used computer modelling to show me how he could make me look like a film star if I'd let him take a bit off the end of my nose and stick it on my chin. He kept on manipulating the mouse until I looked like Steve McQueen. When I told him I wanted to be Cary Grant his face fell, but not very far.

Postscript

In the short span of a broadcast there is little time available in which to cover yourself if you risk an insensitive statement, so I had to leave out of this piece the interesting but desolating information that the Hollywood plastic surgeon, after showing me how he could fix my face, asked me to fix his own life. Telling me that he wanted to move into stand-up comedy, he asked me for my advice, and wondered if I might care to look at a script he had written. My face fell: a sight he would normally have greeted as a business opportunity, but on this occasion it must have been all too clear that what he had induced was dismay rather than hope. I was within an ace of hearing him audition. It was a desperate moment but I didn't want to appear ruthless by saying so on air. For similar reasons, I didn't mention the startling effect of meeting Kirk Douglas face to face, as it were. (Later on, in my book of memoirs *The Blaze of Obscurity*, I did mention it, because it fitted the story.) An actor whose on-screen gurning I deplored but whose intelligence I admired – his book of autobiography is a model of reflective sanity – had turned himself into ... into what? Into a bad drawing of Kirk Douglas. But to prove myself sympathetic as well as observant, I would have needed a thousand words for that point alone, and it seemed more useful to go on stressing the general point that the perfectly sensible work of reconstructing faces blighted from childhood by a callous providence had largely been made possible by the perfectly senseless desire of the spoiled rich to wish Fate undone.

It should be added, however, that a plaything for the rich has by now become a requirement for the poor, in line with the modern mass-democratic tendency for all privileges to be claimed as common property. Low-rent hookers acquire the same face as a goldfish, and in India high-school students have dimples put in because they think it will give them a better chance at university. Almost always the results are too incongruous to be effective, but as with the celebrity culture, there is no legislating against delusion. One can merely hope that the storm will blow itself out. Yet the whole farrago would still be worth it just for making it possible for those children in Africa to have their cleft palates repaired.

FIDGETS ON THE MARCH

Dates of show: 16 and 18 February 2007

I once knew a young man who tapped his fingers on the table while he spoke. He didn't tap them loudly. He just tapped them to accompany the rhythm of what he was saying, so that the general effect was more varied than monotonous. But it drove me crazy, and I went even crazier because I wasn't allowed to say that I was going crazy. In the polite Anglo-Saxon culture from which the Australian culture derives – and I want to examine this word 'culture' in a minute – you don't tell people who have the fidgets to stop fidgeting. This young man was in our house quite a lot, tapping away for a couple of years, and never once did I feel that I had the leeway to tell him to stop doing that or I would arrange to have him escorted outside and inserted upside down into the wheelie bin for compostable matter.

Then he married one of my daughters and I felt free to speak. I spoke gently, trying to leave room for the consideration that I might be unusually sensitive to the fidgets in other people, and might even have a case of the fidgets myself that I didn't know about. The possibility that there are deliberate cases of the fidgets is one that we will have to examine, but surely the fidgets in general are just a sign of nervous energy, and almost all young people fidget. My son-in-law has been exemplary since I finally felt free to explain my point with the aid of a mallet, and lately he hasn't even needed to keep his hands in his pockets during a conversation.

But fidgeting is a bad sign in adults, and the mental version of the fidgets is practically a defining mark of the age we live in now, when the liberal democracies, as if they couldn't count on enough trouble from illiberal forces of all persuasions, nevertheless behave as if they had a duty to demoralize their own populations by changing the name of everything that people have learned to rely on. The excellent social commentator Christopher Booker once called the widespread official urge to change the name of everything that works Neophilia, but I think we need a new name, the fidgets.

Thinking that anything needs a new name is, of course, an example of the fidgets, but in this case I think we need it because the word Neophilia suggested that the urge came from a mere love of the new, whereas I think it comes from something more comprehensive, a demonically playful urge to see how far people can be driven towards insanity before they protest. Not long ago, at Paddington, I ran to catch a train that was called First. The long version of the name is First Great Western, which is already bad enough because it suggests the possible existence of a Second Great Western. But the First Great Western company insists on referring to itself and its trains as just First.

My problem, as I ran with a heavy bag in each hand from the barrier end of the platform, was to find the first second-class carriage in a train all of whose carriages were marked First. I cursed First in the worst language at my command, but my outburst at First was nothing beside the imprecations I rained on One. Yes, what used to be simply called Anglia Railways is now even more briefly but far less simply called One. This leaves the way clear for the railway station announcer to inform potential passengers that one One train will leave from platform two and the other One train will leave from platform three.

If the first One train leaves at twenty to one, it's the twenty to one One train, and if the other one leaves at ten to one it's ten to one on that it's the one One train one actually wanted but one couldn't understand the announcement. What happens when you have to change from a First train to a One train I leave to you, but you might face a situation where you should catch the first First train if you want to change to the one One train that will get you to the mental hospital before you crack up.

Except, of course, that it's never now called a train, it's called a service, just as the passenger is now a customer. Linguistic philosophers have already written theses about how the vocabulary of marketing has invaded the realm of transport, which logically should have no need of marketing, because people know exactly what they want and demand nothing except for the means of transport to be safe, clean and on time. But the language of marketing spreads inexorably because it gives those who use it a chance to be creative, which everybody has been taught is a desirable thing to be.

In fact, the last thing that a passenger who has already been outraged by being called a customer wants to hear when he is sitting, or probably standing, in a train running late, or probably not running at all, is a voice on the public address system calling the train a service, when providing a service is exactly what it is currently in the process of not doing. Nor does the voice on the public address system show any sign, once it gets started, of wanting to shut up. The voice supplies the information that the buffet car is situated in the middle of the service, for the benefit of anyone who thought that it might be travelling along separately some way behind the service. The voice apologizes for the delay caused to your journey, a way of softening the fact that the delay has been caused, not to your journey, but to you.

The voice continues to audition for a career in broadcasting by pointing out that the first One service to arrive at the next station will be the last One service to continue any further until the engineering works have been completed. Where did it all start? Well, it probably started when the name British Railways contracted to British Rail. Contraction of a system's name is a bad sign and rearrangement of the name's components is another. It's a rule that this rearrangement of the name's verbal components should only take place at a time when the system's mechanical components are melting down. London Transport, for example, changed to Transport for London in the very period when the Jubilee Line extension was in a continual process of coming to a halt because its hyper-sophisticated signalling system was doing what state-of-the-art technology always does, i.e. proving that the technology you want is the stuff that used to work. The total cost of changing a logo for an organization that big is so frightening that the figure is seldom published.

Sometimes the total cost happens twice. History has forgotten the brief period when the name Royal Mail, which everyone understood, was changed to Consignia, which nobody understood. The cost of changing the name on every facility and product of the Royal Mail to

Consignia was astronomical, and the cost of changing the name back again was astronomical twice. A country that could do that to itself was ready to construct the Millennium Dome, a monument to the fidgets said to be visible from the moon, an attribute valued by the kind of people who think they have already been there.

But perhaps the most remarkable thing about the Millennium Dome is that it still has its 'the'. The unwanted, unwarranted and unwieldy suppression of a preliminary 'the' is a sure sign of the fidgets at executive level. The Tate Gallery, for example, in either of its main manifestations, Tate Britain or Tate Modern, is now officially not the Tate, but Tate. This leaves the way open to meet at eight at Tate to eat, in which case we ate at Tate, or we were late at Tate and had to wait, and thus missed our Tate-at-eight tête-à-tête.

Such changes of name were once made by freshly appointed executives who wanted to announce their arrival, and who, unable to change what they should, changed what they could. But by now, surely, it's done out of a kind of desperation, as if words can work magic. It happens throughout the culture, and the misguided use of the word 'culture' is a disturbing further development of what is essentially voodoo. Regularly now we hear about young men shooting each other, and sometimes shooting their own girlfriends, as a response to what they call 'disrespect'. The misuse of the word 'disrespect' is just a pitiful sign of the vicious stupidity by which young men demand to be respected when there is nothing to respect them for. But when the upmarket newspapers run worried articles about what they call 'the gun culture', that's something else. Calling it 'the gun culture' not only solves nothing, it actually compounds the offence, by tacitly conceding that the responsible authorities can't be expected to confiscate the lethal weapons from the individual boneheads waving them, but should wait until a complex sociological phenomenon has been explained in the appropriately elevated words. And you can't blame the responsible authorities for waiting. Actually to do something about a young crack-head fidgeting with a gun takes more than high-flown language. It takes bravery. But that's another subject.

Postscript

This broadcast drew a lot of letters – not always with a psychiatric clinic as the sender's address – from people who had been driven nuts by the way the names of trains changed as the 'service' got worse. Calling an actual train a 'service' was, of course, the initial signal that the rot had irreversibly set in. A large public innovation in language is always the sure sign that a damaging alteration has taken place in reality. Most of the alterations come about as a result of rampant managerialism, which is an impulse in itself. It is a universal law that if the new management of a company can do nothing else, it will change the company's name. Later on there was a blatant case when the reliably named Norwich Union building society changed its name to Aviva. Everybody in Britain liked the sound of Norwich Union, and people abroad were proud when they learned to pronounce it, but it was decided that a group with global ambitions needed a name equally and immediately impressive in all countries. That the new word 'Aviva' was no more impressive that the strangled cry of a drunken Spanish football fan was not held to be relevant.

FLYING PEOPLE, FLAGRANT PIFFLE

Dates of show: 23 and 25 February 2007

A journalist who lives near Clapham High Street in London recently wrote a piece in which he wondered why that famous street was turning into what he called a demilitarized zone. Judging from the context he so frighteningly evoked, I think he must have meant a militarized zone, but he could be excused for losing his grip on the English language. Stray into the wrong side of that road and you can be in gangland. The now commonly canvassed idea that the nation's youth is sinking into a state of hopelessness just one step away from open warfare is hard to accept, but only if you haven't actually seen one young man being assaulted by a couple of others, or, more likely, by half a dozen others.

The best way not to see it is to live somewhere else. I myself spend a lot of time in south London, but so far it's the right part of south London. The chances of getting mown down in the cross-fire between permanently dazed crack-heads accusing each other of 'disrespect' is still quite low. The only thing to be afraid of is that I might meet Danny on the bus. Danny, who has been named and shamed because Britain lacks the means to send him into orbit, is barely tall enough to nut you in the groin, but he has accumulated so many ASBOs for meaningless violence that he is no longer allowed upstairs on the bus, where, apparently, his meaningless violence is especially likely to be unleashed. As far as I can figure out on my pocket calculator, this altitude restriction on Danny's activities increases my chance of meeting him downstairs when I struggle aboard. Meaningless violence from Danny has driven a lot of people to fear for their sanity already and I'd hate to be in a position where I would have to use my martial arts skills on one so small.

My martial arts skills were learned from martial arts movies. Nowadays, having attained the status of black belt with gold tassels and diamond clasp, I no longer need to watch these movies, but they're everywhere and some of them are disguised as art, so they can sneak up on you. An art martial arts movie, or martial arts art movie, makes meaningless violence meaningful, or so we're told. I was able to test this claim all over again the other night, when, still shaking from a newspaper close-up of Danny's face, I accidentally tripped the switch on my television set's optical fibre sidereal satellite cable box and was confronted once again, on channel 723, with the allegedly classic martial arts movie *Crouching Tiger, Hidden Dragon*.

Many film critics, not all of them on medication, think that *Crouching Tiger, Hidden Dragon* is still the acme, apex and apotheosis of the Chinese meaningful violence martial arts art movie, mainly because of the purportedly balletic beauty with which its featured personnel run up the sheer walls of the Forbidden City and along the treetops of the enchanted forest while slicing at each other with whirling swords made from fragments of a meteorite forged in the book-lined cave of a Confucian philosopher, with extra boiled rice.

Ancient Chinese swords, despite the legendary sharpness proved by their ability to purée a passing butterfly, rarely make contact with swordsmen, or swordswomen, in such a way that the victim loses a limb or even a little finger. Two opposing swordsmen or swords-women – let's just call them swordspersons – will emerge untouched from a fifteen-minute stretch of virtuoso choreography, a *pas de deux* for interlocking whirlwinds. If, after all that spinning, diving, somer-saulting and grimacing, a sword strikes home, it makes only a small neat puncture which in no way lessens the loser's capacity to speak that special dialogue from the Orient that actually sounds *more* Chinese after it has been dubbed into English.

'Your skills are great,' says Falling Snow. 'Your sword was quick,' says Rising Cloud. 'Your quest is finished,' says Passing Wind. Passing Wind is Rising Cloud's mentor. Passing Wind is old, older than the hills, visible in the background for purposes of comparison. Yet he, too, can fly. He's been flying since before the Wright brothers. He's been flying since long before mainland China started turning out sword operas with flying people in them, and you probably remember him from the very first such epic that made an international hit: 'Flying People, Flagrant Piffle'. He was a veteran even then, and by now he has run up every wall in China. All the young swordspersons fall to their knees before Passing Wind.

The sub-genre of meaningfully violent martial arts art movies grew out of the sub-sub-genre of kickboxer movies. Ever since Bruce Lee was at the height of his histrionic powers back in the early seventies, kickboxer movies have been coming out of Hong Kong like a trail of oil behind a sampan. Those who believe that Liberace was a better actor than Bruce Lee tend to neglect the fact that Bruce, though unable to narrow his eyes without flaring his nostrils and vice versa, had hidden powers of hypnosis. A dozen assailants, strangely unequipped with guns, would corner Bruce in a car park behind the studio and sportingly give away their numerical advantage by running at him one at a time, shouting so as to ensure that he could see them coming and kick each one of them in the chin with the sound of a slamming door.

As each assailant reeled back stunned to be replaced by the next, a close-up on Bruce's face revealed that his narrowed eyes and flared nostrils had been joined by pursed lips. Try it with your own face and you'll find it isn't easy, but when I saw my first Bruce Lee movie in its place of origin, Hong Kong, the whole audience was doing it. Needless to say, they were all young men, and suddenly I got the point. They were just ordinary, hard-working stiffs in suits, like those many millions of Chinese young men, everywhere in the world except in China, who had a good job and a mobile telephone.

Mobile telephones were as big as lunch-boxes in those days but the jobs were already proving that you could have a salary and still feel powerless. Soon, most of the jobs in the developed world would feel like that. And what do we dream of when we're powerless? We dream of having amazing personal martial arts skills. The same dream spread to the West, as it were, when oriental martial arts started invading Hollywood B-movies. It was bad enough when they invaded television in the form of a long-running American series called *Kung Fu*, starring David Carradine as a saintly oriental figure who would withstand an hour of provocation by hoodlums armed with rocket launchers before he finally cut loose with the barefoot martial arts skills taught to him by a master even more ancient than Passing Wind.

But it got worse when the saintly figure was Jean-Claude van

Damme. Once again he didn't want to fight, but when bad people opened up on him with a four-barrelled 20mm cannon he was forced to kick them in the chin. Jean-Claude's face is a bodybuilder's bicep in worried search of its original arm but he looks like Bertrand Russell when compared to Chuck Norris. With two eyes sharing the one socket, Chuck is an action hero whose countless movies kick their way straight to video. Master of every military weapon, Chuck would still rather fight barefooted, which gives you a clue. Personal, stylized cinematic violence is really a way of giving you a holiday from the world in which guns are decisive.

Much further upmarket than Jean-Claude and Chuck, it happened again in *An Officer and a Gentleman*, when Richard Gere, who was born with narrowed eyes, was a trainee jet pilot who turned out to have kickboxing skills hitherto unsuspected until he and his girl were harassed by provocative hoodlums. Soon he would be flying a Tomcat off the deck of the USS *Nimitz* with enough firepower under his wings to melt a city, but now he was kicking the eyebrows off a bunch of bar-room thugs. And they all picked themselves up and slunk off to their lairs, and not one of them came back with a gun.

And that's what the bare hands are all about, and it's even what the swords are all about. It's even what the movies with guns in them are all about, because Hollywood bullets swerve around the star and anyone on the feature list that the audience might like. Real bullets don't do that. Real bullets don't care who they hit. Real bullets fired by a real gun turn your highly trained kickboxing feet into instruments for running away with if you're lucky. You don't get to rise into the air, spin around, and elegantly kick the weapon from the nerveless fingers of the awed assailant. It's a lie to suggest otherwise, and we could tie ourselves in knots worrying about how a free society can persuade its most powerful medium of entertainment to stop peddling drivel, but there's at least the bitter consolation that the people who most terrify us are probably the ones who spend least time watching exquisite mid-air ballets of acrobatic combat. They're out there on the lower deck of the bus, heading for the demilitarized zone.

Postscript

As with the previous broadcast, the underlying topic here is about our helplessness in the face of youthful violence in the streets. Despite continual assurance from the police that the incidence of adolescent gun crime was going down, everybody knew that it was always going up: not in your street, perhaps, but in other streets you'd heard about. You don't, however, need to see a gun in order to feel uneasy. It is enough to have your home burgled a couple of times. Ours was burgled twice, and neither time was I at home, or I would have ... would have what? A favourite newspaper horror story is about the homeowner who retaliates and is jailed for excessive violence against the thief. Though this apparently inverted judicial procedure is not without merit – electing yourself as the executioner of some dolt who nicks your videos does seem a touch excessive when you come to think about it – dreams of retaliation are hard to quell. But unless you really are a master of martial arts, you lack the means. So the dream machine takes over.

NOB VOICES, YOB VOICES

Dates of show: 2 and 4 March 2007

Helen Mirren deserves her Oscar for having learned to sound like the Queen, but the Queen should get two Oscars for having learned to sound like Helen Mirren. It took Her Majesty a lifetime of study but she finally managed to overcome her origins and start making the same sort of noise as any other well-brought-up girl from the Home Counties. She and Dame Helen might not precisely be two Essex girls together, but they share roughly the same distinction, dignity and air of authority, although I suppose Dame Helen is still the one that springs to mind when, if you're a red-blooded male with propensities towards larceny, you think of the detective inspector you'd most like to be arrested by.

It's nice, though, to see the class business losing its sting. When I first came to Britain forty-five years ago, there was still a class gap, not to say a class gulf. Most countries bigger than an atoll have different social classes but what makes for a really noxious class divide is that there are feelings of inferiority to match the feelings of superiority. In Australia, there are plenty of people who feel superior, especially if their share of a race horse is big enough to run on its own, but hardly anyone feels inferior: they're all in it together. In Britain, the same is at last more or less so. The homeland has caught up with its colony. But when I first came to London, there was still plenty of quietly simmering resentful envy going on from the lower class towards the upper, which only increased the arrogance of the upper class towards the lower.

A measure of arrogance is that you really don't care what the people around you think of the way you sound. Still lingering, in the early 1960s, one of the main differences between the working class and the middle class was that working-class married couples would rarely raise their voices to each other when they fought in public. Middle-class married couples, on the other hand, would bellow at each other as if nobody else was there, which is the true sign of unshakeable class confidence, because if you're that arrogant, nobody else *is* there.

One of my first visits to the West End theatre was to the Aldwych to see a Peter Hall production of *King Lear*. Paul Scofield played Lear in a leather outfit that squeaked when he walked. I got so obsessed with the sound of his leather trousers squeaking that I missed most of the words, but I would probably have missed them anyway, because he had pitched his voice very low. He was a gravel-voiced, nearly inaudible Lear. Even going mad on the blasted heath, he didn't howl, he growled.

In the foyer afterwards there was a lot of polite murmuring and I started to wonder if I hadn't come to a country that had lost the power of speech. Then, through the crowded foyer, there strode towards the street a very suave well-brushed couple who had clearly come in from the stockbroker belt for their weekly culture ration. As the female stalked away towards the exit she shouted back over her shoulder, 'I'm not your slave, John.'

But it wasn't just the volume of her voice that made it stick in my mind. It was the elocution. The full cut-glass number, it was what I had come to London expecting to hear a lot more of. In Australia I had been brought up on the sort of British movies where you could identify everyone according to class by the way they spoke. You couldn't do that in American movies, but in a British movie like *In Which We Serve* you knew that Noël Coward was upper deck and Richard Attenborough was lower deck. Upper deck had a stiff upper lip and lower deck had a trembling lower lip. In *Brief Encounter*, Trevor Howard and Celia Johnson were doomed never to consummate their passion but you could tell they were made for each other by the way they spoke.

Celia, even more than Trevor, had that wonderful clipped eccent by which all the vowels were formed in the beck of the mithe and the lips never went sleck. I'm bound to say that when women were speaking the upper-class British accent it turned me on a treat, but my arrival in London seemed to be the signal for the whole thing to disappear. All the women from the north started sounding like Rachel Roberts in *Saturday Night and Sunday Morning* and nobody in the south sounded like Celia Johnson any more except the Queen, who still, when addressing the nation at Christmas, sounded as if she had only recently attended her own coronation and been stunned by the spectacle of the Archbishop of Canterbury in full drag.

The history of Britain since that time can be roughly summarized as the successful attempt to persuade the monarch to approach, from the top down, nearer to the happy medium that linguistic experts call standard English, or received English, or even BBC English, although you might wonder how there can be such a thing as BBC English if someone like me is on the BBC. The BBC, along with the nation's broadcasting system in general, has been instrumental in this change. Regional accents were correctly judged to be worth hearing.

A mistake, however, although not the biggest mistake, was to suppose that the regional accents were all equally understandable. I could gladly listen to Ken Stott reading the whole Bible aloud, but even a short reading by Jimmy Nail would leave me puzzled, and not just because I'm an Aussie. It's because a Scottish accent is inherently more intelligible than a Geordie accent, except, perhaps, from Ruth in *The Archers*. By intelligible I mean intelligible to other English-speakers. Americans, wherever they come from, almost invariably pronounce the whole word. So one of the secrets of American cultural power is that all Americans understand each other instantly across three million square miles and everybody else in the world who speaks English can understand them too, whereas there are plenty of British people who can't understand their own countrymen across a distance of a hundred yards. But let's suppose, for a moment, that all British regional accents were equally easy on the general ear. The biggest mistake was to think that yob is a regional accent as well.

But the yob voice isn't regional. The yob voice doesn't come from a geographical division. It comes from a social assertion, the way that the upper-class accent once did, and a sure sign of the yob voice's deliberate aggressiveness is that it's produced with even more effort. It once took a lot of energy to speak like Sir Alec Douglas-Home. You practically had to swallow your own mouth. It takes the same kind of effort to produce the yob uproar, whose sheer volume is the chief sign that what's really happening is a newly dominant social force arrogantly asserting its privileges. But the privileges aren't class privileges. This is a different thing.

Yob privileges are classless privileges. One of them is automatic individuality. In the age of universal stardom, everyone has a right to stand out even if he has no detectable characteristics. With half the consonants missing, the sound the voice makes is telling us that it doesn't matter if there is no information to be conveyed, as long as the message is heard, and the message is 'this is me'. The angle-grinder loudness of the voice serves to amplify the message 'this is me', even if the person shouting it might himself doubt the validity of that statement when he looks into a mirror. On a train, you will hear just how classless yobbery can be, when every carriage except the quiet carriage is occupied by yobs with jobs, important men who are proving it by using their mobile phones as megaphones. The quiet carriage is full of them too, conveying the further message that your space is their space if they say so.

It's an ugly sound they make, and any dreamy-eyed social pundit is foolish who asserts that all voices have equal value. He would be closer to being right if all voices had equal volume, but the loudness is still the tip-off. Once it was one bunch who didn't care what you thought, and now it's another. It's a change for the better. Long ago, Sir Alf Ramsey was mocked when he went into secret training to pick up his dropped aitches. But he was right to believe that there was indeed such a thing as being well spoken. There still is. When some commentators correctly decided that what Jade Goody said about Shilpa Shetty couldn't have been a race thing because racism is an idea and Jade hasn't got an idea in her head, they incorrectly decided that it must have been a class thing. But it wasn't. It was just that Shilpa sounded like Zeinab Badawi and Trevor McDonald and all the other people who grew up speaking a reasonably pleasant-sounding English, and poor Jade didn't. She had plenty to resent, because nothing makes you nervous quite like knowing that you get on other people's nerves. Not that we should encourage the idea that changing the way you sound is an easy trick for an adult. It can take years, even if your face is on the stamps. But it can't be that hard to just turn down the volume.

Postscript

Even today, when the reaction has set in and a return to decorum is thought desirable by almost everybody, you will still hear the proposition being advanced that the idea of a received standard pronunciation is a phantom. But the proposition is the phantom: we pay attention, find friendship, fall in love, and even marry, always with the proviso that the voice we hear is tolerable. Even the most stridently confident ladette knows that she has missed out on something by not sounding like the voice of that effortlessly classy woman reading out the information on the London Underground. When the luscious courtesan Abi Titmuss came to prominence, it was instantly clear why so many quite intelligent men were keen to know her. To go with her appearance, she was well spoken, and they were at least as interested in a leg up as a leg over. The same quite intelligent men rarely feel the same way about Katie Price, because she sounds as rough as a gravel road. There are no prizes for pointing out that the proper names of these flamboyant women are already fading on the breeze, but at the time of my broadcast they were common currency, if 'common' is the word we want. In the case of Abi, one would have thought, it isn't: there is no gainsaying a pretty knack for speech. The ability of a model for proactive lingerie to sound better than at least one ranking duchess would have given William Blake material for a poem about the death of England.

I was a bit premature in declaring that the strangled tones of the upper class vanished from Britain at the same time as I arrived from Australia. But there can be no doubt that the tones of the middle class were already sounding more, well, *normal.* When I was a TV critic you could still hear the beautifully spoken presenter Vanya Kewley on television every week, and one night in Stratford, at the opening night of *Les liaisons dangereuses*, I thrilled to the delicious voice of Lindsay Duncan. But her voice would not have been so lovely if she had not pronounced the words so well. No form of enunciation that mangles the language can ever be attractive, and it is a mark of sentimentality to suppose it can. One of the disastrous consequences of the BBC's elevation of Estuarine English to the status of a legitimate regional dialect was that scarcely any new female recruit to the BBC television screen sounded bearable unless her parents came from the

Indian subcontinent. Nor is America exempt from the rule that a lack of vocal education is tough on the listener's ears, mind and nervous system. Mira Sorvino sounds good in *Mighty Aphrodite* only because Woody Allen sounds so bad. How should a man sound? At the time of writing there is no man in Britain who sounds quite as good as the Archbishop of Canterbury, not because of his Christian principles but because of his precise articulation, although his naturally deep timbre helps.

In the text, where I mentioned the Peter Hall production of *King Lear*, I should have said Peter Brook. The error got all the way to the air because I spoke with such confidence nobody thought of checking it. So much for the fidelity of memory.

BECAUSE SHE'S WORTH IT

Dates of show: 9 and 11 March 2007

Let us imagine that a hundred miles north of Anchorage, Alaska, there is a little town called Moose Tooth. When the air base was still open, a few miles even further north into the snow and ice, some of the ground crew for the supersonic delta-wing bombers would come into town on Friday nights to tie one on, and the population of Moose Tooth, in order to service this sparse traffic, gradually climbed from 126 people to 214. Then the base closed and Moose Tooth shrank again to its present size. There are seventy-three people over the age of twenty-one and most of the kids who go away to get educated never come back. It's headline news in the single-sheet local paper when one of them does.

Nothing happens in Moose Tooth, or it didn't until this week, when it was announced that Moose Tooth would be one of the few places in the world where Elizabeth Hurley would not be staging part of her marriage celebrations. Another place was the two-house town of Bindiai, South Australia, population four people; but Bindiai never had a prayer because it hasn't got a newspaper. Moose Tooth, as we have seen, does have a newspaper, the *Moose Tooth Truth-teller*, and therefore it was in with a chance. A cruel deprivation, then, that Liz Hurley and her husband Arun Nayar probably won't be turning up.

Indeed, we should be serious here and concede that this wedding has been a comparatively modest affair, mainly confined to parts of Britain and most of India. The British part of the wedding, the opening ceremony of the ceremony, as it were, took place, as you may have heard, at Sudeley Castle in the Cotswolds. Paparazzi from all over the planet gathered around the outer perimeter of Sudeley Castle to be told to their surprise that they would not be allowed in.

Psychologists are baffled as to how so many otherwise intelligent adult males equipped with expensive cameras could harbour the delusion that the couple about to be married had not done a deal with *Hello!* magazine and that they, the paparazzi, would be allowed in.

Was it a collective delusion that they would all be allowed in, or was it an individual delusion, multiplied by the number of paparazzi present, that they would each be allowed in, one at a time? Was it possible, scientists wondered, that Signore Massimo Intrusione from the distinguished Italian foreign affairs magazine *Il Pesto* honestly envisaged a scenario in which a heavily built security man would say, 'Seeing it's you, Massimo, come right in. Miss Hurley's waiting for you beside the swimming pool in a vestigial bikini. Kir royale?'

But the paps, as always, were prepared for a long siege with nothing to sleep in except a ditch. These are men whose digestive systems are in a state of training beyond anything demanded of the SAS. These are men who can sustain life on a cockroach fry-up while they wait for a shot of Pete Doherty falling out of a window at the Priory. Only one thing breaks their spirit, and that's when their quarry refuses to play fair. So, alas, it was in this case. It turned out that the event the paps were not being allowed in to see, the wedding ceremony, had actually taken place the day before. So what they weren't being allowed in to see now was what was happening the day after the thing had already happened that they hadn't been told about. They were angry in sixteen languages. Some of them were so angry they missed Elton John's secret arrival, vertically out of the sky in a purple helicopter.

But enough of hiding the wedding's light under a bushel. Onward to India, and the first day of a promised week of celebration. The couple came ashore in Mumbai, the new name for Bombay. In new Mumbai as in old Bombay, the Taj Mahal Hotel is the centre of the action. I stayed at the Tajma myself once, and on my first walk along the waterfront I saw a snake-charmer in action. Squatting on the pavement with the yogi-like suppleness that snake-charmers acquire after decades of practice, he played his flute above a wicker basket. A cobra came up out of the basket and bit him.

Apparently it hardly ever happens, and back in the Tajma I became famous for what I had seen. It was my brush with celebrity. But I wasn't there this week when Liz Hurley and Arun Nayar arrived in the hushed anonymity of a silver Bentley to occupy the royal suite of a Tajma entirely walled in by paparazzi, and I'll never get over that until my dying day, which I could feel getting nearer every minute as I continued reading about their wedding.

After Mumbai the festivities moved on to Jodhpur, and this is where security really got tight, because it is comparatively easy to close down a hotel, but to close down a whole bunch of palaces and forts all in the one city takes what the Indian newspapers, still masters of journalistic English like old Fleet Street used to make, call a 'ring of steel'.

Apparently the ring of steel mainly consisted of a ban on mobile phones, lest one of the phones be used to snap an illicit picture and thereby pre-empt the aforesaid *Hello!* exclusive, making it no more exclusive than the Catherine Zeta Jones and Michael Douglas exclusive that got hijacked by *OK!*, back in the prehistoric days before telephones could take pictures. What made this ban newsworthy was that it extended even to the Maharaja of Jodhpur, who might ordinarily have expected his word to be taken that he would not be pointing his mobile phone at Miss Hurley and snatching pictures on the pretext of calling directory enquiries.

In view of the massed muscle of the inner ring of steel, the Indian press concluded that Jodhpur would be, and I quote, 'more secure than during the Mughal invasions', unquote. That sounded pretty secure until you googled the Mughals and found out that in 1561 they went through the defences of Jodhpur like a scimitar through butter, but let's not quibble. Sufficient to say that at Jodhpur's magnificent Bhawan Palace hotel a sacred fire was ignited. Amid Vedic chanting, Arun's shawl was tied to Elizabeth's veil, or it could have been that her veil was tied to his shawl. Either way, they had time to sort it out as they circled the sacred fire seven times in a shower of rose petals. My notes say 'road metals' but in the excitement of not being there I might have sometimes misheard the odd phrase while taking notes in front of a television set in London while an understandably excited woman in India was describing a scene that she couldn't see either because she hadn't been allowed in.

The next bit that nobody was allowed to see was, one can only imagine, awe-inspiring. Arun placed on Elizabeth's wrists a set of red wedding bangles washed in milk – just what she'd always dreamed of.

In the background, screaming paparazzi fell to their deaths from the castle walls as their aluminium extension ladders melted in the heat of the sacred fire. It reminded me so much of my own wedding, when we circled the sacred Barbie seven times, but only because, the first six times, our friend's camera didn't work. There was meant to be a little red light, and it didn't go on.

There's no reason why Liz Hurley's wedding shouldn't continue touring the world indefinitely. It might be the best way to stay married. Certainly the wedding should become a movie, and that's where the bride could really come into her own. I always liked Elizabeth Hurley. Nice voice, real figure, lovely face, what was there not to like? She was sometimes knocked for her acting but she never got much of a chance to do it. As a producer, however, she had her name on a movie that came close to being really worthwhile. It was *Extreme Measures* and it had a good role for Gene Hackman. If Hugh Grant hadn't been in it as well, the critics might have been able to raise their brains slightly and mention the fact that she had proved herself at a difficult task. But it didn't happen, and she went on to another kind of production, the celebrity caravan in which she now stars.

She's good at that too. And if we're really worried about the celebrity culture, she's the one who's already thought of the answer. One of the things she's celebrated for is inventing a category of people called 'civilians', by which she means people that the fame machine should ignore, because they never wanted that kind of attention. She did want it, and she's good at it. You won't get any Britney Spears moments from her. Kate Middleton, on the other hand, doesn't want it. Whether the media should be allowed to chase her anyway is a question about press freedom that we can examine another time, perhaps after the findings of the MPs' current deliberations on the subject have been digested and we've all decided whether allowing a prospective princess to be hounded like a fox is really such a good idea, or whether putting an official stop to it might not be an even worse one. But for now let's just enjoy the spectacle of the circus running as it should, with the clown paparazzi going crazy in pursuit of a woman whose wedding would be ruined if they left her alone.

Postscript

I wasn't kidding when I praised Elizabeth Hurley's off-screen role as the producer of *Extreme Measures*, but some of my friends thought I was, and got indignant when they found out that I meant it. Their reaction was natural: the idea that someone caught up in frivolity might occasionally do something serious is a hard one to process, because the attractive neatness of categories always tends to prevail against nuance. In a nation stupefied by cheap journalism, no pigeon flies far from its hole. Anyway, the young lady soon reaffirmed her allegiance to the celebrity culture, to the extent, alas, of doing something weird to her mouth: or perhaps my vision had begun to blur. I never met her, even in my role as a television interviewer. Nor did I meet her erstwhile steady date Hugh Grant; but, the celebrity culture being what it is, I somehow felt that I knew him, and when I bumped into him at a summer lawn party I played hail-fellow-well-met. Seeing the shock in his eyes, I recognized it as the same terror I felt when, on my lesser scale, someone did the same to me. The celebrity culture distorts everything, even the simple process of saying hello. It consists entirely of distortions. The terrorists who attacked the Taj Mahal Hotel the following year would not have done so had it been less well known as a stopping-off place for celebrities. They picked the stage on which to make themselves famous, even though most of them remained anonymous.

GOING FOR GOLD

Dates of show: 16 and 18 March 2007

After the success of the Sydney Olympic Games in 2000, the Australian media instantly forgot that they had spent four solid years predicting doom and disaster all the way up until the opening ceremony. The same scenario was played out in the prelude to the Athens Olympics in 2004, with the whole world's media running unending stories about unfinished buildings, until finally it turned out that the same people who had built the Acropolis could still build a basketball stadium, even if they had to set the concrete with a hairdryer.

In both Sydney and Athens, the Olympics went off as well as the Olympics ever do. Not even Atlanta in 1996 was quite the shambles that the world's press made out. Most of the facilities in Atlanta were actually finished, even if a few of the buses from the Olympic village delivered some of the athletes to the stadium after their event had started, or to Mexico after it was over. For reasons of newsworthiness the press would always prefer it if the Olympic Games collapsed in utter chaos, but with the understandable exception of Munich in 1972, they haven't done so yet. Why is it that one feels that if they do, it will be in London in 2012?

Well, the chief reason one feels they might, is that they're already facing the prospect of a gargantuan overspend. Let's say, for purposes of illustration, that there is a sport called piano-lifting, and that the new Wembley piano-lifting theatre, to a design by the internationally famous maverick architect Nestroy Berserk, had an initial budget of ten million pounds. Now, with only a few stacks of bricks and a concrete mixer actually in evidence on the site where the magnificent building is destined to stand, it turns out that the cost has already gone up to twenty million pounds, because nobody had told Señor Berserk that the floor, which he had designed to be built out of Peruvian balsa, would be required to bear the impact of pianos dropping vertically when the piano-lifter failed to complete the required clean and jerk.

Offended by this philistine insult to his artistic vision, he resigned in a huff, to be replaced by the even more volatile post-modern, pre-sane architectural genius Whacko Rubric. Herr Rubric, having disdainfully scrapped everything that had already not been built, has started again, not building something even more expensive, a translucent carbon-fibre cube with a randomized laser-lit roofline that reflects the resonance of a Croatian piano-lifter's bulging neck as he holds a Bechstein concert grand briefly aloft.

And the piano-lifting theatre is just a minor example. Don't even ask about the synchronized underwater squash court, which, after three years of digging, is only six inches deep, and is costing a million pounds a week to keep free of water while scholars argue about whether the Roman ruins that have been uncovered were once a temple, a military brothel or, as the majority opinion now holds, a synchronized underwater squash court.

The second reason for the prevailing pessimism is closely related to the first. Ever since World War II, big British projects have acquired a reputation for not only going many times over budget, but for not actually getting done. Unless you're my age or even older, you probably won't remember Britain's post-war ground-nut scheme. You certainly won't remember the nuts, because hardly any nuts were produced. What was produced was a large deficit, thereby establishing the rule that a bad project takes longer to stop if the money being spent previously belonged to the taxpayer.

Private enterprises like giant aircraft went badly enough, however, and almost always there came a time when the government had to support them with public funds, pending the day that they could go into service and start losing money on a commercial basis. The Bristol Brabazon and the Saunders-Roe Princess double-decker flying boat – I can remember the names because even in faraway Australia I was collecting pictures of them – never got beyond the stage of being photographed. The prototypes would appear at Farnborough year after year, always in a different livery to suggest that all the world's airlines were clamouring to buy them, while elsewhere the Americans were getting on with the business of dominating the sky. The biggest airliners in the world but also the slowest, the Brabazon and the Princess laid down the development pattern for the fastest airliner in the world but also the smallest. Concorde eventually got into service, but only after going monumentally over budget while failing ever to be a viable financial proposition for the luckless airlines that got involved with it.

As for the British weapons systems, if you regard war as a bad thing you should be pleased at how often the country's defence contractors built weapons that didn't work. Blue Streak, Blue Steel, Skybolt: always the impressive name, rarely the effective result, and never a prayer of being either on time or on budget. This was the culture that eventually led to the Millennium Dome. The soaring ambition and the technical expertise were always there. What was never there was the clear-sighted ability to put together a good committee. British committees had once successfully fought the German bombers, night-fighters and V1s by sheer analytical brain-power. But somehow, in the post-war era, that ability had been lost. Which makes it all the more remarkable that one of the Millennium Dome's most stalwart apologists, the writer Simon Jenkins, has come up with the answer, or part of the answer, to the Olympics fiasco.

He loyally went on calling the Dome an exciting construction even as its empty interior resonated to the hollow whistle of a billion pounds being sucked into oblivion. But uniquely among his fraternity, he gained in wisdom from his discomfiture, and he now points out that the way to forestall disaster with the Olympics is to put up fewer new buildings and rely more on the fact that the television trans-mission is what counts. He's almost right. He'd be completely right if he said that the trick is to put up no new buildings at all and think in television terms exclusively.

That last part is really what happened in Sydney. I was there to cover the Sydney Olympics, and I soon found out that for the city's population the cool thing to do on a hot night was to watch the show on the giant screens in the streets. Apart from the tourists, nobody went out to the stadium except old-age pensioners and the unem-ployed, and really not even the opening ceremony needed a building that big. There was no reason why the whole thing couldn't have been staged entirely to suit television, and there's no reason why London shouldn't think that way now. After all, London's already got the games. The International Olympic Committee might threaten to take them back, but the International Olympic Committee could always be told to take a running triple jump. The only true internationalism of the Olympic Games, after all, lies in the beauty of human bodies. In 1936 in Berlin, Hitler got stuck with staging the Olympics, because the date had been set up before he came to power. He didn't like internationalism. He liked nationalism, and the more racist the better, but for once he had the sense to soft-pedal the mania and let Leni Riefenstahl shoot whatever she liked. She paid particular attention to the supreme physical beauty of the American black athlete Jesse Owens. The enchanting spectacle of Owens on the move was the central motif of her film *Olympia*, and it's still true today that the Olympic events that count are the ones that look good.

I invented the sport of piano-lifting because I didn't want to insult people who are sincerely interested in weightlifting, but I've never met any except people who are weightlifters themselves, and you don't have to be in the same building with many of them before you realize that there's not much room for anybody else, and you don't have to watch them in action for very long before you come to the conclusion that weightlifting is of interest only to weightlifters and the people who marry them. Nevertheless I'm sure that the weightlifting venue for the London Olympics will be built on time, will be an inspiration to all the world's weightlifters, and will come in useful in the future as a facility for turning young people away from knives and guns and towards lifting weights. But I'm equally sure that when you add up the cost of all the new Olympic facilities, it will turn out to be a very expensive way of regenerating the area they cover.

With the money you saved from not building hopelessly specialized facilities for sports more boring than a shopping channel for machine tools, you could actually regenerate an area on purpose instead of just incidentally, and you could also put on a really good-looking televised Olympics. I don't mean with a lot of close-ups of girl gymnasts sticking their toes in their ears. I'm past all that, and the Russian girl gymnast I used to be crazy about is somebody's grandmother by now. But I do mean that the Olympics have to be made less like the Academy Awards, where even the grace is ruined by the vulgarity, and money gets into everything like a drug. But we won't even mention drugs.

Postscript

This was a rather grudging piece, whose tone I now regret. As an Australian I might have been carried away by the universally acknowledged success of the Sydney Olympics in 2000, although I had not forgotten that they, too, had suffered from the kind of pre-emptive press reception that thrives on pessimism. Assigned to cover the Sydney event as a visiting fireman, I arrived from London just in time to witness how the massed ranks of the Australian press changed overnight from merchants of doom to celebrants of a national triumph. Not having forgotten that low moment, I did my best to allow for the possibility that London might come through with something like the goods. But below my opinion, and affecting my tone, was a more general pessimism arising from Britain's poor performance in major projects since World War II. Sometimes it seemed as if no technical effort instigated by a British government had worked since the campaign against Hitler's V-weapons. Would the London Olympics buildings be finished on time and within a reasonable multiple of the initial budget? When, later on, during early 2010, it emerged that they indeed might, some of the newspapers had to report, with barely controlled rage, that the London Olympics situation wasn't as bad as had been feared, or hoped. I felt a twinge of guilt at having gone along with a manufactured mood, when the aim I had set myself for these broadcasts was to avoid any such servility – always the close consort of opportunism.

BLACK DESTINY

Dates of show: 23 and 25 March 2007

About ten years back there were a few newspaper stories in Australia about a young Aborigine woman – in the Northern Territory, I think – who had graduated in law. In addition to her cleverness she was very good looking. Stand by for the media brouhaha. If the young and gifted are black too, they don't often get to choose the rest of their destiny: for good or ill, they become representatives. But not much more was heard of the young lawyer. The media somehow forgot her, and eventually so did I, until the whole subject came alive for me again this weekend when Britain's new star racing driver Lewis Hamilton, in Adelaide for the first grand prix of the new Formula One season, and the first grand prix in which he had ever driven, got a podium finish.

It takes a petrol-head like me to fully appreciate how unusual it is for a driver of any colour to do this on his first drive. Even a non-car-nut will appreciate that it can't be easy, because all those other drivers want it too, and they can all drive. There were other British drivers who finished further down the field who had been at it for years and had never done what young Hamilton did. Two of them had won F1 races but they hadn't reached the podium on their first time out.

Jenson Button, who has spent seven years in harness and won only one grand prix so far, could console himself that some very good drivers go their whole career and never win anything, but there he was down there in Adelaide getting nowhere in his eco-friendly Honda that apparently offsets its carbon emissions by going slowly. And David Coulthard, who has won thirteen races in his time, is now in a car that seems to have developed a passive-aggressive personality.

A nice man in real life, David Coulthard will live to laugh at his bad day, but at the moment he probably doesn't find anything very amusing about the spectacle of yet another young Briton taking his turn as Britain's boy wonder. And this boy wonder automatically gets more press than any previous British boy wonder of whatever height, class and degree of good looks, because this boy wonder is black.

Luckily, for the other drivers and for everybody else in the Formula One world, skin-colour won't enter into it. Race has got nothing to do with racing. For a long while there wasn't a single black contender to help prove this to be so, but finally there is one, and he seems to have all the other qualities too: qualities which drivers as gifted as he is usually develop later, or never. Naturally wise, considerate and modest, he's as graceful in his deportment as Denzel Washington. He hasn't even got Barack Obama's ears problem. But there's the potential problem for him, because the press, regaled with such an impeccably wrapped package, will find it irresistible to make him a representative. It will be his destiny. A black destiny, however, can be a tough destiny to have.

To put any doubt of that at rest, there was the case of young Adam Regis, a fifteen-year-old black London schoolboy who was stabbed to death recently. Young Adam was understandably written up as a young man with a future. He was a reading mentor at school, and came from a prominent sporting family. He was going places. Young people who stab people are going nowhere. Young Adam represented black hope. Young people who stab people represent nothing except what the press usually calls the gun culture, unless, as in this case, there are no guns in evidence, whereupon it gets called the knife culture.

After these ghastly events there was a lot said by black people in the area about how the young lack role models. Yet young Adam was a role model, and he got killed. It's a fair bet that his very qualities made him a target. If young men who carry knives are to put the knives away and follow the glorious course of Lewis Hamilton, they will need a lot more than to be told that the knife culture is a dead end. Ron Dennis, the boss of McLaren, Hamilton's wealthy grand-prix team, laid down the law: if Hamilton didn't study, he couldn't drive. But who will lay down the law to the young and stupid? Can the role model do it, just by example? It sounds a heavy burden.

When the graceful and gracious black American tennis player

Arthur Ashe became Wimbledon champion he found no lessening of the pressure on him to be a perfect character as well as a perfect stroke-maker. He could go as far as his great talent could take him in the direction of money and prestige. That kind of discrimination was over, and there was no longer any danger of second-class treatment. But the first-class treatment came at a price which was a kind of discrimination all on its own. He couldn't go as far as behaving like John McEnroe. If Arthur Ashe had thrown a single tantrum, he would have been headline news for a week. A single swear word to an umpire would have brought on a debate in Congress. It was because he was a representative.

Arthur Ashe has gone now but Tiger Woods, in another sport, has risen in his place to adopt the duties of the black champion who wins everything but is also the perfect gentleman at all times. Just occasionally he allows himself to bounce a misbehaving putter off the green but if he even once called it a dirty name he knows what would happen next. He'd better not be caught eating even one extra hamburger. There are white American golfers who can barely fit into the bunker along with the ball, but Tiger has an obligation to go on looking gorgeous, and, above all, behaving like a saint.

The part about the behaviour applies equally to our newscaster Sir Trevor McDonald. The late Reggie Bosanquet used to read the news when he was as drunk as a man can be and still speak, but if Sir Trevor ever availed himself of the same privileges, he would be forcibly reminded of his duties as a representative.

When I was still working full time in mainstream television I had a lot of stars for guests and a few of them were hard to handle. Diana Ross was one of them. If you wanted her to cross the studio diagonally, her lawyers had to agree to it beforehand. Later on, when she got officially hassled at Heathrow, I found myself chortling at the news. Then I reflected that it had probably been a few experiences like that early on that had made her so touchy. So I got my opinion of her back in balance, or I thought I did. But then, just the other night, I realized all over again that where it belonged was out of balance. I was watching one of those cable channels where they run hits for ever, and one of them had a compilation video of Diana Ross singing 'Chain Reaction' at various times in her Tamla career, and she was so terrific that I was out of my chair dancing as if I could still dance. So she was never a black obliged to behave well even when whites behaved badly towards her. She was never a representative of a race. She was an individual, and gifted beyond belief.

You can't really say that last thing about Naomi Campbell, who has just started a stint cleaning floors in New York to pay off the misdemeanour of bouncing her mobile phone off somebody's head. While cleaning the floors she will have to walk up and down, which is really what she does for a living, apart from looking lovely. But I did a TV show with her once, and I saw her in tears, and it wasn't because she'd just read her own novel for the first time. The attention – the extra attention because she was a black model in a snow-white world – had got to her all over again, and it's not much of a defence of our callousness to say that she asked for it. So did Cathy Freeman, the Australian 400-metres champion. She wanted to be hailed as a winner. But at the Sydney Olympics she was asked to win not just for herself and for Australia but for Aborigine destiny. She won anyway, but I'll never know how. I have noticed, though, that since her Olympic triumph I've ceased to notice her. I'm not even sure she's still in Australia. She's worked the disappearing trick. She's managed to come back from where that young law graduate never went.

She should be famous, that young lawyer: famous for being not famous. Somehow she staved off the over-meaningful life where everything you do isn't just for you, but for all the people who look even vaguely like you. It's too big a category. The biggest fight that lies ahead for Lewis Hamilton will be to prove that he doesn't want to make it as a black driver, any more than I want to make it as a bald broadcaster. That's why we call it making a name for yourself.

Postscript

Like a Ming vase so precious that you always think of it falling to its doom no matter how substantial the plinth on which it has been mounted in the museum, the image of Tiger Woods was shattered late in 2009, on the night of Thanksgiving. Since the great champion has more or less asked to be given it in the neck, one doubts if he felt any great bitterness towards the media, even though he had courted their approval from the beginning. Sad on his behalf, I saw no reason to accuse him of hypocrisy – certainly no reason strong enough to offset my admiration for him as a great athlete. A bargain with the media had been mandatory since his dazzling boyhood. He would be perfect, and everyone would praise him. But the basis of the bargain was that he should be an ideal representative, or at least seem so. It might have worked for ever, except that there was eventually more seeming than could possibly survive in the light of the facts. As to that, he probably judged himself comparatively virtuous because the temptations he succumbed to were far outnumbered by those he turned down. In the mind of the philanderer, such self-exculpation is a common trait, and surely endemic at the champion's level of fame and glamour, where, as with a male film star, women who would not normally dream of being available decide to make an exception. Poor sap, he had plenty of competition for bad behaviour from the white golfers around him. But his lapse from grace was potentiated by his representative role, which always carried with it an unreal requirement for moral perfection. Very few press commentators had the nous to pronounce themselves relieved that a paragon had been let off the hook. Almost all of them preferred to cluck: an exhibition far more dispiriting than Tiger's adventures on the tiles, or even than his subsequent apology, whose most nauseating aspect was the implication that his wife must have been a helpless dupe. Meanwhile Barack Obama has become President of the United States, a breakthrough which ensures that no black man will ever have to be perfect again. But at the time of this broadcast, perfection was still a requirement.

TORTURE ON *24*

Dates of show: 30 March and 1 April 2007

Somewhere in the San Fernando Valley in Los Angeles there is a nondescript building where the giant creative brains get together who are responsible for creating the TV show *24*. The show stars Kiefer Sutherland as Jack Bauer, the counter-terrorist who has only one day, spread over twenty-four episodes each an hour long, to stave off the latest threat to civilization mounted by terrorists whose sole trace of human consideration is their willingness to mount threats that will exactly fit the production company's format of twenty-four hour-long episodes minus time for commercials.

Richly rewarded in their task by a huge flow of international revenue and the admiration of ultra-right-wing boneheads everywhere who think the show is an educational tool, the masterminds who produce *24* have been having a more than usually good time recently, because their show, which has always been prominent in the TV preview pages wherever it screens in the world, is now in the news pages as well. The news stories focus on the show's alleged fondness for torture scenes in which counter-terrorist Bauer extracts from the terrorists the necessary information to disarm the ticking atomic bomb or the ticking bio-war canister or whatever else is ticking. Alert to any ticking threat, Bauer would drive a Humvee through your bedroom wall to disarm your alarm clock. Bauer doesn't really want to torture the heavies but he has to or else the microbe bomb will go off right there in Los Angeles and there will be no more seasons of *24* or hope for mankind.

The torture scenes where Bauer has to get ruthless and grit his teeth even more than usual – and there's another question. How hard can an actor grit his teeth before they shatter? Kiefer Sutherland's father had long teeth even when he was young but he merely bared them, he didn't grit them. Kiefer grits them to the point where you imagine a Ming vase in a vice. When will they explode? Twenty-four hours from now? – But back to the first question.

The torture scenes where Bauer has to get ruthless and grit his teeth even more than usual have always been a standard gimmick in *24* but recently they've been headline news because the West Point military academy has asked the producers of *24* to tone the torture theme down. Apparently West Point cadets think the show represents their country's real situation in a dangerous world and they have started to envisage themselves as counter-terrorists first, soldiers second, giving scant thought to the exam question about what Custer should have done at the Little Big Horn and looking forward instead to the first time when they will be obliged to grit their teeth and torture one or more ethnically named terrorists in order to find, or locate as the Americans say, the microbe bomb that will go off in twenty-four hours.

Even more disturbing than the possibility that officer cadets might be thinking like this is that the men they command might be thinking like this. American troops are apparently surging into Iraq with DVDs of *24* stashed in their kit. It was this last part that made my jaw drop. You mean there are still people who actually care enough about *24* to carry a DVD of it? I thought that anyone with a brain in his head quit watching *24* after the first season, when it had already become clear that Jack Bauer's daughter was going to go on getting kidnapped as often as she escaped. Admittedly she wasn't always kidnapped by exactly the same bunch of kidnappers, but that was what was so strange. She would get away from one bunch of kidnappers and run towards another bunch of kidnappers. Eventually you figured out that this was what united all the world's terrorist groups whatever their professed religious loyalties or political aims: the desire to kidnap Jack Bauer's daughter.

When it got to the point where Bauer could never pick up the phone without being told all over again that his daughter had been kidnapped, I gradually stopped watching *24*. After half a dozen seasons had gone by, I was tuning in only for the final hour when Bauer, having determined the location of the anthrax missile after torturing everyone else in the cast who was still alive, arrived in slow-motion counterpoint against the last seconds of the countdown with his gritted teeth poised to cut the red wire instead of the blue wire, or the blue wire instead of the red wire, but anyway it was bound to be the right wire because the information had been yielded to him along with the last agonized breath of the chief terrorist and therefore had to be true.

That last part is open to question even on the practical level. People in the business of extracting information are united in the belief that pain is a clumsy inducement and that persuasion works better. People questioned under torture will make up the wrong answer if they don't know the right one. And they can be quite resistant to torture, and even welcome it, if they think that the fact that you are torturing them proves that you are indeed the devil painted in their propaganda. It really is a better plan to try proving to prisoners that they will eat better in your prison than they do at home. The only conceivable circumstances when torture is the only way is when time is tight, and the creatively fertile writers of 24 have to invent those circumstances because the ticking clock scenario is unlikely in real life. Terrorists usually take their time. The real problem is with people who want to be torturers.

These include nearly all terrorists, but they also include, unless we're careful, far too many people in the home team. Abu Ghraib under the Americans would have been regarded as paradise by anyone who was in the same place under Saddam Hussein, but it has to be faced that the soldiers who were subsequently convicted of abuse weren't alone in their dumb eagerness to turn up for work there. There is always a supply of sadists in any army. The thing to avoid is creating the demand. Instructive, then, that West Point doesn't want the maniacs to be encouraged. When democratic states favour torture, either directly by themselves or indirectly by rendition – a fancy word for handing over people you suspect of loathing you to people you know you loathe – it not only destroys the credibility of any claim you might have to be defending a value, it also encourages the formation of a gung-ho, pseudo-realist, would-be-warrior caste that thinks the ruthless is not just permitted, but desirable, in order to rule by fear.

But rule by fear works only if it's total. In the old Soviet Union, whose regime did rule by fear right to the end, there would have been no question of the Red Army politely asking a Moscow television station to tone down its twenty-four-part show about Janko Baurovitch torturing the captured CIA agent in order to locate the nerve-gas capsule buried under Red Square. The state would simply have declared its will. The US, despite what its countless enemies think, is not a state that can simply declare its will, which is the very reason why we aren't wasting our time when we vocalize our scorn after Vice-President Cheney's wife plays hostess to the creators of *24* as if they were a school of philosophers.

For the US, flirtation with torture would be a terrible strategy simply for the way it squanders the last of the goodwill that the Americans still had going for them at the end of World War II, when the Germans surrendered in their direction and even the Japanese got the point instantly when the first stick of gum appeared. In the US there has always been torture on the screen, both large and small. In *NYPD Blue*, a genuine television creation in a way that *24* conspicuously isn't, Andy Sipowicz routinely battered the truth out of the villains.

Whether what happens on the screen is a trigger for what happens in real life is a big question, but it turns out that even West Point thinks it might be. West Point representatives, when they go to Los Angeles to plead their case, have no weapon available to them except persuasion. They are up against one of the many drawbacks of a free society, which wouldn't be free if it weren't full of things we didn't like. In a free society, creative types are free to explore possibilities. One of the possibilities the *24* masterminds feel free to explore is the possibility that a state based on legality might not be strong enough to defend itself. The same possibility preoccupied Lincoln. The question might never be settled. But the question about torture was settled more than two hundred years ago, by Montesquieu. The first great exponent of multiculturalism, Montesquieu hailed its variety as a fact but also saw its drawback as an ideology. He could quite see that torture might be functional in some cultures, but he said it was wrong in all of them.

So it is, and we'll just have to find another way of getting at the truth if we are to foil the most frightening plan of the Universal Blessed Jihad against Jack Bauer's Daughter – to develop a microbe bomb that will blow up in twenty-three hours.

Postscript

During World War II the British never officially tortured their prisoners, but obtained a lot of information just by putting them together in the one place and listening surreptitiously to what they said. It was the imaginative option. Eventually the imaginative option becomes too widely known to be useful, but a liberal society can be partly described as one that goes on finding the imaginative option without lapsing into the common delusion that cruelty is the only answer. Even supposing a ticking-bomb scenario did occur, it would surely be more effective to threaten the jihadists with luxury than with agony. An earthly paradise could easily be arranged, complete with the promised seventy-two virgins. A dozen such squads of interrogators could be recruited in Las Vegas alone. Surely it would take only a few hours of concentrated blasphemy before the desperate young men would be saying anything to stop the pleasure. One doesn't like to be flippant on the subject, but the posturing pseudo-realism of the torture fans seems even more flippant: an ugly reminder that although the left wing has dissipated into fatuity, the right wing retains its concentrated virulence. As for the lamentable *24*, it looked like the height of frivolity even at the time, when the bitter facts of insurgency and counter-insurgency (or, much more commonly, terror and counter-terror) were fully on display in Iraq. It was mainly a matter of thousands of soldiers having to be brave all at once and every day, with no chance of help from a super-hero. If it took dreams of a super-hero to boost morale, then there was no point in sneering, but nor was there any point in pretending that Kiefer Sutherland was satisfactory in the role. He impressed Dick Cheney's wife, though.

CONGRATULATIONS!

Dates of show: 6 and 8 April 2007

Congratulations! You have been chosen to hear a ten-minute speech by a professional Australian author. Yes, as a result of your application being successful, you are eligible to listen free of charge to an address by an experienced Australian writer and broadcaster whose computer skills bring him into contact on a daily basis with both in-coming and out-going e-mails. This author has noticed that no matter how often updated his computer security system is, he is still regularly bombarded with variations of the Mk II Nigerian scam. The in-coming e-mail of the Mk II Nigerian scam always starts with the word 'Congratulations!'. Here, with no obligation on your part, is a precis of a Mk II Nigerian scam e-mail letter that this Australian author received yesterday.

Unlike earlier versions of the Mk II Nigerian scam approach which usually came from Nigeria, this one was datelined the Department of Lotteries and State Loans, Madrid. But like them it started with the word 'Congratulations!' before it went on to say, 'our international marketing department works in conjunction with world residential white papers, humanitarian organizations, and the help of embassies and chambers of commerce in countries in Europe, the Pacific and Australia.'

But the suggestion that there could be other countries within Australia would have aroused our experienced Australian writer's suspicion if it had not already been aroused by the phrase 'our international marketing department', which is standard in the Mk II Nigerian scam pitch, as if the institution in the headline also had a national marketing department, as if his suspicion had not already been aroused by the word 'Congratulations!'.

The Australian writer was then informed that simply by existing he had won a prize in the third category. The implication that there must be a second and first category in which even richer prizes might be awarded was once again a standard corroborating device in a Mk II Nigerian scam sucker play. The third-category prize was announced as being 615,810 euros. That tagged-on ten was again a subtle touch, as was the information that there were sixteen other winners to be congratulated, all of whom had won the same amount, thereby sharing a total of seventeen times 615,810 euros, a very large sum for any institution to be giving away unless it was involved in funding the Millennium Dome or the London Olympics.

'We ask,' the letter asked, 'that you keep this award away from public notice until your claim had been processed and your fund remitted to you, as this is part of our security measures.' To get the fund remitted, it was merely necessary to contact Señor Carlos Alfonso by a certain date, otherwise the funds would be sent back to Ministry of Economics, presumably to swell the pot for the next disbursement staged under its ministerial auspices, which didn't sound very economic at first blush, but there could be no quarrelling with the name and rank of the official in charge, billed as Dr Antonio Gomez, Vice President.

The doctorate wasn't a bad touch and the Vice Presidency was masterly. Calling him President would have been too much, whereas calling him Vice President suggested that the Ministry of Economics might actually have been engaged in this philanthropic activity as part of some incidental arm of government policy, the kind of thing a Vice President would handle down there in Madrid, if not in Lagos or in a small basement flat somewhere beneath Brixton with an old sofa in the garden for the Ministers of Economics to relax in with a beer on a spring day.

Like most writers, whether Australian or otherwise, I'm pretty good at rearranging the facts on paper to make them more interesting. It's a habit that can spread into real life if you aren't careful and I would have made an accomplished fraudster except for one thing. I don't like fraudsters. I never did like the idea of fooling people, maybe because I don't like being fooled. I don't even like practical jokes. To be a good sport about being done down, you need a lot more natural dignity than I possess. If it's different for you, Congratulations!

The Mk II Nigerian scam might seem a comparatively mild form of fraud compared with the Mk I Nigerian scam. In the Mk I Nigerian scam, they want you to send them some money until Thursday so that they can free their blocked funds, from which they will give you back ten times as much money on Friday. If the flim-flam man is sensible enough to offer you a return of only twice as much, the scam might even work, and I was once defrauded of a heartbreakingly large sum by a fellow writer who was smart enough to offer no return at all. True to her word, she didn't return my money either.

Later I found I was just the latest on an honour roll of sympathetic writers all over Europe that she had been stitching up for years. But at least she wasn't after my identity. In the Mk II Nigerian scam, they're after your details, and once they've got those, they've got you, and they can get going with the business of helping you to rob yourself. Some commentators regard fraudsters as romantic types more interesting than poor old plodding us. These commentators say that few of these frauds would work without our greed. Perhaps not, but none of them would work without the propensity of the fraudster to lie. Admittedly the liar sometimes doesn't have to do much lying. In America before World War II one sharp character made a lot of money in a hurry by placing a classified ad that gave nothing but his post office box number and the instruction in capital letters: HURRY LAST CHANCE TO SEND IN YOUR DOLLAR. I might have sent in my dollar as a tribute to his simplicity.

Hoaxes work. It's a good reason for not liking them. Virginia Woolf and her friends once dressed up as Arabs and successfully inspected the fleet at Spithead. They spent the rest of their lives giggling about their triumph but how hard was it? Evelyn Waugh and his friends invented a modern artist called Bruno Hat. Everybody fell for it, but why wouldn't they? And speaking of Bruno Hat, is it any wonder that so many people have bought Joyce Hatto's CDs under the impression that she is actually playing on them, when all the stolen performances are so good? William Boyd, whose fictional works I admire, recently promoted the works of a non-existent American painter. Boyd must have soon realized with a sickening sensation that people were going to fall for it because they had no reason not to.

In Australia during World War II, a couple of established poets invented the supposedly nonsensical works of a fictitious poet called

Ern Malley and used them to discredit the modernist pretensions of the young editor who printed them. It never occurred to them that as writers of talent they were not in a position to suppose that they could deliberately write something perfectly meaningless. It probably did occur to them that the success of their venture would entail the ruination of the young editor's career. They were talented men, but they were also sadistic, a characteristic inseparable from the hoaxer's personality.

I was part of a hoax once. A bunch of us from Cambridge Footlights pretended to be a team of explorers, visited a local school and bored the sixth-formers for an entire evening with lectures about our adventures in the upper Brazilian hail forest. After the first half-hour I started feeling queasy, and had difficulty looking any of our dupes in the eye. But after an hour I could see what was really wrong with our plan. It was bound to work. There was no risk involved. The world runs on good faith. If all of us had to spend our whole time questioning the credentials of everyone we met, life would come to a halt. Later on, as a parent, I remembered the Brazilian hail forest when I faced that awful moment when a responsible father has to tell his daughter that she must never, ever get into the stranger's car even when he swears blind that he has been sent to take her home.

I suppose there's something to be said for debunking authority, and the celebrities who fell for television satirist Chris Morris's assurances that there was a dangerous new drug called Cake on the loose were proving that we should all be more sceptical. But I think he was also proving that there is a streak of the self-congratulating fraud in every hoaxer, and I found it hard to admire him for his supposed coup. Rory Bremner I really do admire, but I wonder how well he has been sleeping if he actually did hoax Margaret Beckett into saying derogatory things about her colleagues. I have a news-paper quote from him right here. 'I just rang up and said I was Gordon Brown.' Yes, but suppose I just rang Rory up, said I was his bank manager, told him I had just handed all his money to a man from Nigeria who promised to quadruple it by Friday, and said Congratulations!?

Postscript

People who have had their houses robbed seldom feel charitable towards the robbers, and not long before I wrote this piece I had been defrauded by an acquaintance, so I was not feeling charitable towards fraudsters. I'm afraid the rancour broke through, and when I read the script again now, and especially when I listen to it on my website, I detect a note of hysteria. The text almost asks to be acted out, with rending of the garments and beating of the breast. Knowing myself to be a very bad actor, I usually tried to avoid, in these broadcasts, writing anything to be said outside the framework of my own character for more than a sentence at a time, but sometimes passion exerts so strong a grip that you go haywire.

What I like least about fraudsters is their belief (which always shows up when they are caught on camera) that they have a right to the hard-earned money of other people, either because the other people are too stupid to be left unpunished or because they themselves are working quite hard as they duck, weave, fiddle and cheat. If we could maintain a sense of proportion, we would realize that whatever punishment we dream of for the small-time operator who talks the old lady out of her nest-egg should be scaled up many times for the Bernie Madoff types who rip off millions from more successful citizens. (And of course Bernie Madoff is less deserving of retaliatory torment than even one wife-beater.) But our self-deceiving mental mechanisms come into play, and we ourselves start believing that the more successful citizens were asking for it. We would not be telling ourselves that if we were one of them. We would be telling ourselves that what the big-time operator needs is his yacht, jet, houses and cars all rolled into a bundle and shoved up his rear end. Almost always, violence is in one's mental picture of a suitable reply: the tip-off that fraud is in itself a violent act. As I write this, my computer is working properly, but a man keeps ringing up to assure me that it is malfunctioning and that he is ready to call on me and fix it. I would like to meet him at the door, let him in and chop off both his hands. But I won't, because I belong to a culture that has got beyond retributive tantrums. I belong to it, even if he doesn't. So I think I'll just shoot him.

2007 – SERIES TWO

MAN-MADE BEAUTY

Dates of show: 22 and 24 June 2007

Jeffrey Smart is one of several great living Australian painters who have continued the success of their now-deceased role models in carrying our unusually productive little nation's name into the international world of art. Among the illustrious dead are such names as Sidney Nolan, Russell Drysdale and Arthur Boyd. Among the resplendent living are Margaret Olley, John Olsen and Jeffrey Smart. They are all getting on in years but they have that unquenchable sprightliness that painters so often seem to have, possibly because they lead more enjoyable lives than writers.

This last opinion of mine might have something to do with my own temperament. I would have been a happier man if I had been a painter and indeed a happier man if I had been a gravedigger – a very useful occupation, in my view, as it was in the view of the gravedigger who met Hamlet. From the inside I don't actually feel like a wet weekend. But apparently I strike other people that way. This raises large questions about our responsibility for the image we project: questions that I propose to address from time to time in this next, intensely serious series of ten programmes. Have we a duty, for example, to paste on a smile and reassure the young that life is worth living?

Recently I published a large book whose name I won't mention here, and it has been reviewed in all the English-speaking countries, sometimes by reviewers whose names I won't mention here either, until my security staff have rounded them all up and consigned each of them individually to a glass tank full of small undernourished Siamese fighting fish. But some of the reviews were gratifyingly thoughtful and one of the most thoughtful was by that sparkling young British journalist Johann Hari, whose work you may have seen, and if you haven't you should. Although he holds certain political opinions that I don't share – he was careful to point these out in case I had forgotten them – I thought his reaction to my book was a good part of the reward for having written it.

To inspire such keen interest in a bright young person is surely part of my mission when dusk falls on the glittering city and I don the tightly fitting costume of the caped cultural critic to go swinging high above the teeming streets on the lookout for fallacious arguments to counter and damsel-like humanist values to rescue from durance vile. So I took advantage of the marvellous new technology and added Johann Hari's review of my book to my website, whose name I can mention because it's not a business that makes money.

Anyway, clivejames.com now features, in its Recent Books section, a link to Johann Hari's review as posted on his personal website. But at the bottom of Johann Hari's review there is another link, provided by himself, which leads you to a piece he wrote when he was even younger, as if that were possible. Most people younger than him can't write at all except with crayons, but apparently he once interviewed me. No doubt dragging his school satchel, he turned up at my place expecting to meet the sun-soaked spirit behind the merry columns, programmes and articles that he claimed to have been enjoying ever since he was a child, several minutes previously.

I read on past the second paragraph of this interview and I was suddenly appalled. The encounter had taken place about five years ago and obviously it had depressed him deeply, perhaps permanently. The picture he painted of me was of a desperately unhappy and self-questioning paranoid sad-sack. After that it got less funny. It seemed that I not only had to fight back tears as I choked out my defensive answers, but that I started to bleed spontaneously from the scalp. Across the years I think I can dimly remember that when he rang my doorbell upon arrival I brained myself as usual against the sloping roof of my study, but it could well have been the result of one of those occasions when I open the refrigerator door to get out the butter that I'm not supposed to have, drop it on the floor, and then stand up suddenly without having remembered that the door is open. Well-adjusted people don't do that sort of thing even once.

No wonder I had forgotten ever reading the interview, let alone giving it. It was a wonder that I hadn't gone somewhere shortly afterwards to lie down in a bus lane. Unfortunately for me, reading the piece now, I can see that my disappointed young admirer quoted me accurately and that every impression he reported was soundly based. I'd like to think that he caught me on a bad day but I'm afraid that he caught me on a typical one. If that's the way you come over, that's the way you are, and as I speak to you now I am consumed with this latest reinforcement of a recurring notion, the suspicion that I don't spend even a tenth enough time recording the fact that I actually do enjoy those features of existence that don't drive me to mumbling pessimism.

And so I ought to enjoy them. I'm well aware that I'm a lucky man leading a lucky life, at a lucky time in history blessed with the presence of penicillin, painless dentistry and *Team America* on DVD. I do feel gratitude and I ought to show it. But somehow I lack the knack for that. If young Johann is correct, even my jokes drip acid rain. It can't go on like this, or the carbon emissions from my personality will cause the wheels of baby carriages to rust in the street. So let me promise that from this moment I will try to generate the capacity for saying positive things about those few facets – wait a second, about those many facets – of the world that should be celebrated out loud, on the spot and at the time, if only on behalf of the young.

Already, we are told, there are young people who can't sleep at night because they are convinced that before they reach adulthood the house they live in will be twenty feet underwater and that Al Gore, at the tiller of his hydrogen-powered ark, may not have room for them and their families. If I can't generate the capacity to offset such nightmarish pressure on my own account, I'll try to borrow the capacity from others: people who, without being simpletons, nevertheless have the trick of sounding glad to be here.

One of them is the aforesaid Australian painter Jeffrey Smart. He is getting on in years, as I said. He is already a bit older than he was when I started to introduce him at the beginning of this programme. But he is one of those men on whom age looks good. I won't start another digression about how bad age looks on me, because really I am glad to have lived so long, so why complain? Certainly Jeffrey Smart has the energy of a much younger man: much younger than me, in fact. Not that I'm complaining.

He also writes very well, which is a bit steep when you consider how well he paints. Once, when he was quizzed about the high-rise skylines and the airport technology that so often form his subject matter, he said something that I wished I'd said. He said: 'The world has never been so beautiful.' Now that's the kind of thing I've got to get better at saying. Because I've always felt that. When I was still in short trousers I used to walk from my house near Botany Bay all the way to the airport so I could watch the Lockheed Constellations and the Stratocruisers come in from America and line up in front of the terminal.

I found those first airliners of my life, long before I had ever stepped aboard one, as purely beautiful as I now find a late Beethoven quartet. A very late Beethoven quartet, Opus 131 for instance, is practically a musical rendition of a medium-range British airliner called the Airspeed Ambassador, one of the loveliest things that ever flew. I got the same impression when I reached Italy in the early 1960s and hitched a ride in an Alfa Romeo along the beautifully engineered Autostrada del Sole, the Highway of the Sun.

It was the built world that Jeffrey Smart has always loved to paint. Just at the very time when I was writing my first bad poems about the modern Italian landscape, Jeffrey Smart was painting his first good canvases on that very subject. I have a right to my sadness that my poems failed to convey the joy I felt. But all the more reason now to insist on the intensity of the joy. Nature is wonderful but human creativity is part of nature and the two things aren't necessarily at war.

Of course we can't drive, fly and build anywhere and as often as we like. But not to be thrilled about what humanity can create is a kind of wilful sadness. I don't really suffer from it and I shouldn't allow it to be thought that I do. Perhaps I will just have to stand up more carefully under the open refrigerator door, just in case there is a young reporter waiting in the corridor whose world view will be irretrievably soured when I bleed all over him.

Postscript

Most of my earliest aesthetic thrills had been generated by machines, if that does not sound too sinister. I grew up surrounded by flowers but never noticed them until much later. When I was given a tin model of a Spitfire for Christmas I noticed its beauty immediately. I held it aloft to revel in its lines as I ran around the backyard trampling the flowers. Even now, in old age, one of my chief concerns as a critic is to find a rational basis for my lifelong feeling that planes, trains and automobiles, when viewed as human creations, are as interesting as poems, paintings and pieces of music. The subject is vast but the underlying impulse is quite simple: it is the impulse of appreciation, by which it is recognized that mankind has various ways, some of them too technical to register as art, of adding to the store of beautiful created things. In modern times, however, another impulse has shown up in the realm of intellectual affairs and grown steadily stronger: a much more complex impulse whose tendency is to wish that human achievement might be undone so that mankind's existence could revert to something less pernicious.

This train of thought, in my opinion, would be worth opposing if only because its effects, if it could get its way, would be the opposite of benevolent. Many of the modern world's problems undoubtedly do spring from human achievement: local overpopulation, for example, is partly the result of advances in medicine. But the answer lies in further achievement and more thoughtful advances. Nobody who has taken a look at Le Corbusier's horrible plans for a modernized Paris could doubt that there are some advances which are too destructive to be allowed, but the question turns on the merits of the individual case, and not on the principle. On the whole, it is the built world that has made life bearable. The hankering for a return to nature is suicidal. Yet it is widely shared among people not otherwise unintelligent, and marks our time as surely as it marked Rousseau's. Despair is in the air, even in the lands of plenty. But surely it is more sensible, and better manners, to examine the possible deficiencies of one's own temperament than to start teaching nihilism to children. The urge to brainwash the next generation in its tender years is surely at the heart of the totalitarian impulse, whose depredations form the binding theme of *Cultural Amnesia*, the book I was not allowed to mention in the broadcast. The BBC's rules are the same for everybody – no plugs – but like any author I couldn't help dreaming of the sales that might have accrued if an exception had been made in my case.

REFLECTIONS ON A DIAMOND SKULL

Dates of show: 29 June and 1 July 2007

By now the momentous advent of Damien Hirst's diamond skull is already retreating into the past, like the unveiling of the Millennium Dome and the archaeological discovery of Tracey Emin's bed under the shards and remnants of a civilization. To avoid charges of timidity, I should give my own critical reaction to the diamond skull straight away. I find it a superior work of communication to the proposed logo for the 2012 London Olympics, because the logo, based on the figures composing the date 2012, fails to convey that information in immediately apprehensible form. You have to be told by some other means the very thing that the logo sets out to tell you, which is that the London Olympics will take place in 2012, or as near to that date as can be managed by the kind of people who can't organize a successful T-shirt.

You don't have to be told by anything except the skull that the skull is a skull, studded with small glittering objects. You do have to be told that these small glittering objects are real diamonds, because fake diamonds look exactly like real diamonds to anyone but an expert, and that many diamonds all in the one place are almost always fake, unless they were once used to weigh the combined tonnage of the old Aga Khan or appliquéd to the doorknob of Saddam Hussein's eleventh gold bathroom in palace number 17.

It's a matter of context. A knock-off designer bag looks exactly like the original but its presence on the arm of a downmarket female sex worker leads you to believe that it might not be genuine. When she produces the receipt, however, the evidence begins to accumulate that she has made an investment purchase.

Back with the skull: once you have been told that the diamonds are real even though they look phoney because of their context, it's easy to believe that the materials of this otherwise unremarkable bibelot cost somewhere above ten million sterling and that the selling price will be nowhere below fifty million, which sounds like a profit for somebody. We can only hope that the artisans who put the diamonds into position with tweezers – presuming that Mr Hirst didn't do this himself – were being paid better than the workers who build the hotels in Dubai. Those workers get fifteen minutes for lunch. But the skull isn't out to pose satirical questions to corporate capitalism. The skull takes corporate capitalism for granted.

In fact the skull exists in order to make corporate capitalism feel artistic. It's unlikely that any single individual, no matter how well off, will be in the market to buy the diamond skull. Not even Madonna, who might like the skull to go with her Frida Kahlo paintings, which it rivals in its kitsch shock value – although the skull, unlike a Frida Kahlo open-heart self-portrait, has no moustache – not even Madonna would be able to pay the tab without feeling the pinch.

There is an Indian zillionaire who regards the Hinduja brothers as poverty-stricken. *He* could afford the skull, but it would cut into the fund he keeps for getting a flying-saucer pilot to defect. What he wants is an operational flying saucer, not a tarted-up prop from the Ghost Train. Damien Hirst's manager, who knows an awful lot about money, has deliberately priced the diamond skull out at the dizzy limit where individual wealth must bow to the wealth of institutions.

Even if Michael Jackson buys the thing for a paperweight, I'll be surprised if it isn't soon passed on at yet another huge mark-up to its true destination, the area between the atrium and the boardroom of the London or New York headquarters of some organization with a name like Merrill Stanley Morgan Lynch. Shining like a compressed constellation on its marble plinth, the skull will have the task of being talked about by the board members as they make their stately progress into a meeting and do a bit of international bonding before getting down to business.

The director from Oslo, in English, points out to the directors from Lima and Kuala Lumpur that the skull is the product of the same English artist who cut a shark in half. The Japanese interpreter points out to the director from Tokyo that the skull is the product of the English artist who was cut in half by a shark.

Everybody has relaxed. They have talked about art. The diamond skull has fulfilled its destiny, which is to be a talking point, what used to be miscalled a conversation piece: a way of chattering about art for people who know nothing about it. And that gives us a clue.

Because even if you do know about art, you can't talk about it socially. You don't talk about that bit in Botticelli's *Primavera* where the Medici prince reaches up for the orange or that bit in the *Birth of Venus* where her neck would look wrong if her shoulders weren't wrong too. It would be a conversation killer if you did, except among a gathering of Botticelli experts. That level of art is a different kind of event, and a much slower one. In the early nineteenth century a Botticelli could be bought for peanuts. The painter's commercial value, which is infinite, took a long time to catch up with the value placed on him by those who understood him.

Eventually the big Botticelli pictures were so identified with the soul of their country's heritage that Hitler buried them in a salt-mine with orders to destroy them if he lost the war. The pictures were saved by some Nazi officer who loved them more than his ideology. But when it comes to art, we don't talk about serious matters like that at the dinner table unless we know each other well enough to risk being boring. Instead, we talk about the nonsense. Salvador Dalí became a celebrity because he was more than half talking point. He could paint, but he was serious mainly about publicity. Tracey's bed was all talking point. I'm not sure who has it now. I think it burned down, unless I've got my stories mixed up. What I am sure of is that I have inhabited beds in far worse condition than Tracey's. But Tracey's bed is the one we all know.

This is where the mass media come in, as they once came in for Morecambe and Wise when everybody watched their Christmas show on television and every newspaper talked about it afterwards. For a certain period, the mass media give subjects of common speech even to people who fancy themselves above the mass media. Damien Hirst's shark was a common talking point for a time, and so will the diamond skull be: for a little more time, perhaps, but not for ever. The Botticelli paintings are for ever because they aren't talking points. The difference is absolute. For the diamond skull to be immortal, the culture it expresses will have to become immortal, and that culture is the celebrity culture. It might happen. I'm being positive in this series, and I have to admit that lately I've begun to feel uneasy about the low view I've always taken of celebrity claptrap.

The guilt I started to feel about questioning the achievements of Posh Spice or Britney Spears should have tipped me off. The secret of criticism is to know what your real feelings are before you try to express them. My real feelings were crystallized by that delicious comic moment when Paris Hilton emerged from the slammer to pronounce herself grateful for what she called her 'learning experience'. At last I realized that I didn't really disapprove of her at all. She's too valuable. She's our example, today, of the person who exists to prove that wealth for its own sake is utterly pointless.

And that's the very culture that the diamond skull expresses. Most of the Aztec crystal skulls that were once so popular in the world's major museums have by now turned out to be fake, but when they drew crowds it was because the Aztecs, though horrible, lived long ago, and the skulls were therefore thought to express a vanished culture, if nothing else. But the diamond skull expresses a culture all our own: the celebrity culture. Glittering, hollow and perfectly brainless, it reflects spendthrift emptiness with its every facet.

As with the culture itself, so with this brilliant symbol, we are left with almost nothing to say, but we can all say something. We might say that all the skull needs is Snoop Dogg's shades, David Beckham's earring and a wig styled like whatever that is on top of Donald Trump's head, and then it would reflect our whole existence. But that wouldn't be quite right, because one of the things we want is art for all.

The diamond skull wants that too. You can tell by the device on its forehead: a kind of cartoon cartouche with a touching subtext saying: this isn't just a skull covered in diamonds in your bog-standard manner, a certain amount of contrivance went into it as well. And even though that touch of decoration is actually no more subtle than the bogus coat of arms on a 1950s Cadillac, it sends out a message to every viewer. The diamond skull wants you to know that art isn't just money after all. I'm delighted to agree, just as I'm sure that the merry miners all over the world who dug out the original diamonds have now realized the pettiness of any thoughts about a rise in salary.

Postscript

Damien Hirst's occasional appearances on television, in his role as the rough-hewn chap being pitilessly questioned about what it is like to be a genius, are enough to prove that he has his charms. Similarly, I was pleased to exchange an air-kiss with Tracey Emin when I met her at a reception, and for those who know her better she must be fun to talk to: her celebrated description of herself ('Body from *Baywatch*, face from *Crimewatch*') is a true epigram. But the key word is 'celebrated'. These are famous artists, but their art is a commodity before it is a creation. The painter Sarah Raphael, who was lost to us tragically early in what was already a great career, made works of art. There was a reason why people paid high prices for them: because they didn't want to live without them. People who pay a high price for a diamond skull just don't want to live without the visible proof that they can afford the tab. By the time of this broadcast, the air was starting to hiss out of the notion that international corporate greed might have a beneficial collective effect in patronage for the arts. It was not yet seen that the collective effect of corporate greed was going to be a hard lesson for the world's financial system, but the bloom was off the rose. Or to put it another way, the shine was off the skull, which proved to be Hirst's last venture in the field of the impossibly priced no-no. After that he went back to repairing his own sharks, which, to the disappointment of their injudicious owners, were proving more resistant than Lenin and Chairman Mao to the preservative properties of formaldehyde.

GLIDER SHOES

Dates of show: 6 and 8 July 2007

The youngsters who wear them call them wheelies or Heelys, but to avoid any evocation of the dreaded wheelie bin I prefer to call them glider shoes. I saw my first pair of glider shoes several weeks ago on a slightly sloping stretch of brick pavement beside London's City Hall, which is not far up river from my office. Or rather I saw the small boy wearing the glider shoes. I noticed him before I noticed the shoes, which is the whole idea.

Like anyone in the vicinity of the City Hall building at any time, I am always on the lookout for something pleasant to look at instead. Ken Livingstone works in City Hall and I would almost rather look at him than look at his building. As I recall, he had a similar opinion to mine about the appearance of that building before he was obliged to move into it, but after he was, his opinion abruptly changed: a measure of his pragmatism.

Anyway, less of that for now, because I want to be positive in this series. Let's just say that there I was, walking up past City Hall towards my favoured branch of a certain famous coffee-bar chain where I get my morning grande decaff skinny latte to stay – the same establishment is patronized also by Ken, but he never stays, he always goes – and as I walked I was looking around trying to avoid any view that included City Hall, which for now I will deliberately avoid describing as a magnified flounder's eye in lonely search of its missing twin, when suddenly, or rather gradually, this child glided into view.

Not yet an adolescent but bigger than an infant, in the Victorian era he would have been described as an urchin. But the Victorian era never produced an urchin who could glide forward without moving his feet. This kid moved silently past me and on down the very slight incline as I stopped, swivelled, and marvelled. It was a dream come true.

About fifty years ago when I first saw Jean Cocteau's film about Orpheus, I had been especially taken by the way the characters, on their way into the underworld, glided forward without moving their feet. But I knew that to be film trickery. This was real life. The slope of the pavement was just detectable enough to suggest that gravity was doing the job of propelling this little bloke across the earth's surface, but even more startling than the absence of motion from his shoes was the absence of noise.

If there were a hundred ball-bearings under each shoe, they must be of a new kind. I would have liked to ask him, but at my age you don't want to be seen breaking into a run in pursuit of a strange child, or you can end up on a police register. So I contained my curiosity until I was among my family a few days later. Among my family there are sources for all knowledge. Knowledge, for example, of how to save the earth by separating compostable and non-compostable waste matter into dedicated wheelie bins. Knowledge beyond my ken, and, I suspect, beyond Ken's ken.

But it soon became apparent that on the subject of glider shoes they were merely guessing. They hadn't seen underneath a pair, although they could report numerous sightings of tots going eerily past without any obvious outlay of power: the ideal means of locomotion at last, emissions nil, the zero footprint. There were various guesses as to the means, from multiple nylon wheels to a caterpillar track suspended on liquid-filled tungsten bearings. One suggestion involved two tiny hovercraft connected electronically to travel side by side, but the proponent of that theory was at a loss to explain the absence of dust or indeed any measurable impact on the environment.

All were agreed that this latter characteristic was a good thing and the sooner that the President of the United States and his entire entourage could travel from the White House to Andrews Air Force Base by glider shoe instead of motorcade the better for mankind. But this consensus had yielded more emotion than information, and I resolved to arrange things in the near future so that I could find out how a glider shoe worked.

While waiting, I had ample time to review my life and decide that one of the many things that had gone wrong with it was that I have never managed to realize this very dream of frictionless, effortless motion despite many attempts. Early in my career, at about the age of ten, I was bought a pair of roller skates by my mother, but they were not very satisfactory. I could go down our street at a fair clip in my feeble pram-wheeled billycart, but on the skates I might as well have been going up the street as down.

The skates were a kind of framework with wheels. The framework was extensible, to fit any shoe by gripping on to the edge of the sole with adjustable grips. It was my first lesson in the lifelong necessity of avoiding anything extensible with adjustable grips. Later on I was to ruin my spearfishing career by paying extra money for a pair of adjustable flippers. They weighed a ton and were the main reason why I never speared anything except a friend.

The adjustable skates made a heck of a row and they didn't work, so I was an uproar going nowhere. Later on the same sort of thing went wrong with my ice skates. They weren't adjustable, but one of them kept coming detached from the boot. If they both had done that, at least symmetry would have been maintained. At the Glaciarium I learned nothing except how to go quite fast around the corners.

There was a fifteen-minute interval in every session during which a trainee figure-skater performed. One of them was called Jacqueline and I fell in love with her. She wasn't just beauty, she was beauty going sideways without effort. Something deep within me, at the level of dreams, responded to the idea of this effortless transition through space. I tried to explain this to her later on when she was circulating with the crowd but I didn't get very far before I noisily fell over, with that desperate last attempt to save one's balance which on ice sounds so exactly like a frozen lettuce being cut up with a buzz saw.

The amount of effort I always had to put into the supposedly effortless was demoralizing. The same applied much later, when I first went skiing in the Alps. Instead of hiring my skis like everybody else, I made a bargain purchase of a pair of skis with adjustable bindings. The results were predictable and often inverted. It finally ceased to be astonishing how often I ended up upside down. Once again, there was a lot of noise involved, and scarcely any impression of a smooth transition across the surface. I made one transition across a ski instructor and was sent back to the baby slope, the oldest person there by twenty years. I conceived at that point a tremendous envy for small people gliding without effort.

And now here they are again, and they haven't even got any paraphernalia under their feet. There is nothing between them and the turning earth except a mystery.

Last week I solved it. Once again I was passing City Hall, having just seen Ken arrive with his haversack, all set to sit up there in his office and ask himself, well what is it today, the congestion charge or global warming? I had lots of reasons to be looking away, and thus it was that another glider-shoe urchin, a female this time, sped silently across my vision.

But this time my quarry was speeding towards a pair of proud parents, who gathered her in and showered her with praise, as one does with one's children when they defy the law of gravity. I asked to see how the shoes worked, and there was the secret. There was one wheel in each heel. The wheel was made of some tough plastic and the bearing was frictionless. So all you had to do was lift your toes and you were on your way.

You could tell instantly why there had never been any Victorian glider-shoe urchins. This was state-of-the-art technology. Not that it will change the world. The shoes will work on a flat surface if their owner skips along a bit at the start, and on anything a bit more inclined the effect is automatic and addictive. But on a too steep hill the heels dig in automatically and everything stops unless the human projectile leans right forward.

So the glider shoes would be good in Milton Keynes but hopeless in Edinburgh, fine in Perth but dangerous in Sydney, and in San Francisco they would produce the world's first supersonic child. There has already been at least one serious glider-shoe accident and I suppose that when the first glider-shoe child goes under a bendy-bus, Ken will ban the shoes instead of the bus, and that will be that. But for now, it's bliss if you're the right weight and the right age. Watching, I can remember being both those things. I suppose the secret of life is not to miss the fun now of thinking how much fun you would have had then.

Postscript

Several pedants wrote in to point out that a frictionless bearing was impossible. I knew that, but I was writing a lyric, if not a lament. The less-exacting listener could hear bubbling, not far under the surface of this broadcast, my genuine sense of having been cheated by time. Had roller-blades been available when I was young, my skating career might have been different, with less humiliation and fewer bruises. I can still remember the year when I visited New York on assignment and found the pathways of Central Park functioning as promenades for roller-bladers by the swarm. It was the ethereal ease of their progress that did my head in. Where were the curses and the beads of sweat? But this feeling of having been born too early for the best fun needs careful watching, or we will end up with bile-ducts corroded by envy of our own offspring. And anyway, it's a kind of recompense that the offspring sometimes lose out by the advance. Young people born to the cassette and then the CD never knew the thrill of revelling in an LP's artwork and liner notes, and now there are young people with hideously leaking earphones who have never touched a CD. Music comes to them through the iPod, with not a word to be seen. Through the iPad (is it wise for the name of each product to look like a misprint for the other?) words will come to the next generation with not a book to be seen. Or at any rate that's the theory. But the theory might be worthless, and actual physical books might become more and more desirable and cherished. All we can be sure of is that the pleasure principle will rule. A questionable impulse, no doubt: but it built the Alhambra.

WIMBLEDON WISDOM

Dates of show: 13 and 15 July 2007

As yet another Wimbledon fortnight drains away into history, let us contemplate the receding waters and try to draw some useful lessons. I leave aside such questions as: why is either of Rafael Nadal's upper arms thicker than Tim Henman's neck? I'm being positive in this series and I want to look on the bright side, which was briefly visible on the final Sunday when Nadal and Federer miraculously encountered no moisture except their own perspiration for the length of an entire match.

But it's the invisible bright side that I want to look at now. I mean the commentary. Once again, the Wimbledon television commentary hit its peak on those days when there was no tennis at all and you were regaled with long stretches of American ex-champions talking. John McEnroe and Martina Navratilova are so interesting when they talk about tennis that they scarcely need to be accompanied by an actual match.

Admittedly things on the commentary front were rather spoiled on the last day when the mind-bending struggle between Nadal and Federer was accompanied by the voices of John Lloyd and Jimmy Connors. Jimmy Connors is another American ex-champion and like the rest of them he is full of real information, but he also suffers from an excess of good manners by which he feels it incumbent upon him to ask John Lloyd for an expert opinion. John Lloyd is indeed an expert. Like the other high-profile British commentator Sue Barker he is no stranger to Centre Court. But also like her, he is a stranger to actually winning the championship, which Connors did twice. As I remember it, Connors was thoroughly obnoxious in his behaviour while doing so, but nowadays, as an elder statesman, he has acquired humility.

It isn't humility that we want in a commentator. We want the confidence of distilled wisdom, and from the other American commentating ex-champs we get it. Even Tracey Austin, still a slip of a thing, can dish out her fund of knowledge like Aristotle. And there lies my theme: the wisdom of the great sportsmen, and how, if they can express what they know, they can tell us about life in general as well as their sport in particular. *The Wisdom of Wimbledon*, by Martina Navratilova and John McEnroe. It could be a book. It wouldn't even have to be a picture book, which is lucky, because a lot of the pictures would be of the covers getting dragged on only minutes after they had been dragged off.

Let's begin in brief with McEnroe, so we can finish by praising Navratilova at length. McEnroe is so far and away the supreme male Wimbledon commentator that the TV camera snatches pictures of him when we aren't allowed to hear his voice. On the final day, as always, he was commentating for American television, but a British camera snuck shots of him through the front window of the commentary box, so that we could see his mouth move. Almost certainly it was saying something fascinating. When Federer had that uncharacteristic mental excursion in the fourth set and tried to convince himself that the Hawkeye replay must be wrong, was McEnroe saying, as Federer mopped his boiling head with a towel, that Federer would be better off if he let all his anger out in one go? That's exactly what we heard Connors say, and it's exactly what Connors used to do, but not even Connors did it on the Krakatoa scale of McEnroe. It would have been valuable to have McEnroe's opinion.

As things were, we got his opinion mainly on days when there was no tennis at all, owing to that intermittent Wimbledon drizzle which would be put down to climate change if it was ever any different. But his comments, as always, were nearly as good as watching him play used to be, and a lot quieter. He has become a philosopher. You can put inverted commas around the word if you like, but so many of the phrases we now use when we talk about tennis were invented by him. McEnroe was the first commentator ever to say that a certain champion would soon be a step slow. It was his way of saying that the champion, although he could still hit everything, was a tenth of a second slower at getting into position to hit it. Ever since I heard McEnroe first use that phrase in a Wimbledon commentary, I have used it myself to describe the erosion of my own faculties and capacities, although 'a step slow' often demands to be modified. Ten yards slow? A mile slow?

However you phrase it, the idea enshrines a central and sad truth about physical achievement at high level. It depends on the body. When McEnroe, his stomach still flat and his formidable mouth only at the beginning of its development curve, found that he was moving a step slow, he transferred to the seniors. There's a lesson there. Be the first to decide that you've been up there too long. Which brings us to Martina, who was up there for a generation, still collecting doubles titles after she grew a step too slow for the singles. But she knew how to quit when the day came, because there's nothing she doesn't know about the sport she dominated. Billie-Jean King dominated it before her, and Billie-Jean is another inspiring case of what brains can do for a sportsman. On one drenched day of the tournament just past, Billie-Jean and Martina were both giving us their opinions to fill up the time until the All England Club gets its roof built, and to hear them talk was a reminder of what Virginia Wade was once up against, because Virginia had nothing to back her up except the British press, whereas the American women had the whole American culture of unblushing self-belief to drive them forward.

Unblushing and articulate. Martina wasn't even born American, but she realized that mastering the local language would be part of the job, and she did it the way she did everything else, thoroughly. In fact she did it to the point where you could take the inverted commas off the word 'philosopher' and simply admit that any analytical statement she made was worth writing down. After one of her countless Wimbledon victories, she once answered a not very interesting question with a very interesting answer. 'What matters,' she said, 'isn't how well you play when you're playing well. What matters is how well you play when you're playing badly.'

I wrote that down at the time and still haven't seen a neater way of expressing the truth that a high average is what counts. At this Wimbledon she was easily the sanest voice in the perpetual discussion about whether Maria Sharapova should be allowed to grunt so loudly. In case you haven't heard her in action, Sharapova, when she hits the ball, makes the same sort of sound as young adolescent males make when they first see her stretching up to serve. Some journalists describe the noise she makes as orgasmic but they must be very lucky in their love lives. The noise has an element of agony, and often there is a matching reaction on the face of her opponent. Should Maria be allowed to do it? Martina settled the matter in a way that you and I couldn't, because we haven't played in a grand slam final. When one player grunts, she said, the other player can't hear the racket hit the ball, and is thus deprived of a vital item of information about how the ball will behave next. In other words, the grunter is taking an unfair advantage. When it was put to her that some people might not be able to help grunting, Martina pointed out that if Federer didn't have to grunt, then nobody did.

And indeed Federer doesn't grunt. I hadn't noticed, so common has grunting become. For too long I have been buying the notion that some players have to. Connors certainly grunted, to the point that Bjorn Borg started to grunt back. And Monica Seles, cruelly deprived by a madman of her good chance to be up there in the all-time rankings with Billie-Jean and Martina, was the first big grunter in the women's game. But Federer doesn't grunt, so nobody needs to. The case is closed.

Finally, as Martina said, it's a matter of fairness. For years now we have lived in an era when fairness needs to be explained, and indeed there was something stuffy about the time when everybody took it for granted. You could just about say that men's tennis took a step up when McEnroe first yelled at a Wimbledon umpire, although it isn't only the Aussies who think that there was never such a thing as a step up from Rod Laver, who would have rather died than yell at anybody.

But sport without sportsmanship is indeed a dreary prospect. Perhaps sick of losing, the rest of us tend to call such ruthlessness the American approach. But it isn't fair to say so. Martina Navratilova is all American except for her birth, and even McEnroe, in the heyday of his apoplexy, knew that the rules of behaviour were there, even when he was testing them to the limit. The champions give it everything, and if they are gifted as well with the ability to speak, they can tell us a lot about life. Or else they can be like Borg, who was there on the last day and said nothing. Which tells you something too.

Postscript

Probably I was too nice about Jimmy Connors. From Andre Agassi's excellently ghosted autobiography, Jimbo emerges as an ogre. But even if he had the personality of John Dillinger, he would still rank high among the American ex-champions who grace Wimbledon with their presence in the role of commentator, or even, as in the case of Connors, just as a guest who occasionally says a few words. Back in the 1970s, I can proudly say, I laid the foundations for the academic discipline which went on to establish that the Wimbledon commentators could be clearly ranked by national origin, with the Americans at the top, the Europeans (Boris Becker, for example) coming next, and the British at the bottom. Partly it was a matter of whether they could speak the English language. It was always an axiom that any American sportsman spoke better English than the English. With time it also became clear that the same applied to sportsmen from continental Europe. Any tennis veteran from Romania, even if he never left his country except to play on the tour, will speak English with more fluency than John Lloyd.

But here one strays dangerously into the minefield of possible insult. For the truth's sake as well as for gallantry, it might be wise to say that the British commentators are inhibited by diplomacy as much as by their native inarticulacy. Not just in the technical sense, there is a limit to what Virginia Wade can say, because she is speaking for the All England Club, whereas the wonderful Tracey Austin is speaking for herself. When praising the pattycake serve of the newly emergent Czech teenager, and remarking how it will have to land in the correct court a bit more often if she is to 'go through' to the next round, Virginia can't tell you that the delicate young creature, if she 'goes through', will find Serena Williams waiting like a Tiger tank in the middle of the road, traversing her turret and calibrating her sights in preparation for the upcoming thirty minutes of horrendous violence. Tracey Austin, on the other hand, *can* tell you that Maria Sharapova, while developing her service action, endlessly watched a video of Pete Sampras. But the main criterion dividing the tennis commentators into two clear groups isn't so much national as philosophical. There is a difference between informed opinion and polite flannel. The first occupies your mind, and the second merely occupies air-time.

HELPLESSLY ADVANCED

Dates of show: 20 and 22 July 2007

Stories on the inside pages of the newspapers can tell you a lot about a larger subject than the one they purport to be dealing with. I was reading a story recently about car theft. There was the usual stuff about cars being stolen, instantly supplied with stolen documentation, and sold back next day to the original dealer, or something like that. Not finding any kind of thief glamorous, even if he looks like George Clooney and steals all of Las Vegas, I was paying only vague attention until I got to a paragraph about a bunch of young American thieves who broke into a parked luxury car by night with the intention of driving it away.

They didn't drive it anywhere because none of them knew how to work a manual gearbox, or stick shift as the Americans used to call it when such a thing was still manufactured. I imagine the three desperadoes were still sitting there cluelessly stirring the gear-stick when the police arrived, responding to complaints from neighbours that somebody was using an angle grinder in the car park.

It would have made a good comic scene in a frat-house movie, except that those movies, aimed as they are at hyper-hormonal teenagers, draw little of their revenue from people old enough to remember what a gearbox was like when it wasn't automatic: when, that is, it didn't do the whole thing for you. So there would be nobody to laugh, and the post-pubescent audience would drum their heels impatiently on the heads of the people in the row in front, waiting for the next scene when the frat brats fight to take a peek through the knot-hole in the wall of the girls' washroom. Thus our path moves on irretrievably into technologically determined time, as Confucius said when one of his acolytes invented the pencil.

Then again, the current issue of the seriously intellectual Australian magazine *Quadrant* has just carried a disturbing article by a University of Western Australia mathematics teacher recounting how some of his pupils have emerged from the high-school system unscathed by any requirement to do simple mental arithmetic. Equipped with electronic calculators since the cradle, they enter university, and even penetrate as far as the second year of a mathematical subject, unable to multiply 8 by 4 without mechanical assistance. Asked to multiply 4 by 8, they complain about having been set two problems instead of one. Most of these unwitting victims of a permissive noneducation will graduate, because there is no machinery by which they can fail, and the machinery which helps them to do their set tasks in arithmetic, the machine that does it all for them, will always be on hand.

Presumably when they move on to become air-traffic controllers or risk-analysts at the nuclear power plant they will still always have calculators in their pockets. But it's daunting to think of the calculator getting stuck in an air-traffic controller's pocket when he suddenly needs to figure out roughly how long it will take one blip on the radar screen to coincide with another. One of the many advantages of learning your tables by rote and being able to do mental arithmetic is that you know what order of answer you are after for any given question. If you buy eight dinner plates at four pounds each, the total outlay will be something like thirty pounds, but nothing like three pounds or three hundred pounds, and if the salesperson, staring dimly at the figure beeping up on her till, says the price is thirty-two thousand pounds, you'll know that you should think twice – that's two times once – before handing over your credit card.

But without the benefit conferred by a headful of thoroughly memorized relationships, the air-traffic controller will be lost, and eventually some of his pilots will get lost, not to mention their passengers. And if the pressure in the condenser pipe is rising by 4 psi every eight minutes and there are only 32 psi of tolerance left before structural failure, the man at the desk had better realize that he hasn't got all day before he scrambles the reactor.

These are fantasy scenarios on my part, but Mike Alder, the sardonic mathematics teacher who wrote the article, thinks that the whole of modern society might soon come flickering and fizzing to a halt because the people who make and work the miracle machines can't add up in their heads. He sounds at least as convincing a doomsayer as those who hold that we'll end up under twenty feet of water dotted with the corpses of roasted polar bears.

Speaking of which, it almost happened to me on a recent rainy weekend. I was away from my office for most of it. On the Monday I came back to London from Wales in the back of a car. I'm used to being in the back because I don't drive on the public roads owing to a nervous condition which other drivers contract when they see me coming. But the upside is that I can work. Reading and writing are what I do for a living, and while travelling as a passenger I can do both. I had an article to finish that day for a magazine in Chicago. Drafting the piece in my notebook with a biro, I got most of it done during the trip, which took about three and a half hours. As usual I spent almost no time reflecting that the same journey would have taken Jane Austen more than a week, and that covering the same distance was even slower before the invention of the horse. I took the speed for granted, and if we had been slowed up for an hour by the rain I would have thought that abnormal.

We weren't. I got to my desk safely by early evening, and I sat down at my computer to begin the task of transforming the draft in my notebook into a document, which I could do the final work on before sending it off by e-mail to Chicago, where it would arrive at the speed of light before close of business in the mid-West. I pressed the button that lights up the screen and nothing happened. Strange, I thought. All the diodes are glowing correctly and I can even hear the thing hum. I poked around among the cables and sockets, testing with my fingertips to make sure everything was a tight fit. It was only then that I noticed the whole thing was wet. I looked up and saw that the rim of one of the recessed light fittings in the ceiling was stained with water. At this point a director of a frat-house comedy would have staged the scene differently. I would have found out that I had my hands in a lake of electricity when I lit up all over with crackling blue cobwebs and was blown backwards into the closet where my room-mate was hiding with my naked girlfriend. What happened instead was a mental revelation, much harder to film. I realized that the technology was miles ahead of me. I barely knew how to switch the stricken monster off, and had no idea at all of how to fix it. I thought briefly of aiming my microwave oven at it.

During the rest of that week, before I left for a business visit to

Australia, I slowly grasped that I was more helpless than I had ever thought. The hard-drive eventually got saved by my young friend Idris. His principal instrument of salvation was a hairdryer, which personally I thought only one step up from my microwave notion, but Idris knows how a computer works. Since I don't really know how a hairdryer works, I needed this harsh reminder of just how irreversible the road has become. As the proprietor of a state-of-the-art, multimedia, money-losing website I'm in awe of the new technology, but I'm also in almost complete ignorance of it.

For day after nail-biting day I couldn't send or receive e-mails. Finally I had to fly to Sydney with no clear idea of whom I was supposed to meet at the other end, because all my schedules were attached to e-mails I couldn't read. Getting to Australia and back in roughly the time it took Magellan to leave harbour, I regained my office to find a new flood ready to hit my computer – all the e-mails that had piled up in cyberspace over the past fortnight. There were more than a hundred and fifty of them, practically all decorated with that little red exclamation mark that looks like the droppings of an angry sparrow.

Yes, I could have accessed them in my Sydney hotel, but I didn't know how. I don't know how to do anything the machine does and there's a limit to how far I can go back down the one-way path. I can still write an article by hand, but do I really want to copy it onto a typewriter, and then mail the typescript, and then wait? I can't go back to all that, any more than the young mathematicians can go back to doing arithmetic in their heads, or the young car-thieves can go back to treading on the clutch pedal before shifting the gear-stick, and then – this is the hard part, as I remember – letting the clutch pedal come up slowly while they steadily tread on the accelerator. All too primitive. So we let the machines do it, and more and more they make us feel powerful enough to forget how helpless we really are. Let's call that a plus.

Postscript

How young do you have to be before you feel that the latest model of the iPhone is not beyond you? You are probably already too old at the age of ten. Having received a new iPhone just before I was due to leave for New York, I looked forward to conducting all my Internet business on it while I was away. Then my secretary told me what it would cost to do so. After I shrieked at her to switch off those functions immediately, she told me that when I was abroad some of the functions, unless I knew exactly how to disable them, would go on racking up costs even if I didn't use them. Finally I plugged the new phone into its charger – is that the right terminology? – and left it sitting there on the kitchen counter. When I got back from my trip I still left it there. Six months later it is still there. By now it has grown obsolete, after a career of never having been used. Probably I have always had the wrong temperament for advanced technology and should never have fooled with computers at all. Some of the brightest people in my generation won't touch the things. Neither Les Murray nor Tom Stoppard composes on a computer or can even be contacted through one. It doesn't seem to slow them down, but I suppose it would be the sheer speed of getting the donkeywork done that I would miss most if I had to go back to carbon paper and stamps.

Nevertheless, though I couldn't do without the Internet, there are whole sections of it that I avoid from instinct. There is something wrong with Facebook and Twitter. People who think they are that interesting are usually to be avoided, unless they are Stephen Fry. And anyway, my own best sentences and phrases come after long consideration: the last thing I want to do is send out a text version of something I just thought of. Occasionally, when on stage, I think of something nifty on the spur of the moment, and the audience might even seem to enjoy it, but I would still like to keep it for a while before committing it to print. And print, where these machines are concerned, means for ever: unless you can arrange an incandescent death for your hard-drive in an atomic furnace, not even the 'delete' button will bury anything you write beyond retrieval. The computer's insistence on committing the ephemeral to eternity is what makes it an instrument of the devil. And now the same applies to the telephone. The instinct of self-preservation should be enough to make us steer clear of every new breakthrough until it has been proved innocuous. Until then, wiser to assume that a private phone call plugs straight through to a universal broadcasting system and an ineradicable archive. Wiser, indeed, not to say anything to anyone by any means, and live as the Romans did under Tiberius.

HARRY POTTER ENVY

Dates of show: 27 and 29 July 2007

If asked whether I suffer from the condition commonly known as J. K. Rowling Envy, I can't say no. Like any other writer who is not J. K. Rowling, I can't say no because my teeth are so tightly gritted in a smile of good sportsmanship that tiny fragments of enamel are given off into the atmosphere, and if I opened my mouth any further a long howl of anguish would be released, tapering into a convulsive whimper, punctuated with deliriously mumbled statistics: 325 million copies; 65 languages; a thousand million dollars; a million billion roubles. Gazillion fantabulon megayen . . .

Yet mine is only a mild expression of J. K. Rowling Envy. Some clinical psychologists insist on referring to J. K. Rowling Envy under its full technical name of *invidia rolinosis potteritis* but those are the psychologists who get the job of trying to restore sanity to writers who have plunged into a canal with a word processor to weigh them down or who have turned up gibbering at a Harry Potter midnight book launch and thrown themselves on a burning pyre of their own books screaming, 'What about me?'

As we go to air, the latest, and avowedly the last, of such Harry Potter book-launch events is allegedly retreating into the past. This contention that the Harry Potter continuous book-launch era is now over for ever is one we might well view with scepticism, but let's suppose for the moment that it's true, and return to the question of whether a writer should be without J. K. Rowling envy. It seems to me an impossible requirement. As I've stated several times in earlier broadcasts, I set out to be positive in this series, but there is such a thing as facing inconvenient truths, and I think we should admit that there is no point in presuming to condemn an envy so deep-seated.

The requirement is to control it, not to eliminate it. For any writer of almost any type, there is no prospect of eliminating it: it burns too deep, like a fire in the hold.

You will notice that I say *almost* any type, so as to allow room for the occasional altruist author who is not out to make a hit. Take Dr Roger Bannister, the man who ran the first four-minute mile. I think of him most mornings when I'm out doing my exercise walk which culminates in a sprint phase of a forty-minute mile. I can remember watching the newsreel when he ran the first four-minute mile and thinking, well, the old country might not have an empire any more but it isn't finished yet.

But in the long run, if that's the phrase I'm looking for, it was Bannister's brain that mattered. Later on he co-authored the standard medical textbook on neurology, which has gone on selling all his life and will probably remain on the medical school curriculum far into the future. The book has sold thousands of copies over the years but he wouldn't want it to be a bestseller, because for that to happen there would have to be a superfluous supply of neurologists.

In other words, he did it for love. He is not in the business of maximizing his sales, and the same could be said of all other authors who work to satisfy the requirements of a limited market. But most writers of books are out after the biggest share that they can get of an unlimited market, and this is where J. K. Rowling Envy comes in. She's actually done what every writer dreams of. What every writer dreams of is of everybody reading the book. I speak approximately, of course. I personally don't read Harry Potter books because I was inoculated, very early in life, against all forms of magic and elfin whimsy, even when convincingly disguised as literature.

I still haven't forgiven C. S. Lewis for going on all those long walks with J. R. R. Tolkien and failing to strangle him, thus to save us from hundreds of pages dripping with the wizardly wisdom of Gandalf and from the kind of movie in which Orlando Bloom defiantly flexes his delicate jaw at thousands of computer-generated orcs. In fact it would have been even better if C. S. Lewis and J. R. R. Tolkien could have strangled each other, so that we could also have been saved from the *Chronicles of Narnia*. But there is one grown-up member of my family who would regard this opinion as hopelessly restrictive. Having read everything including Tolstoy and Jane Austen, she still has time for

elves and wizards, and reads all the Harry Potter books as if they had
been designed for adults as well as children.

Perhaps they have. Certainly the total readership for the Potter
sequence far exceeds the number of literate young people on earth.
JK doesn't need me reading her too. She's got the planet, and all its
treasure. In getting that, she is also getting the other thing that any
writer dreams of. She is getting a torrential stream of income, from
royalties beyond the dreams of royalty. Not even the Sultan of Brunei
actually makes money on the scale of JK. He accumulates it somehow,
but he doesn't make it. And recently, when his ex-wife went crazy
with the credit card and squandered a couple of million quid, he
noticed. Judging from his track record, he should never have noticed
a little thing like that. This year JK gave at least ten times that much
to charity, and we presume it barely dented the bank.

This is hard to take for most writers because most writers don't
even make a living. Although the occasional book of mine does
reasonably well – about, say 0.003 on the Rowling scale – I'm always
careful not to tell a journalist how many copies it has sold, because
the journalist invariably looks unimpressed. Journalists are too used
to hearing that Jeffrey Archer or John Grisham sold a million of
their latest book in a week. But the average book doesn't sell even
a thousand copies in a year. The average book is lucky to sell a hundred in its lifetime. The average book doesn't even get published.

Until recent times the average writer could always tell himself
that he was suffering for his art and that the blockbuster bestselling
author was merely cashing in on a formula. The writer of the serious, sensitive novel that came out, rolled over and sank could always
say that John Archer and Jeffrey Grisham were peddling a gimmick,
or that the Bond franchise will sell shed-loads anyway, no matter
who writes the actual words.

But JK blew that consolation away. She was so obviously working
from creative inspiration, and her global audience so obviously loves
the stuff. The profile journalists who write about JK's houses all over
the world would dearly like just one of those houses for themselves,
but the days are gone when they could delude themselves that a thick
volume of chick-lit written a paragraph at a time before breakfast
would get them off the piece-work treadmill.

Now they know that they have to come up with something
inspired. Inspiration being what they have always been short of, they

succumb to such an intensity of J. K. Rowling Envy that they buy a copy of one of her designer evening gowns and stage an imaginary tête-à-tête dinner at home with George Clooney. If the journalist is male, this is likely to cause trouble at work.

If would-be writers aren't capable of writing a book for its own sake, they shouldn't be writing at all. I speak as one who would have found it hard to make ends meet as a writer if I had not been wearing another hat in show-business. I can't honestly whinge about having pushed my pen in vain but if I had done nothing else except write books I would be raking the leaves on one of JK's front lawns by now, and glad of the gig. And I'm one of the lucky ones. The thing to grasp is that if you're getting published at all, you're one of the lucky ones. You're expressing yourself, and the bookselling business is still willing to take a chance on someone like you. The publishers are still looking for a hit, and one of the reasons they are doing so is JK. No matter what you hear about the depredations of mass merchandizing and the destructive effect of supermarket discounts, her success gives a lease of life to a whole industry.

It also gives a lease of life to the allegedly threatened activity of reading – reading worldwide, in all languages, but especially in English. Which puts Britain back in the middle of the action. It's another four-minute mile, a flying of the flag for a post-imperial empire in which personal initiative counts for more than social position, a glorious act of individuality. JK might even be a key player in a whole new historical development. What if, by aid of the globalized entertainment industry, the world's evil could turn into a fictional spectacle in which real people no longer form the cast and almost everything bad that happens happens in a book or on a screen? Would that be trivialization, or the opposite? Either way, it really would be magic, but as countless Harry Potter fans will tell you, magic has already happened seven times. Whether they can live without Harry Potter we will have to find out. Personally I miss Biggles.

Postscript

There must be something to it. Even now that they are adults, my two daughters, who read everything of quality and are not to be fooled by mere fashion, will actually fight to be first with the new

Harry Potter book. Perhaps there is more to magic than the spells. Among the best-read men I know, Anthony Lane and Adam Gopnik both think I must be in the grip of madness when I refuse to rave about Tolkien. They might be right. There is such a thing as a blind spot. I know that I have a blind spot about food, in which I can't get much interested beyond its function in sustaining life. Yet I have friends who read, and write, books about it. Some of those who write books about it get quite rich, wherein lies the real topic of the above broadcast. In pronouncing the importance of controlling one's envy for those who sell books in huge numbers, I should have been more clear that everything, in the publishing world, depends on such people. A wise writer in any genre, if he sells merely by the thousand, would do well to spend the late part of each evening on his knees and praying to heaven that his publisher will discover a new Dan Brown.

The serious writer who vaunts himself on not being a commercial prospect had better realize that his publisher can afford to publish him only because some other writer of less refined ambitions is earning cash. From the publisher's angle, the difficult question, when it comes to the next Dan Brown, is how to spot him. If you yourself were picking talent for a publishing house, you would be inclined, on the basis of his manuscripts, to report that the next Dan Brown could scarcely write English. You would be right, but you would be wrong. The executive who turned down the Beatles had tastes too fastidious for the job. It follows that the most vital piece of recruiting a publishing house can do is to choose the dim but keen editor whose heart genuinely races when the manuscript of the next *The Da Vinci Code* is carried in. Somewhere just below board level in every successful publishing house there is at least one chump. These chumps can be most easily identified by their excellent tailoring and large cars.

SMOKING THE MEMORY

Dates of show: 3 and 5 August 2007

At my age, achievements become few and small. One enters the era of tiny triumphs. The other morning, as I walked along slowly beside the Thames on my way to my favourite coffee bar – walking slowly because I was deliberately minimizing my impact on the environment – I reflected, in the style of one of those old essayists who were always reflecting on narrow areas of experience that turned out to have a wide area of implication, I reflected, as I walked slowly upstream beside the south bank of the Thames and turned up the spanking new glass-lined avenue that calls itself More London, I reflected that the now virtually complete restrictions on smoking would have driven me to violence if I still smoked, but I don't, so they haven't.

I did it. I finally quit. Two and a half years ago I smoked my last tin of cigarillos, and although I still dream of taking them up again on my death bed – more of that later – I am now at one with the non-smoking world. I almost pity, instead of envy, those who are still caught up in it. Outside the entrance halls to the tall glass buildings of More London – what a name, so exactly conveying that it has less of everything – there were groups of people smoking at each other. Occasionally they talked to each other as well, but you could tell they were talking about smoking. Some of them were arriving late for work and were having a quick one before they went inside. Some of them had arrived for work earlier and had come back outside for the first smoking break of the day, or perhaps the second.

Cigarette butts surrounded each group in a sort of fairy ring. Already these fairy rings seem to be moving further away from doorways, and one foresees the day when the fairy rings disappear altogether. In California it was already happening ten years ago when it was decreed that you not only couldn't smoke in the outside section of the restaurant, you couldn't smoke within fifty yards of the entrance. When the entrances were less than fifty yards apart, smokers in Bel Air had to walk to Hollywood Boulevard before they could light up. Now it's happening in Britain. It's already happened in Scotland, where any space with three walls is designated a non-smoking zone. After that law came in, you could see otherwise sane-looking people counting walls and you knew that they were smokers.

I was just such a smoker from my early teens until my early thirties, quickly working up from a twenty a day habit to the dizzy eighty a day peak that some so-called experts declare impossible because you would have to wake up in the night. But of course I woke up in the night. It was an expensive habit but I never subsequently thought of suing the manufacturers to get my money back. Revenge on the tobacco companies was always a branch of the compensation culture that I thought especially ungracious, like suing a host for having served you champagne before you fell into his swimming pool. At the age of eleven it was already clear to me that inhaling cigarette smoke was likely to do to my lungs the same thing that it had done to my Uncle Harold's.

Coughing himself inside out, Uncle Harold would reach for the next cigarette. By the time I quit, I was doing the same. Impressed by the news that if I stopped cold before I was thirty-five it would probably undo any damage I had already caused, I didn't have another drag for thirteen years. But I missed it every day, so how, you might be asking – and if you're trying to quit you'll certainly be asking – how did I manage it?

I used the offset method, i.e. I spent the money on something else, something that I could see accumulate instead of burn away. The same amount of money I would have spent per week on cigarettes I spent on recordings of classical music. They were all on vinyl in those days and eventually I built up a collection weighing a couple of tons, almost as much as the pyramid of the butts of all the cigarettes I had ever smoked would have weighed if they had been swept together in the one place, which would have had to be as big as Trafalgar Square. As I sat there listening to, say, the Mozart String Quintet K 516, I could reflect that its limitless sublimities almost outranked the pleasure of sucking on the fiftieth filter tip of the day.

But there was the catch. I was still thinking of that pleasure, and eventually I took up smoking again, but this time with new hopes of smoking in moderation. I had been impressed by the way Clint Eastwood in the spaghetti Westerns chewed a cigarillo instead of saying anything. Taciturnity had always been among those dreams for myself I knew to be hopeless, but I correctly assessed that he smoked far fewer cigarillos than he would have smoked cigarettes. Alas, the same was not true for me, and within a year I was chain-smoking the little cigars, often carrying a third tin of ten for when the first two ran out.

So it went on for a further twenty years on and off, and usually more on than off, while the final whistle was blowing for smokers in the Western world. The cigarettes which had been the only stable European currency in 1945 gradually but inexorably became branded as evidence of the lethal conspiracy of big business against populations helpless to choose their own fate, and the freedom to choose death was rolled back under the imperative to lead a healthier life.

Eventually even I was convinced, and I gave up again, partly because of my job. Flying all over the world to make films for television, I was sometimes faced with thirteen hours in the air without a smoke. The thirteen hours might as well have been thirteen years. After most of the airlines turned on the non-smoking signs for keeps, a smoker who wanted to keep his fires burning had to plot a circuitous route across the globe, and often he would have to fly with an airline that allowed not only cigarettes in the cabin, but live chickens.

There was also the matter of a cough that became harder to conceal from my family. The smoking I could conceal, or thought I could, by going out into the garden for a quick dozen drags before always burying the butt in the soil of the same pot plant and sticking a peppermint in my mouth. Why a man thinks the sweet stench of peppermints from his mouth will offset the foul reek of smoke in his clothes is a question that has so far puzzled science. Anyway, it soon transpired that only I was fooled.

So I would give up for another year, offsetting the money this time with a plan to spend the same amount on health food in order to halve my weight. Having doubled it, I would hit the cigarillos yet again. Finally it was the Australia run that spelled the end of my smoking career. After thirteen hours we arrived at Bangkok airport and I raced for the smoking room. Smoking room was a big name for a small Perspex cubicle that was opaque from the outside because of the grey pressure of the fumes within. I opened the door, saw all the other smokers sitting there face to face in two tight rows, and I realized that I would have to smoke in the standing position. Then I realized I didn't have to light up. All I had to do was breathe in. It was the moment of truth.

But then, I had always known the truth. The truth is that I love smoking. Hence the failure of all my attempts to give it up, because every method I used was predicated on the assumption that a desire could be eliminated once it was seen to be absurd. I tried nicotine patches and kept sticking them on until they joined up at the edges. I looked like the flesh-pink version of the jade warrior. There is a book out now which teaches that every cigarette you have from your second cigarette onwards does nothing for you except raise your nicotine level up to what it was. Possibly so, but in my case it also satisfied a deep longing, the memory of which lingers like lost love.

So how did I finally quit? I learned to smoke the memory. When the longing hits you, don't try to repress it. Savour it. The actual thing wouldn't be any better. In fact it wouldn't be as good, because it would last only as long as the cigarette or the cigarillo, whereas the memory lasts as long as you like. Reflect on the frivolity of your desires all you wish, but you will never conquer them unless you first admit their urgency. And since I'm being positive in this series, let me record that I feel better. I still quite like the idea of taking a crate of cigarillos with me when I go into the nursing home, but that day will be further off now than it would have been if I hadn't stopped lighting a fire in the lower half of my face every few minutes. I would have been in the same condition as the pot plant. The pot plant died.

Postscript

This broadcast has a sad resonance for me when I read it again and I can scarcely listen to it without tears of shame. Within a year of having written the script, I was smoking cigarillos again. And this time, having made such a public boast about my powers of self-control, I was obliged to smoke in secret. There was many a furtive disappearance on many an absurd pretext. Remorse, however, was not the worst consequence. On the first day of the year 2010 my lifetime's dereliction caught up with me, and I was diagnosed for COPD. This fancy set of initials sounds like an American television police series but the quickest way to explain it is that it used to be called emphysema. I was lucky it was only that. Judging by the cough I had developed, I was fully expecting that the X-rays would come back as a picture of lung cancer, but it seems that I am one of the lucky two-thirds of smokers who don't get it. (Readers who are relieved by those odds should try expressing them another way, and contemplate the proven fact that a full third of smokers do get it: a pretty ominous statistic to be fooling with.) My lung X-rays were scarcely a clean sheet – they looked like a battlefield on the moon – but there was no cancer. So I got away with it after all. It's a little stroke of luck to be blessing myself about as I lug an oxygen tank onto the aircraft when I want to fly anywhere. Apparently the chances are good that I will be able to ditch the tank soon. I'll try not to celebrate by lighting up. No, smoking was never worth the money, and certainly not worth the danger. But my real trouble was – I tried to be honest about this – that I liked it. Loved it, in fact. At the time of writing, when I haven't had a smoke for an entire year, I'm on seven different medications per day. Two of them are inhalers, and guess what, one of them gives me a blast not very different from those first few hundred cigarettes I smoked when I was still in short pants.

DESIRABLE DEVICES

Dates of show: 10 and 12 August 2007

On my way to work I made my weekly stop-off at the mega-super-hypermarket in the shopping area-precinct-mall just between the motorway exit from the north and the outer rim of the congestion charge zone. As I chose a shopping trolley from the ranks of hundreds of shopping trolleys in front of the vast retailing edifice, I at last realized the significance of the sign on the trolley that said it would stop when it got to the red line.

I vowed to be positive in this series and yet it's taken me all this time to notice the most positive sign of the lot. For years I have been disgusted by the sight of shopping trolleys poking some of their structure above the surface of otherwise pleasant brooks and creeks in which they have been merrily immersed by the nation's infinite supply of casual vandals. How can this be fixed? I would ask myself. It can't, I answered, because so large a proportion of the population can't be re-educated. But here we are already, looking at the day when nobody will be able to wheel a shopping trolley any further away from the supermarket than the red line before the wheels lock and the trolley stops. Unless the shopper wants to pick up the fully laden trolley and carry it to his boombox car, that's where the trolley will remain. Triggered by the signal from the red line, the microchip built into the trolley has done its job. A problem posed by technological advance has been solved in the best way: by more technological advance.

Surely the best answer to the plastic-bag plague also lies in physics and chemistry, rather than in a change of morality. Ireland has got its total number of plastic bags down by about eighty per cent just by taxing them, but the twenty per cent left over are still enough to make the landscape hideous. Also it's undoubtedly a huge fuss always to remember to take your durable shopping bag with you to the store.

I can't remember whether I've said this before, but I'm getting to the time of my life when I can't remember anything, and although I can see myself buying a designer-label permanent shopping bag, I can't see myself remembering to have it with me. What I want, what every sensible person wants, is a plastic bag that biodegrades. Some of them claim to do that already, but only by a percentage. Again, it's usually twenty per cent. If the bag starts its twenty per cent biodegradation immediately, you're left holding eighty per cent of the bag, with one hundred per cent of your purchases all over the road. If the process takes time, then the effects will make little aesthetic difference. Nobody's going to look at the hedgerow lining a narrow country road and cheer that twenty per cent of each plastic bag has gone, while there are still the usual few thousand plastic bags almost entirely present.

What industry has to do is come up with a bag that turns to a puff of dust after a certain date, preferably some time before the sea rises to drown civilization. It shouldn't be all that hard and I'm sure some great globalized company is already working on it. Until then, boneheads with boombox cars will go on loading a dozen bulging plastic bags each into the back after the trolley has been abandoned, and will make sure, when they unload them, that the plastic bags are added to the landscape as usual. If people who travel in boombox cars were open to rational persuasion not to dump their junk, they wouldn't be driving around in a broadcasting station.

What should be done, then, about boombox cars? Only a few days ago the car I was a passenger in was trapped just behind a four-by-four boombox car in a traffic jam. The bass notes of the witless hip-hop anthem it was transmitting along with its emissions hit me repeatedly in the stomach. When I was young I might have walked up and said something to them and got hit in the stomach for real. As things were, I sat there planning the technology to retaliate. It needs to be introduced into the boombox car at the point of manufacture. There will be set levels of volume and duration so that the prospective purchaser and his dreadful friends can briefly get the stimulus they find necessary to life, but at anything beyond those levels the air-conditioning system will instantly lower the temperature by 150 degrees centigrade. Suddenly they'll be sitting there in a block of ice, silent for the first time in their benighted lives.

Public silence is a dying concept, as we know. We'll never get it back if we rely on the return of good manners, because the people who make a lot of noise have no idea that they are crossing a boundary: they think they are exercising a freedom. People who yell into mobile phones would look sincerely puzzled if you dared to interrupt them. How can you be bothered by a little thing like noise? Only last week I was making a long train journey and there was a man in my carriage who maintained his cacophonous part in a single telephone conversation for a hundred miles. During this intermittent uproar I feebly worked on mental plans for the kind of Heath Robinson device that would deal with him.

The carriage would need a noise detector that reacted to any violation of a set limit by tripping a switch under the perpetrator's seat that would eject it and him through a flap in the roof and out into the speeding landscape. But fitting every seat in the train with such a facility would cost too much, and there would be the problem of littering, as the plastic bags in the hedgerows were joined by all those startled bodies.

No, once again the matter will have to be dealt with by a technological advance included at the point of manufacture. What every new mobile phone needs is a small, simple, retractable hypodermic syringe to inject barbiturates into the phone user's earlobe when he or she exceeds the volume limit. The howling monologue would thus rapidly be replaced by a deep silence. There could be a problem about the same system if the user is at the wheel of a car, because innocent people might be involved in the resulting crash. I'm still working on that, but there is no reason why competent engineers and pharmacologists should not be working already on the technology.

Public-address systems in the park are another threat that could be easily neutralized. The park in front of our house would be bliss in summer if not for a rising incidence, on the weekend, of pre-charity-run gatherings in which the chief irrepressible enthusiast of the local community-spirit committee asks the assembled multitude if they are all right. For some reason this worthily motivated pest always asks crowds of any size the same question, and at the top of her voice. She is already yelling when she asks this question of a group of three people she meets in the street, and when she is turned loose behind a microphone in front of three hundred people in the park she makes so much noise asking whether they are all right that she can probably be heard on the moon. What she needs is a microphone with a small attached reservoir primed to react to excess volume by plugging her mouth with a squirt of quick-drying polymer.

I should hasten to say, at this point, that I am not against charity runs. I am just against any attendant noise pollution, which exemplifies the difference between something we hope does good and something we know does damage. The polymer mouth-plug could be removed upon receipt of a written guarantee of silent behaviour and an undertaking to wear the plug prominently displayed, as a sign of repentance. Quite often the public nuisance is so dumb that he agrees to wear such a sign in advance. This is the useful aspect of the continuing tendency towards flaunting a face full of metal studs. People who do all that are telling you they are imbeciles from a hundred yards away and all you have to do is turn down an alley.

Another case of visibly identified imbecility concerns Lindsay Lohan, who has taken positive steps to redeem herself through technology, or anyway steps have been taken on her behalf. We are told that an anklet was fitted to Lindsay Lohan in order to monitor how much she drinks. Before I could figure out whether the anklet told the police or Lindsay Lohan, there was news that some of her fans were already copying her anklet. This seems likely to be the anklet's most desirable function. The anklet was already useful to help tell us that Lindsay Lohan was in the vicinity, if we hadn't already been tipped off by the approaching press conference, and now we will know if anybody who admires Lindsay Lohan has just joined us on the top deck of the bus.

Put your trust in our powers of invention. If the can of fizzy drink pointlessly carried by every cockily shambling young male dimwit could be rigged so as to degrade suddenly when the can was still half full, the disposal problem would be solved and the trousers of the can's proud owner would be soaked in a suitably punitive manner. I can't imagine that this smart-can technology would cost any more than redesigning the London Olympics logo.

Postscript

Under the froth and bubble, the solemn undertow of this and several other broadcasts over the course of three years was my growing dread of the possibility that the concept of private space might disappear altogether from modern society, yielding nothing except a supposedly democratic 'community' in which nobody would be left alone because it would not be understood why anybody should want to be. Political theorists call such an alteration a 'change of consciousness'. Sometimes a change of consciousness is for the better – it is an unmixed blessing, for example, that lynch law is no longer common in the United States – but a change of consciousness by which privacy has ceased to be conceivable is a threat to civilization. Nor do you need to be a fuddy-duddy to find it so. All you need to be is sensitive. Unfortunately (one of the key considerations in this matter) the sensitive are the people least likely to protest. Their silence is interpreted as assent, and so the depredation goes further. Not that they would have much effect if they spoke up. At best, they would be thought to have some mysterious illness.

The assumption that there should be no such thing as private space is intimately connected to the assumption that there should be no such thing as private communication. When one of Prince Charles's private phone calls was printed in the newspapers back in 1992, not even one article was written about the only real ethical question involved, which was whether intercepted private phone calls should be treated as news. It was simply, and universally, assumed that they should be. The community, it is thought, has a right to know. Community rights trump individual rights every time. But what Alexander Zinoviev once said about the repressive system in the old Soviet Union applies equally, if in less immediately lethal form, to our fine freedom: any society in which collective rights outrank individual rights is a lawless society, and that's that.

CLICK ON THE ICON

Dates of show: 17 and 19 August 2007

The word 'icon' gets tossed around like the term 'Renaissance man'. Just as any actor is called a Renaissance man if he can play three chords on a guitar, so the photograph of any face becomes an icon if you can still attach a name to it after its owner is dead. But the original icons had nothing to do with photography. They were pre-Renaissance religious images usually depicting Jesus and scenes from his life or death, with his mother Mary often figuring prominently. The amount of information in the icon was often quite restricted, and that's the element that now fascinates us most. Some of the pioneering modern artists picked up on that very element of minimum information, maximum suggestion. An icon often had little more to it than the curve of a mother's weeping cheek.

When modern painting tried to return to the icon's simplicity, it was in search of that characteristic of pre-sophisticated, often pre-competent art by which the viewer's imagination is drawn in to fill a space, instead of shut out by a display of technique. Here lay the power of the photograph. It could register a form but simplify its content, especially if the image was in black and white. In Hollywood, there had been many famously beautiful faces before Greta Garbo arrived from Sweden, had her teeth fixed and became the world's biggest female film star. But Garbo was the first to realize that the very idea of a face could be beautiful. A woman much more original than she is often given credit for, Garbo knew that any kind of camera, whether cinematic or still, always lies, because it gives a single figure far more importance than it can have in life.

She also spotted that nothing was more important to a female movie star than the studio publicity stills that went into the newspapers and magazines all over the earth. Garbo would dictate the lighting in her stills sessions until the frame contained the bare minimum of information about her face: it was just eyes, a mouth, and a shadow. Often the nose was just a pair of tilted nostrils.

Garbo was well aware that she was a bit of a lump in real life. This even became apparent in some of her movies. Watch her dance in the role of Mata Hari and you wonder why the set doesn't shake. But in the stills she always looked ethereal. By now there is a whole generation of people who have never seen Garbo in a moving picture. They should. In *Ninotchka* she shows you how graciously funny she could be, and you can guess that she was called boring in real life only by people who were scared by the way her lovely face stirred their imaginations to expect so much that they couldn't value her down-to-earth common sense. But one of the reasons that their imaginations were stirred is that they were meeting the icon, which, with the aid of her own cunning, had been shaped and projected by the studio publicity system.

Since Garbo, every female film star has wanted the same for herself. Louise Brooks achieved iconic status without making many films that a mass audience ever saw, and nowadays almost nobody has seen any film she made, yet she is instantly recognizable by her hairstyle, which in itself gets described as iconic. By the time the movies got as far as me, there were female icons to burn. I grew up watching Linda Darnell, Rita Hayworth and Kim Novak. I thought Linda Darnell was the loveliest but I lost my heart to a single photograph of Rita Hayworth. The photo was a studio still taken by 'Whitey' Schaefer and I didn't know, when I first pasted it to my wall, that the star had had her hairline lifted by the studio so that her forehead would reflect more light.

Rita Hayworth could dance. If she had been an inch or two shorter, she would have been an even better partner for Fred Astaire than Ginger Rogers was. But Rita Hayworth's abilities meant nothing to me beside her looks, and Orson Welles, who was married to her briefly, probably felt the same way. It wasn't what she could do, it was what she seemed to embody: beauty itself.

Kim Novak was the extreme case of that. She didn't even have to act, which was lucky, because she barely could. She just had to stand there looking out of this world, so that James Stewart, in *Vertigo*, could believably go out of his mind for her. It was always tough on the real actresses that so many mere beauties became icons, but it was inevitable because men are born idealists, and usually stay that way most of their lives.

Occasionally an icon could act. There was an actress called Janice Rule who was so lovely that she overwhelmed any part she was playing, but in a Western called *Invitation to a Gunfighter*, which only a few people have ever seen, she is the plausible reason why Yul Brynner goes mad to possess her, shooting up the whole town. A woman who could drive Yul Brynner to achieve acting must really have had something. For a while I collected Janice Rule movies. She was in *The Chase*, with Marlon Brando and the young Robert Redford, but for me there was nobody on the screen except her. I feel the same way about Natalie Portman now, as long as she isn't dressed up as Amidala, Queen of Naboo, the bad-hair planet.

Mention of Marlon Brando reminds us that there are male icons too. In the thirties the publicity stills of Johnny Weissmuller proved him to be the most beautiful man on earth, the title that Denzel Washington holds now. Weissmuller had the kind of classical face that was probably non-existent in ancient Greece but which was born again in Brando and Elvis Presley. Take a look at a publicity still of Brando and check out the sculptural perfection of his mouth.

Unfortunately Brando did the same, and became so fascinated with the orifice he ate with that he tried to give it a life of its own on screen by pouting. Antonia Quirke, in her highly original novel *Madame Depardieu and the Beautiful Strangers*, is very perceptive about the faces of the male screen stars but sometimes underestimates the degree to which they are hamming it up. Trying to improve on their natural blessings, they tend to mug. Even Tom Berenger, blessed with the nearest thing to a perfect face in recent times, ended up doing strange things with his mouth, and still stranger things are done by actors who would like to be icons. I call it mouthing and I say that it should not be tolerated. Popcorn should be hurled at the screen until the practice ceases. Otherwise Bruce Willis will go on thinking that he is being charming when he purses his lips.

He has been pursing them until they bleed ever since his first days in television, and he is still pursing them as he comes swinging in through the plate-glass window to mow down a row of central European heavies in *Die Hard All Over Again*. Even Harrison Ford, otherwise excellent icon material, holds his mouth half open in the mistaken assumption that he looks more thoughtful that way. All the icons have to do is just be while we look at them, but not even the smart ones are content to do that, and there are real dummies who don't fit the icon frame at all but think they might if they do enough work with their mouths and the way they stand.

Between *NYPD Blue* and *CSI Miami*, something happened to David Caruso which his admirers call a movie career but I think might have been a brainstorm. Some internal blunt-force trauma convinced him that if he pouted thoughtfully enough while taking his dark glasses off before putting them on again, we might finally register the iconic perfection of his face. On screen he stands sideways no matter what, just so that we can see his face from all angles. The director, perhaps per contract, cooperates by closing in until Caruso's face fills the frame. It remains, however, just a face, which is the very thing that the iconic face refuses to do. The iconic face is radiant with the incorporation of the ideal. Its owner can be as dumb as they come and have no acting talent at all, yet somehow the fearful symmetry comes shining out.

It's because our imagination is pouring in. There's a moment in *Camille* when Garbo, at the theatre, turns around to smile at Robert Taylor, who was handsome but might as well have been carved out of wood, like a cigar-store Indian. Garbo's face seems to flutter as she turns, as if the film has been double printed so that one still succeeds another. I can remember my own gasp the first time I saw her do that. There was a similar moment in *Rear Window* when Grace Kelly leaned across the screen to kiss James Stewart. Why wasn't she kissing me? I was already in long trousers. She looked pretty good in real life, but on screen, lit so her face was just radiance and an outline, she was an icon.

Postscript

Some listeners thought that I was being more self-indulgent than politically exploratory when broaching this subject, but I thought I was being both. The appreciation of human faces has become part of the celebrity culture, and no topic of modern times could be more political than that, especially by the extent to which it does not appear to be political at all. (Naomi Campbell thought it had nothing to do with politics when Nelson Mandela sat her down at the same table as Charles Taylor, erstwhile President of Liberia. Actually she had been put right in the middle of the battle for Africa's future.) Just as we rank prospective friends and life-partners by their voices, we rank them by the faces they appreciate. It's one of our first clues to their aesthetic sense. The power of the film-star face – often, to a large extent, a constructed myth – to influence reality was the most original part of the story line of the movie *L.A. Confidential*, which turned on the unsettling paradox that a young woman who looked like Kim Basinger might be induced to look like Rita Hayworth. So far, the best book on the subject isn't about the faces of female film stars but about the faces of male film stars. It's the novel I referred to in the text, *Madame Depardieu and the Beautiful Strangers*, by Antonia Quirke. The novel's narrator sees the surrounding world entirely in term of iconic male faces. Without the author's wit and gift for analysis, it would have been a story riddled with madness, but as the clock ticks it seems less mad all the time – which might mean that we've all gone mad. I must be one of hundreds of male readers who thought immediately of writing a counter-novel about female film stars, but I gave up the idea after clicking through about three pages of the Tea Leoni images on the web. At my age, it would so clearly be the work of an obsessive. And yet 'obsession' is not far from being the right word when our minds are being navigated by an ideal perception. You start thinking that a small woman in a raincoat half a mile away in the mist might be Ludivine Sagnier.

Iconic faces may be shorthand but they are a real notation, and social progress can be measured by how they rise in favour. Nowadays it is quite possible to imagine that a white young man, let alone a black young man, might want to look like Denzel Washington. This is a clear improvement on the time when Michael Jackson wanted to look like Elizabeth Taylor. On the same theme but in another part of the forest, what is most frightening about Japanese pornographic comic books is not so much that the female figures are schoolgirls in bondage, as that they are still given Westernized features. All those young blondes with pointed noses are tokens of cultural discontent.

CLAMS ARE HAPPY

Dates of show: 24 and 26 August 2007

In an early Robert Redford starring vehicle called *The Candidate*, which is now largely forgotten but shouldn't be – watch and marvel as he uses all four facial expressions – there is an interchange of dialogue which encapsulates a nagging philosophical problem. Redford has pointed out that if he runs for office he will never be happy again, and his prospective campaign manager says: 'Clams are happy.'

Redford decides that he is a more complex mechanism than a clam – some critics of his acting might think he reaches this decision too hastily – and runs for office. The implication is that happiness, in itself, is no worthwhile aim in human life. Certainly T. E. Lawrence didn't think so. It was T. E. Lawrence who bowled over the young C. V. James by insisting in print that happiness was 'a by-product of absorption'.

Peter O'Toole didn't actually say this when he impersonated T. E. Lawrence on screen in *Lawrence of Arabia*. Always one of the most cultivated among actors, O'Toole, as his autobiography *Loitering With Intent* proves, wields a prose style considerably more notable for clarity and rhythm than anything Lawrence could muster in his much-praised but seldom-read masterpiece *Seven Pillars of Wisdom*, a magnum opus which has all the characteristics of a sand-dune without the sense of humour.

But the producers of the movie wanted their Lawrence to lead memorable charges across the desert, not to utter penetrating philosophical truths. He was allowed to proclaim the secret of stoicism, but only when putting out a match with his fingertips. Film producers want the visual element. If somebody says that no man is an island, they want to see a man and an island.

So O'Toole's Lawrence of Arabia got no chance to tell his co-star

Omar Sharif, who really was 'of Arabia', that happiness was a by-product of absorption. In real life, Omar Sharif was under the impression that happiness involved champagne, cigars and a blonde on each arm. He might well have looked nonplussed at the word 'absorption'. But the off-screen Lawrence wasn't proposing that the human soul should model its aspirations on the properties of an aspirin. He was saying that if you were absorbed enough in some worthwhile activity, happiness might be the spin-off.

A corollary to this fine idea was that there might be no time to enjoy the happiness, because you would be too busy being absorbed. I myself, during a long career separating an idle and misspent adolescence from my present state of incipient disintegration, usually found that I had almost no time to stop and examine what might well have turned out to be a period of happiness, and that, when I did, the happiness soon struck me as so absurdly self-centred that it made me unhappy to think about it.

I also found that it might be taken as even more self-centred to voice this conclusion. The people who are sharing the raft on your course through life's rapids, notably your immediate family, are unlikely to burst out cheering if you say you can't be happy for five minutes without thinking of all the people who aren't. They might be quick to point out that when you talk that way, the people who aren't include them, and that they might perhaps come first in your thoughts, to the extent, at least, of your trying not to bore them with expressions of your misery just when everybody is settling down to watch *The Sopranos*.

When I set out to be positive in this series I guessed that the question of the legitimacy of personal happiness was bound to come up, but I kept putting it off. What makes the question so tricky is that we're given both the capacity for personal happiness and the sense of proportion to realize that it's an offence against common reason. The capacity for happiness works the same way as the capacity for misery, in that it refuses to be relative. If you have made a loved one miserable, it's useless to tell them that many thousands of people are currently dying by violence. In fact it's another form of violence to say so. Misery can seldom be reasoned away. But happiness, though just as pure a feeling, can often be reasoned away in an instant.

Nowadays I try not to let that happen. Not long ago I was in New York on business and the weather was getting hot enough to make you walk on the east side of the avenues in the morning and the west side in the afternoon, so as to keep in the shadow. If you're anywhere near Central Park, it's the ideal weather for a take-out deli lunch. You don't have to eat fast food in America, because between every two fast-food emporia there's a deli full of good slow scoff. Armed with about ten bucks' worth of unimpeachable nutrition, I went into the park, sat on a rock, got started on my salad, and contemplated existence. I saw an old guy hobble past who was what I will be in about ten years, if not ten minutes. He looked happy and suddenly so was I.

For once I managed to hold back the thoughts of how few deli lunches had been eaten that day in Darfur, and I savoured the moment along with my slice of watermelon, which took me back to when I was a kid in Australia. It was sixty years since I first had a slice of watermelon wrapped so far around my head that it chilled my ears. That time, I hadn't questioned the legitimacy of my happiness, and I tried not to this time either. But I had to try, that was the difference. I don't think it's true that the underdeveloped world starves because the developed world doesn't, but there's just no denying that you can't eat your fill without insulting a lot of people who have nothing to eat at all.

You find that out when you grow up. Finding that out *is* growing up. Life makes us melancholy, and the melancholy comes from the realization that your moments of happiness are not only fleeting, but meaningless in the context of the sufferings of others.

Melancholy will find us. We don't need to seek it, and it's definitely no virtue in itself. By her own account, Shakespeare's Beatrice was born under a dancing star, and she's the brightest of her bunch because she has the impulse to be merry, even though, being so brilliant, she will see the world as it is and it will make her sad. Meanwhile she will correctly judge any man proud of his own gloom to be a crashing bore.

We owe it to the next generation to behave as if life were worth living. It is, even when we hear that yet another child has gone missing. It is even for the child's parents, although to them it might not seem so ever again. But the little children want your smile, or they get scared. In my own family, in which I used to be a member of the second generation but have now been promoted to the first, a third-generation member has recently established herself as one of the leading footballers in her age group.

Her age group is two minus. But she can not only kick a ball, she can link the kicks into something indistinguishable from ball control. She is never not moving. She is also hardly ever not smiling, except when you aren't. If you frown, she will catch the frown, and would tell you off if she had the words. She already has words in a scarcely credible number, and only last weekend she came up with her first complete sentence. Dare I say that it was a philosophical aperçu comparable with 'happiness is a by-product of absorption'? With several adult witnesses present, she said: 'The wanting, and the more, and the porridge.'

Move over, Seneca. Step aside, Pascal. Now this is philosophy. For indeed there is the wanting: and sometimes the wanting is for means of sustenance tragically unavailable. And then there is the more, and there will always be the desire for more, as with Oliver Twist, who did not have enough, and as with the glutton, who has too much. And then there is the porridge, the irreducible essential which must be provided or else there can be no real choices.

Whether or not this young philosopher is providing us with a coherent picture of the world, I am happy to hear her speak. But the question remains of what the happiness is worth. It's impossible to be compassionate for all the suffering individuals in the human race, and Dickens was only one of the great writers who noticed that those whose hearts are always with unknown thousands of people abroad are often the most indifferent to the fewer people nearer home who might benefit from practical help, starting with their own children, bouncing down the stairs unattended even as the philanthropist histrionically weeps for larger disasters far away.

We should do what we can, but save our sadness that we can do no more. Because eventually disaster will draw close enough. Dealing with it will demand a sense of proportion, which is always a balance between good cheer and realism, and can't be resolved entirely in favour of either term, lest our view of life be either inane on the one hand, or heartbroken on the other. And so saying, he vaulted to the saddle of his camel and rode away.

Postscript

The fashion for melancholy often returns when there is a sufficiently glamorous figure to lend a style to a despair. Churchill's 'black dog' wrote a licence for many mini-Churchills, and in our time Stephen

Fry has been an influential melancholic. Nobody very much cared about Spike Milligan's melancholia because he broke the furniture, but Fry makes it look as if sufficient sadness might produce a sonnet sequence. The fashion was already well entrenched when Pushkin made the hero of his long poem *Eugene Onegin* a model of gloom. A close reading reveals Onegin to be a bit of a pain and one is tempted to conclude that Tatiana had a lucky escape. In twentieth-century America it became axiomatic that melancholic writers drank. Hemingway, Faulkner, Fitzgerald, Agee, Cheever ... the list is endless. The habit was likely to induce depression even if there had been little to weep about in the first place. Drugs were a further development on the theme of the world being hard to bear.

But of course it is, even at its best. One can even be sad at the injustice of one's having been spared the worst. But to become desperate on that account looks very like self-indulgence, and on the whole melancholy is surely best left to those who have really got it. Sometimes there is ample reason: having to look after hopelessly damaged loved ones at the expense of one's own fulfilment must make Fate look like an enemy. Nor can being hopelessly damaged oneself be inducive to merriment. But quite often melancholy is a medical condition that can be treated with drugs. (In olden times they would have been called 'pills to purge melancholy', which then they seldom did, but now they often do.) To treat it with admiration is almost always a mistake. An extreme case of that mistake is provided by the case of Sylvia Plath, a highly gifted poet who took it upon herself to represent the destruction of the European Jews as if it had been an episode in her personal history. It wasn't, and the fact that it wasn't should have been her true subject. She was ill, but too many of her admirers have less excuse for not realizing that there was a blasphemy involved in her undoubted brilliance. Since her death, modern literary history has had to put up with whole generations of literary aficionados who think that poets can't be serious unless they flirt with suicide. Such misplaced enthusiasm is really a form of triviality, another way of not caring very much about the stricken.

2008 – SERIES ONE

PRINCES INTO BATTLE

Dates of show: 7 and 9 March 2008

The British royal princes are brought up with Shakespeare ringing in their ears like an alarm clock they can't turn off. Though they might not get around to reading any of the other plays, *Henry V* is certainly one title that they can't escape. Henry V, known to his familiars as Harry, starts off as a scapegrace but proves his mettle on the battlefield. If a prince's name actually happens to *be* Harry, the Shakespearean role model must be hard to get out of his mind, even if he is not much of a student. Many a line in the play must sound like a prescription for conduct, with the possible exception of the one about 'a little touch of Harry in the night', and even that one was said on the eve of the Battle of Agincourt, where the young king was seen by all to have finally put his wastrel days behind him.

Whatever you think of Prince Harry's adventure in Afghanistan, you can see why he wanted to do it, and understand why he must have been disappointed when the eventual puncture to the press embargo cut the adventure short. But for a while there, he was doing what he most dearly wanted. It's probably what most men want, early in their lives, even when the very idea frightens them. Dr Johnson once said, 'Every man thinks meanly of himself for not having been a soldier.' It's not so much that men seek danger – any fool can do that – as that they feel guilty about not having been tested in mortal combat. There are things you don't know about life if you have never been faced with somebody who wants to shoot you.

I remember when I was doing national service in Australia and we had a spell of so-called 'realistic training' when we had to lie down clinging to the open ground while bullets were passing low overhead. It was scary enough to actually hear the bullets ripping by. But I couldn't help thinking even at the time that there was all the difference in the world between a machine-gunner who was trying to hit me and this machine-gunner, who was trying to miss me, and would probably have missed me even if I had stood up suddenly straight into the path of the bullets. He was the best machine-gunner in the Australian army and he had devoted all his skill for years on end to making sure that not a single mother's son ever got touched. I was grateful, but it did occur to me that the realistic training was unrealistic in a certain vital respect. In the army I learned a lot of things that Harry has just learned. If you don't muck in, you will soon be left out. And there is no privacy in the army, for anybody. Stop to take a dump and all your mates will find you: it's practically a way of being rescued if you are lost in the desert. But he learned one thing I know nothing about. He learned for sure how he would behave when the bullets were looking for him.

The minute he got home, he was in another kind of battle, which one way or another will go on for the rest of his life. You can tell when people are serious about getting rid of the monarchy because they use the humanitarian argument, the argument that says nobody should be a prisoner of his birth. The royal children are born to be theorized about, and there is no getting out of it. To be subjects of press speculation is their destiny. It must be a pestilential destiny to have. Suddenly the press was full of armchair military experts who felt qualified to assure us that Harry's presence among the troops had put them in extra danger. There were suggestions that the whole thing had been a PR stunt on behalf of the army. Further up the line towards Fayed-style fantasy, there were even suggestions that the royal family was trying to improve its image. It was like reading newspapers more than a century out of date. Back then, during the Zulu War, there was actually a case that fitted all those theories to perfection.

Let's roll the tape back to the year 1879, and examine the case of Napoleon III's son Eugène Louis Jean Joseph Napoléon the Prince Imperial, he who might well have become Napoleon IV. For purposes of brevity, we'll call him Eugène. After his father died in exile, Eugène was keen to establish himself as the natural heir to his great-uncle's military genius, thus to prove that he was fit to ascend the throne of France, a seat which still looked available. The new republic was shaky on its base, a fact proved by the press campaigns it was prepared to mount against the pretender's credibility. Eugène, they warned, had no qualifications for the job except ambition.

Admittedly he gave his critics a lot to go on. With the endorsement of Queen Victoria, Eugène joined the British army, where he soon proved himself to be an unmitigated liability. He wasn't just a fool – although he was outstandingly that – he was a busy fool, thus exactly fitting the description of the kind of officer who, the first Napoleon had once said, must be got rid of immediately. Eugène really *was* a danger to his fellow soldiers. He never got the point that there was no such thing as a single Zulu. When he saw a single Zulu, he galloped off to chase him, invariably registering surprise when the single Zulu led him and his small detachment of troops to a couple of hundred other Zulus hiding behind a hill.

Eugène wasn't unique in his stupidity. Most of the British officers made a point of underestimating the enemy until the Battle of Isandlwana turned into a massacre which cost the British expeditionary force 1,300 soldiers dead. The horrified Prime Minister, Benjamin Disraeli, retrieved some of the PR disaster by promoting the immediately subsequent Battle of Rorke's Drift as a victory compensating for the previous defeat, but he knew it didn't. Another victory, no matter how small, would have been welcome.

Keen to provide it was none other than Eugène, at the head of a troop of soldiers which he led twenty-two miles into Zulu country with the intention, apparently, of confusing the foe by having a picnic. Carefully choosing a position where his men could be approached under cover from all sides, Eugène ordered that the horses be unsaddled so that they could rest. He had an experienced British officer with him but the experienced British officer was a victim of social deference, and didn't like to contradict royalty. The Zulus had no such inhibitions. Cutting to the chase, we can say that Eugène might have died a more impressive death if he had not last been seen alive riding *under* his horse, where his hastily buckled saddle had slipped. His body was recovered with eighteen assegai wounds in it. The court of enquiry, which managed to blame everyone except him, never did establish whether eighteen Zulus had stabbed him once, or one Zulu had stabbed him eighteen times.

It's easy to make fun of him now, but the poor sap was chiefly culpable for having wanted to be there. He was trying to prove himself. Even at the time, there were those, especially those who favoured the French republican cause, who said he was there for political reasons. But it seems more likely that it was personal. The precedent puts us at liberty to wonder what would have happened if our current warrior prince had been killed or, possibly even worse, captured. God forgive anybody who isn't appalled at the very thought. But he wasn't, and his experience has given him an advantage that will serve him in future even better than it will serve the army. Now, he knows. His elder brother William would doubtless like to know too, but a potential direct Heir to the Throne is faced with the unwritten rule that he may fly, drive, dive and fire weapons only on the understanding that he doesn't fight.

The same was true for his father. Andrew was allowed to fight in the Falklands but Charles, if he had adopted an assumed name and tried to go, would probably have got no further than the airport. One can safely assume that he must have cursed his fate, because there could have been no sharper reminder that he was its prisoner. He has learned to live with such disappointments, and his capacity to do that will make him a good king one day. One of the things I want to do in this series is ask whether, in this new era of perpetual alteration, it might not be wiser to cherish those institutions that work. I believe that the royal family is one that does, but at a harsh price for those born into it. They are bound by duties they didn't choose, whereas the rest of us choose ours. For just a little while, young Harry chose his. Should he have gone to Afghanistan? Now that he's back safely it's easy to say yes. If things had turned out otherwise, saying yes would have been a lot harder. But he knew that things might have turned out otherwise, and he went anyway. He might have written a five-act history play instead, but Britain has other people who can do that, or at any rate it used to.

Postscript

If the future King George VI had been heir to the throne, he would not have been allowed to go to the Battle of Jutland, where he was mentioned in despatches as a turret officer. Instead, his brother Edward was heir, and was never allowed near a battle. So the most intense experience of Edward's life was Mrs Wallis Simpson, whose occasional bouts of cold anger must have been quite frightening, but were scarcely a matter of life and death. King George VI knew what a matter of life and death was. The same applies to the current Duke of Edinburgh, who was at the Battle of Matapan, where he, too, was mentioned in despatches. Thinkers who would like us to dispense with monarchy can get upset with anyone who talks about the royal family as if they were real people, subject to experience that matters to them and might help form their judgement. But they *are* real people, no matter how unreal their circumstances; and that being so, it is unwise to treat them like living gods. In my own view, Prince Charles should have been allowed to see combat. It was a deprivation for him, not to be allowed to risk his life. The sum of such deprivations can lead whole nations astray. Emperor Hirohito, in his younger days, wanted to dress as well as the aforementioned Edward, Prince of Wales, whom he had met; but the Emperor was too holy for his tailor to touch him, so his clothes never fitted.

Put enough reverential nonsense like that together and you get a man whose inability to cope with reality was instrumental in both initiating and prolonging a war that cost millions of lives. Even in a constitutional monarchy, what the monarch knows of life is bound to matter, if only because, contrary to the fond belief of the theorists, a monarchy is our reality. Those who dream of abolishing the system may fancy themselves to be realists, but in fact they are romantics. Or else they are hankering for America – where they would soon find that the presidential system has all the drawbacks of a royal house with none of the advantages. It's notable that the more determined critics of the British monarchy are often keen to insist that King George VI and Queen Elizabeth either tried to leave London during the Blitz or else actually did, leaving lookalikes behind. This fantasy can sometimes be heard at dinner tables in Australia, where there is a widespread belief among the intelligentsia that the constitutional connection with Britain serves only to delay Australia's graduating to the status of 'mature nation'. But mature nations are careful to tell the truth about their heritage.

PRIVATE LIFE

Dates of show: 14 and 16 March 2008

London's mayor Ken Livingstone has an aide who has recently been busted sending amorous e-mails to a friend. The aide, known in the tabloid press headlines as 'Ken aide', has a few questions to answer about what he has been doing with some of the money entrusted to him. No doubt he will give satisfactory answers, and I, to name only one, will realize that my council-tax cheque has been put to good use under his guidance. But he will find it harder to shake off the accusation that he has been writing besotted e-mails, because the *Evening Standard* printed them verbatim. Andrew Gilligan, in charge of that newspaper's investigations into Ken aide's activities, can congratulate himself that he has caught Ken aide red-eyed with lust, if not red-handed in malfeasance. But I wonder if anyone else should be congratulating Mr Gilligan. Isn't there something wrong about helping yourself to the private e-mails of politicians, the private text messages of footballers, the private phone calls of ... But you fill in the blanks. And to the contention that nothing is private for the prominent, shouldn't we be saying that privacy is for everyone, and not just for you and me?

To say that, however, you have to believe in private life as a value. I think most of us still do, although it may very well be true that a private life is becoming impossible to lead. But just because it's fading from existence doesn't mean that it was never vital. Private life is an institution, like the English language, which is collapsing too, and proving, even as it falls to bits, that it's a structure our lives depend on. Ken aide's friend, prominent in that official field of race relations which is now known as community cohesion, has been quoted as saying, 'I see a time when race policy will be actioned with the sanction of committees.' There could be no clearer evidence that the English language is in a bad way. But I got that quotation from something she published, not from one of her e-mails. If she had said it in an e-mail it might well have raced Ken aide's motor, but as far as I know she didn't. And as far as I know is, I think, quite far enough.

Most of us are capable of grasping that if everyone could suddenly read everyone else's thoughts then very few people would survive the subsequent massacre, which would effectively bring civilization to an end. If you were living alone in a cave, you might just stay alive until the following morning, but only if you were in there alone. To live in society at all, we have to keep a reservoir of private thoughts, which, whether wisely or unwisely, we share only with intimates. This sharing of private thoughts is called private life.

Until recently, the concept of private life was basic to civilization. Its value could be measured by the thoroughness with which totalitarian states and religions always did their best to stamp it out. But now we have to face the possibility that the latest stage of civilization, this era of perpetual alteration that we are living in now, might also be trying to stamp it out. You can still keep your thoughts to yourself – nobody has yet invented a machine that can get into your head and broadcast what it finds – but if you try to communicate those private thoughts to anyone else you run an increasing risk that they will be communicated to everyone.

It doesn't matter who you are, if you are conspicuous enough in public life and use a mobile telephone to transmit a private secret then you might very soon see it printed in the newspapers. You probably remember that when this actually happened a few years back, the press coverage was endless. But I can't remember a single feature article which raised the question of whether the printing of an intercepted private phone call was not in itself far more startling than any secrets that might have been revealed. Partly this was because the press, taken as a whole, had already reached the conclusion that everything was grist to its mill. The British press, even its tabloid basement, could be worse. On the whole it leaves the children alone. But one way or another it will print anything it can get about an adult. What has changed, in recent years, is the range of what it can get.

There was a limit to what it could do with letters sent through the post. It couldn't steam them open. In the reign of the first Elizabeth, her chief spy Walsingham routinely opened every letter that entered or left England, but that was early days. If the press wanted to do that now, it would have to steal letters faster than the post office can lose them: a difficult ask. With the arrival of the mobile telephone, things got easier. I can well remember, late in the last century, a senior executive of one of the big press conglomerates trying to impress me at some reception or other by saying that he had, in his safe, transcripts of mobile phone calls that would rock the monarchy on its base. He seemed very proud of himself, but for a moment I realized what it must be like to be face to face with the head of the secret police in the kind of country where only the police have secrets.

Things have moved on since then. No transcript stays in the safe for long, and now there are e-mails to draw upon. It's been said that nobody sensible confides to an e-mail anything that he wouldn't be prepared to see published in the newspapers, and this might indeed be so. But it could equally be said that nobody sensible puts his money in a bank that might be robbed. There are identity thieves robbing banks every minute of the day without even having to pull on a balaclava. Unless we keep our money in the mattress, we have to trust the bank, which might be hard to do, but would be even harder if the bank-robber could not be classified as a criminal. Pinching private phone calls and e-mails ought to be a crime, but somehow it isn't.

And it probably won't be. There are too many laws as it is; too many of the new laws are useless; and a law against printing anything you can find would probably be seen as an infringement of free speech, even though the unrestricted theft of private messages amounts to an infringement of free speech anyway. After the Ken aide e-mail incident hit the headlines, some commentators were quick to note that if you really want to speak freely in private, the thing to do is write an old-fashioned letter.

Few of these commentators noted that their suggestion came at the very time when Post Office™ – trade marked because it is no longer the Royal Mail but is now a business – is proceeding with its plans to close somewhere between 2,500 and 3,000 post offices. Most of these post offices slated by Post Office™ for destruction are in rural areas. In other words, they serve small towns and villages that are hard to get to, which you would have thought was the very reason why the people in them need to write and receive letters. Post Office™'s rationale for this further truncation of its already abbreviated service reaches a height of absurdity which Jonathan Swift would have hesitated to scale, lest his readers stop laughing and reach for the arsenic. Post Office™ says that it all costs too much. The losses, it says, are 'unsustainable'.

You will immediately spot that Post Office™ is speaking the same new language as Ken aide's friend. The post office, before it was hobbled with its trademark, wasn't a business, it was an institution. An institution is something without which civilization itself is unsustainable. It could be said – no doubt Post Office™ has a management layer in which such things are said full time, as a prelude to their being 'actioned' – it could be said that the old ladies in the villages, who will no longer meet each other at the post office after it is turned into a community cohesion centre, could always send e-mails. They need never leave the house. After all, they've had plenty of practice since Dr Beeching was deputed to annihilate the railway service on the same grounds: unsustainability.

And there is always something to be said for leaving the village behind, if you don't mind waiting for a bus. G. K. Chesterton used to argue that the best reason for moving to the city was that in a village everybody knew your business, so you couldn't lead a private life. He'd find it hard to say the same now. You can be in the biggest city in the world, and every phone you pick up, and ever computer you sit down at, is a direct pipeline to universal publicity for any thought you dare to express. Plato would have been envious. He devised a legal body called the Nocturnal Council, but if its members suspected you of impiety they only wanted to discuss it with you for a few years. And Plato never dreamed that his hideous Republic could be established except by coercion. We seem to be volunteering for ours. But nobody has invented a mind-reading device yet, although I have noticed that some of the latest mobile telephones are small enough to crawl into your ear.

Postscript

In my role as a television talking head I had to sit for a lot of press profiles and I was frequently told by the interviewer, when I tried to hold something back, that the public would be interested. I soon learned not to say: 'If you knew better than I do what interests the public, I'd be interviewing you.' It would have been arrogant, and it wouldn't have been true. The interviewer knows exactly what interests the public. The only failure, on the part of the interviewer, is the failure to draw a distinction between what the public finds interesting and what is in the public interest. The question turns on whether the concept of a private life is vital to the general welfare, and the answer is surely yes. In practice, however, privacy is usually trumped by news, and the ethical quarrel is confined to the question of whether or not the news is true. Back near the beginning of the twentieth century, Roger Casement's diaries, which helped to bring him down, seemed likely to be a forgery put about by the British intelligence service, but the less likely possibility, that they were genuine, proved to be true.

What Prince Charles really needed, in the absence of a law forbidding the publication of private phone calls, was maximum publicity given to a phone call concocted by somebody else. If his call was real, it was grist to the mill. Or at least it was in Britain: if his future job had been King of France, his private life would have been as invulnerable to the press as President Mitterrand's. But during the period covered by these broadcasts, it was becoming evident that civilization in Britain was suffering less from the accelerating indiscretion of the media than from the carefully preserved unfairness of the legal system, which allows an ambitious nuisance from anywhere in the world to sue against the slightest sign of defamation, and win large sums. Under this bad law, a book or periodical doesn't have to be published in Britain, it merely has to be available there in some form and however briefly, for anyone from anywhere to bring an action in a British court against the author of the text that is felt to be offensive. The system amounts to a kind of libel tourism. In this respect if in no other, Britain looks like the dunce of the EU. No British institution is felt to be working well when there is a general opinion that they do things better on the Continong.

STATE OF LAW

Dates of show: 21 and 23 March 2008

Last week the man who wanted £300,000 compensation because he slipped on a grape in the car park of his local branch of Marks & Spencer lost his case. Good news for the rule of law, perhaps, but bad news for those of us whose lives have been blighted by injuries which were never our responsibility. I wept for the man who slipped on the grape, because three hundred grand was the least he had coming. Here was an accountant who, before his shoe made contact with the grape in question, was able to charge £225 an hour for his financial services. After he descended from the lofty parabola into which the grape contact had thrown him, he sustained a rupture to his quadriceps tendon. This rupture led, he said, to a 'loss of confidence', which in turn led to 'adverse psychological effects and depression', which in turn meant that he was unable to recruit new clients and contacts and charge them £225 an hour. On top of that, he was no longer able to ski, play football or play tennis. He was probably also unable to play Monopoly, which can put a terrific strain on a ruptured quadriceps tendon, especially when you are losing. The accountant lost in a big way and ended up having to pay his legal costs. I have been brooding about this for some time and would now like to tell him that I share his pain, even in the area of my quadriceps tendon, which was practically the only part of my body that I didn't injure in the accident that still haunts my life.

Interesting that the grape victim should mention skiing, because it was while I was skiing in Switzerland that I sustained an injury entirely due to the carelessness of an organization from which one might have expected more. Not more than £300,000, perhaps, but something. I typed this script without using my thumbs, and here is why. About twenty years ago, both my thumbs were almost dislocated in a skiing accident. If the accident had not happened, I could have typed this script more quickly, and could have typed another in the time saved, thereby restoring my confidence, not to say replenishing my bank balance. I shall be telling the full story of this accident in my fifth volume of *Unreliable Memoirs*, a work which I am currently composing, to a deadline which I have set according to how quickly, or rather how slowly, I can compose a hundred thousand words using eight fingers.

But a short version of the story will sufficiently indicate that I was blameless in the matter. I was on a black run at Davos and it could be argued that I shouldn't have been there, owing to my inability to turn in any direction at any speed. But no attempt was made by the responsible authorities to ascertain this fact before I started my descent. And the run was open to the public. There were signs to say that the run was open, and the signs had been placed by those in charge of the resort. The run was needlessly steep. Those in charge had bulldozers available and it was their responsibility to level the mountain during the night. They had not done so and I was doing seventy-five miles per hour when I took off from a bump and landed on my nose a hundred yards further on. The manufacturers of the ski bindings had done their job. With those manufacturers I have no quarrel. The skis came off as they should have done.

But the loops on my ski poles failed to detach themselves from my thumbs as I hit the snow, which was packed tight. No attempt had been made to loosen it and I therefore continued going downhill at high speed in prone contact with the snow, my cries ignored. Instantly I felt an acute loss of confidence, compounded by a searing pain in both thumbs. The loops, which should have been designed to detach themselves like the bindings, put a severe strain on both the intrinsic and extrinsic muscles of each thumb. In both cases, the first dorsal interroseus was irreversibly inflamed, and the flexor pollicis longus was impacted with the extensor pollicis brevis, thereby permanently inhibiting my capacity to reach for my wallet whenever it was my turn to pay for something. I had legitimate hopes that the owners of the resort would be doing that for me from then on, but my case was thrown out by a Swiss German judge who spoke no English except the phrase 'in your dreams'.

The British judge who so cruelly dashed the hopes of the grape-treading accountant was not necessarily under the influence of the Swiss legal system. The British legal system is still capable of reaching sensible decisions on its own account. Let me overcome my throbbing bilateral pain for a moment and say that the law still has enough majesty to remind us that we are lucky to live in a country with functioning institutions. Nothing will remind the public that if they lived in a country with no laws at all they would be inconceivably worse off than they are now. Most of us have had no experience of living in a lawless society and we therefore find it difficult to imagine.

The British live in a country that has been ruled by law for a long time. What they can't help noticing is that the law doesn't always work. When Dickens, in his great novel *Bleak House*, painted his immortal picture of the chancery court in which your case would remain unresolved for ever, with more and more lawyers taking your money until it was all gone, it wasn't the law he was against. He was against the law not working.

But the law not working can be quite frightening enough. Admittedly there are newspapers that specialize in encouraging such fears. Often when I read the tabloids I wonder if we might not be living in the last days of the Weimar Republic, until I remember that sometimes when a drunken joy-rider wipes out a family waiting at a bus stop he gets picked up by the police and spoken to quite severely, and might even have his licence withdrawn for a whole year.

But what sometimes saps confidence, inducing an adverse psychological condition, is when the legal system consumes vast amounts of public money in proceedings that seem very slow to proceed. A highly vocal cleric, the enemy of his own religion along with every other aspect of British society except its benefit system, which he drew upon to support his large family, ate up hundreds of thousands of pounds in public money before it was finally decided that he was guilty of incitement to murder. But he had declared himself guilty of that years before. He never said that he wasn't inciting people to murder. He said that inciting people to murder was all right.

The present inquiry into the death of the Princess of Wales will get through at least £10 million of the taxpayer's money before it reaches its decision. It was a good sign when the court rejected Mr Fayed's demand that the Queen should be called as a witness, so as to make up for the absence of testimony from Ming the Merciless of Mongo, Emperor of the Universe. But otherwise the inquiry has been an expensive way of establishing that there was never very much to inquire into except an accident. Whatever happened to those poor children in Jersey plainly wasn't an accident, and getting to the bottom of the matter will be worth all the money it costs, but how much money will be left over for such a necessary thing when an unnecessary one is allowed to cost so much? Or am I all wrong about the public money? Perhaps it is being continually replaced with the limitless funds generated by schemes to charge people for using their cars to deliver passengers at Heathrow when the passengers should be using the Heathrow Express, which will be jammed to the roof because millions more people every year will want to cram themselves into an Airbus A380 and fly somewhere that doesn't allow an ex-wife to even think of charging £125 million for four years of marriage. In the end, Lady McCartney was not awarded quite that much of Sir Paul's money, but she certainly wasted a lot of the court's time.

If the well really is bottomless, it would be reassuring to be told so. It might be timely if someone in the government could address the House of Commons on that issue. On that issue, and with that scope: the State of the Law, in a state where law rules, or anyway it should. While we're waiting, we must content ourselves with these occasional outbreaks of what sounds like sweet reason, and base our hopes on those. The latest outbreak we owe to the judge who, in a blessedly short time, concluded that the man whose shoe hit the grape had been subject to an act of God, or let's call it a grape of wrath.

Certainly that judgement put paid to my own planned venture on the same lines. I had it all worked out. In my local supermarket there is a bin that is always shedding a few blueberries on the floor as clueless people pick up the plastic box by the lid and scatter the contents. Having flagrantly neglected to seal the box shut, the supermarket is incontrovertibly responsible for the spilled blueberries. One of those spilled blueberries is fairly aching for contact with my sandal. I had the trajectories all worked out. Hit the blueberry, up in the air, and I would fly feet first into the manager's office with the word 'compensation' already forming, indeed foaming, on my lips. But the law has spoken, and now I must think again.

Postscript

Not long after this script was broadcast, a professional acquaintance of mine had to deal with the news that his young daughter, who had been standing with a group of her friends at the side of the road, had been killed by a car that had gone out of control. It soon emerged that the young man at the wheel had been out of control for the whole of his short life, too much of which, mysteriously, had been marked by his possession of a driver's licence, which no amount of thefts and violations had deprived him of for longer than a few weeks. This time he was actually banned from driving for a while, but the little girl, it should hardly need saying, was subject to a longer penalty. Even now, when I think of her fate, I can't find the words to evoke my own outrage at the state of the law. As for my acquaintance, when he recovered his ability to think and move, he set about the task of getting the law changed, and by now he is a leading figure in the association of deprived parents that is coming closer all the time to obtaining a result.

Such a task is never easy but perhaps the intricacy of the business has done something to distract him from his grief. The thing to remember – the hardest thing to remember, alas – is that the law's imperfections are tokens of its necessity, not of its uselessness. Speaking as one who begrudges every penny of his tax money that is spent on continued benefits for hate-preachers so that their sons can grow up to be car-thieves, I would like to see all their rights suspended until they can be put on an airliner to anywhere. But the fact that I would like that so much is just why we need to have the rule of law. The theme kept on cropping up during my period as a broadcaster – there was no lack of stimulus – and I always tried to give that message, if possible without repeating the illustrations. Even if the reader doesn't spot that the writer has repeated an example, the writer, in order to do so, will usually fudge his construction of the context. Saying it twice almost always involves saying it loosely the second time. Loose talk leads to easy writing and easy writing leads to mediocrity. Nevertheless, in the course of the decades, I was unable to avoid several invocations, in several different media, of Ming the Merciless of Mongo, Emperor of the Universe, and I have a disturbing premonition that he will reappear in one of the last poems I ever write, the waxed tendrils of his long moustache trailing doom at my deathbed. There's something about the name.

PEDAL POWER

Dates of show: 28 and 30 March 2008

I'm glad I've had a whole week to consider the questions raised by an inspired tabloid sting that caught Conservative leader David Cameron, on his way to work, cycling the wrong way up a one-way street as well as ignoring at least one red light. There is so much involved in this case that an instantaneous response would have been useless. Personal morality versus official responsibility, credibility versus hypocrisy, physical fulfilment versus the duty to reduce carbon emissions: all these things were in play from the moment that the red-top reporter got on his bike and started trailing Mr Cameron in the direction of Westminster, with the impending-chase music from *Bullitt* playing ominously on the soundtrack.

For the reporter, it was no easy job. He had a video camera, so he had to ride one-handed. He had to follow Mr Cameron through a red light and along a one-way street, going the wrong way. At any moment Mr Cameron might have stood on the pedals, calves globular, and streaked out of sight like a sprinter in the last hundred metres of the Tour de France. The reporter also had to be careful not to get run over by the car that might be following Mr Cameron on these cycling expeditions because there is no provision on the leader of the opposition's bicycle for his briefcase, official boxes, sandwiches and, apparently, shoes. Tory Central Office insists that no such car has followed the cycling Mr Cameron for some time now, but you never know when it might appear again.

I recognized the bit about the shoes. Though I myself am no longer a cyclist, at least once a week I walk all the way to my office from the railway station, cushioning my feet with an old pair of trainers. Behind me, at a respectful distance, comes a vintage straight-

8 Daimler shovelling the white smoke of burning oil as my driver, a retired Gurkha who was mistakenly allowed into the country by immigration officials under the impression that he was a terrorist, struggles with the slipping clutch. Beside him, on the front passenger seat, are my shoes. I always suspected that there was something wrong with this picture and now that I've read all the documents pertaining to the Cameron cycling case I can finally see what it is. From the viewpoint of credibility, one is vulnerable if one pretends to be a self-sufficient cyclist when there are actually two of one, the other being the driver at the wheel of the car carrying one's stuff.

But I can't think of any other rules I break as I walk to work. I don't even jaywalk, for fear of being knocked down by some high-echelon politician cycling the wrong way down the street after ignoring a red light. It's the flagrant flouting of the rules of the road that has got Mr Cameron into trouble. His apologies have been touching, if not entirely convincing. 'I have obviously made mistakes on this occasion and I am sorry.' Notice how he leaves the way open for the inference that there have been countless other occasions on which he has not made mistakes. Obviously he realizes he has bared his flank to suggestions that his present behaviour on the road when in charge of a bicycle might throw doubts on his future behaviour in 10 Downing Street when in charge of the country.

Here, I think he and his advisers might take courage from historical precedent. One of the things that made Queen Elizabeth I so great a ruler was that she regularly cycled to work. Her skill at riding a bicycle was kept a secret from her adoring public by the fact that her voluminous crinoline concealed the bicycle. To the common people, she seemed to be skimming along the ground at remarkable speed with her hands in her pockets and almost no expenditure of effort, thereby enhancing her reputation for unearthly powers. Another great bike rider was Louis XIV, who regularly cycled between romantic assignations with Madame de Montespan and Madame de Maintenon. At the peak of his cycling career he was able to get the time down to under ten minutes, so that either woman was able to convince herself that he had not been unduly detained by the other. His collection of bicycles was so extensive that he eventually built the Palace of Versailles to house them. When Cardinal Mazarin borrowed one of the king's bicycles without permission, he would have incurred the monarch's wrath even if he had not crashed making a tight turn into the Tuileries, his cassock riddled with broken spokes.

Mr Cameron's advisers should also draw his attention to the evidence provided by the comparative failure of heads of state and prominent politicians who did not cycle to work. When it was suggested to Napoleon that he should ride a bicycle to the Battle of Waterloo, he proudly refused, with disastrous results. He travelled by heavy coach, turning up hot and bothered a crucial few minutes late to be faced with the spectacle of the Duke of Wellington already in position and fighting fit, the duke having arrived at forty miles an hour on a Raleigh lightweight aluminium racing bicycle with a fully aerodynamic wheel-set and low spoke count. In America, General Custer was proud of his seat on a horse but not at all pleased with his seat on a bicycle. He found it impossible to make a cross-cut swing of the cutlass without slicing through the bicycle's front tyre. So at the Battle of the Little Big Horn he galloped rather than cycled into action, to be hopelessly outmanoeuvred by Chief Sitting Bull and half the Sioux nation all mounted on imported Suzuki trail bikes.

But back to reality, in which, we presume, Mr Cameron might want to go on riding his bike despite the dangers. I know I did. Among the many dedicated bike riders at Sydney Technical High School none had a bike to match mine. It had all the kit. It had the gear trigger positioned just under one of the brake handles so that I could change down in a flash when pounding my way up the hill on the far side of Kogarah Bay. It had the cheese-cutter saddle positioned high on its post so that I could steadily castrate myself while showing the maximum length of leg. There were no Lycra shorts in those days, civilization not yet having come to an end, but I rolled my ordinary shorts right up to give that bulging thigh effect that all true cyclists are convinced is so attractive, just as men whose heads rise from a purple lake of tattoos are convinced that their perfectly ordinary features have somehow been rendered more interesting.

Thus equipped and adorned, I cycled everywhere at blinding speed, my legs a blur as I wove in and out of traffic, diving dramatically past the driver's cabin of the school bus as all aboard put their hands over their eyes. A crash under a truck almost killed me and the sight of me in the casualty ward almost killed my mother, but nothing could stop me cycling for years on end, until the day I realized what was missing. I couldn't read while I rode. I tried it, but

when the Kogarah police caught me reading a novel by Erle Stanley
Gardner as I rode no-hands down Railway Parade I realized that the
game was up, and ever since, for about half a century now, I have
used public transport when I'm in the big city. For someone who
does what I do for a living, public transport is even better than a car.
You can't legally read in a car unless somebody else is driving, and
my Gurkha isn't always available to drive the Daimler, because he's
down at the immigration office being told why having risked his life
for Britain a few dozen times isn't enough to earn him permanent
residence or even a full pension.

So when I'm in London I ride the Tube and the bus, and I
imagine that Mr Cameron, too, is under pressure to forget about the
bike. He could answer that if he permanently nixed the car carrying
his shoes and just rode the bike with his shoes on, he would be doing
even less to damage the environment than if he rode on a bus, and
far less than if he rode in a car. But he might find it hard to convince
the Chinese of that. When and if Mr Cameron becomes Prime
Minister, he will be faced, as he travels by kayak across the globe from
conference to conference, with platoons of Chinese gerontocrat Party
bigwigs who all grew up riding bicycles but now wouldn't be seen
dead on a bicycle even though most of them, by our standards, should
be dead already.

Of the more than a thousand million people in China, a high
proportion rode bicycles until recently, but now they'd rather not.
They would rather go by metro or by bus, or, better than that, by
taxi, or even better than that, by car, preferably a car they own.
Nobody in the West is going to persuade China to find a way of
developing its economy without consuming energy. Even if we
reduced our own emissions to zero, the saving wouldn't amount to
much beside whatever a few hundred million Chinese do next instead
of riding bicycles. The reason for Mr Cameron to ditch the bike is
that he has things to do. He's been given a car so that he can work in
it. Riding his bicycle to work, all he can do is think, and he's already
made it evident that in such circumstances he can't think fast enough
to figure out what a red light might mean if he goes through it with
somebody taking pictures of him. Tony would have made Cherie sit
backwards on the pillion, looking out for spies.

Postscript

At that time, David Cameron was still forming his image. It was no easy task for a man whose puppy-fat features gave the impression that he was still forming his face. On the other side of the fence, Gordon Brown was all face and nothing but. British politics was never more clearly a case of a battle between images, with the points of substantial contention hard to detect. The public greeted this contest between cartoons with heart-warming indifference: reassuring evidence that in a modern democracy the *Führerprinzip* need barely flicker. But on each side, a little more definite personification of the governing principles might have been desirable. In my own house I was told that the Labour Party was marginally more generous with nursery care and therefore still to be preferred. Later on, in 2010, I was asked by several publications both in Britain and Australia to cover the British general election, but luckily I had become ill, and so could plausibly ask to be excused. I have no idea how I would have handled the job. Then as now, I couldn't tell one Miliband from another. But even with the economy in difficulties, it held such abundance that you actually had to be one of the poor to notice any overt worsening of conditions. Members of the middle class who, for the first time in their lives, found themselves unable to meet their bills, suffered in silence, as the middle class is wont to do, and anyway they often had relatives to help them where the state could not. The Gurkhas, on the other hand, had a detectably less certain access to the fountain of plenty. One of the reasons that Joanna Lumley emerged as a political heroine was that she was fighting a clear-cut battle. Had she heeded the siren calls to move up into real politics, we might soon have loved her a lot less. There was a man called Clegg, for example, who was almost as glamorous as the divine Joanna. But he preached the renunciation of nuclear energy, an initiative which, if realized, would remove the only possibility of the country weaning itself off fossil fuels without going bankrupt. Luckily he would never be allowed anywhere near the levers of power, would he?

As to the bicycle of my glory days, it has been returning to me more often in my day-dreams as the chances of ever riding anything like it again grow less. But I go on watching the Tour de France on television every year, and recently I wrote a poem called 'A Dream on Two Wheels', which, in its entirety, I print here for the first time anywhere.

> Contador should be the noun
> For anyone who makes the mountains melt
> And can still win sprints.
> From start to finish in the Tour,
> James was the Contador.
>
> Schleck should be the adjective
> For anyone who looks that cool
> And handsome going that fast
> For two weeks. James the Contador
> Has once again been schleck, indeed the schleckest.
>
> Wiggins is just a name.

TERMINAL TERMINAL

Dates of show: 4 and 6 April 2008

Early last week a body called Ofcom okayed the use of mobile telephones on airliners at any height above three thousand metres. Ofcom said it was up to the airlines to deal with any possible problems, perhaps through setting aside special 'quiet zones' on the airliner. As I read these assurances with due alarm, it struck me that such problems might well emanate from those of us who had previously lived in the hope that the whole airliner might be a quiet zone before we climbed aboard. Already we can hardly bear to travel on trains, owing to the prevalence of the kind of mobile telephone user, usually male, who proves his virility by talking at the top of his voice for the whole journey, a subject on which I may have touched in previous broadcasts, so let me apologize for saying it again: not a request you will often hear from a mobile-phone user.

On trains, some of us who do not use mobile phones have already gone vainly berserk in the effort to shame those who do into shutting up for a few minutes. Now, thanks to Ofcom, we would be entering a whole new realm of irritation where we would be hardly able to bear travelling on planes, and on a train you can get off at the next station and walk. On a plane you'll be getting off at Dubai with your hands locked around a mobile-phone user's throat. But someone in the tele-com industry was quick to reassure us that passengers on aircraft would be more likely to send texts or e-mails than talk on mobiles. He said, and I quote, 'Social norms, as well as excessive background noise, may dissuade most people from making phone calls in crowded planes.'

But I have already met Social Norm, and I know all too well that Social Norm never dissuades anyone from making mobile-phone calls. Social Norm is the one making the mobile-phone calls. The excessive background noise, on any form of transport, is made by a score of Social Norms shouting their thick heads off, and all it does is make them shout louder. I also invite you to note the abyss of misunderstanding that lay behind the telecom industry spokesman's contention that 'most people' would be dissuaded from making mobile-phone calls on crowded planes.

But surely unless everybody can be dissuaded, then it would take only one mobile-phone user to turn a long-distance flight into a journey through Purgatory. The thought of making my next business trip to Australia in the company of Social Norm and his mobile phone, not to mention his vociferous wife Social Norma and her mobile phone, was enough to make me wish that the whole business of flying could be brought to an end. It seemed too much to hope for. But then Terminal 5 happened.

Terminal 5 happened at Heathrow, where so many irritating things happen. Terminal 5 was meant to solve them. Still boiling about the lost bag that wrecked your holiday? Relax. Terminal 5 would have the most advanced bag-handling process known to science. Your bags would get through the terminal faster than you did. Passengers would be dumbstruck by an unprecedented level of efficiency, fully in keeping with the staggering beauty of a building which Lord Rogers had designed to express the full lyricism of air travel. All these things were announced before the building opened. A spokesperson for BA, or it could have been BAA, said, 'We want to give fliers an experience they'll remember.' A spokesperson for BAA, or it could have been BA, said that the new terminal would 'put the fun back into flying'. And they both got their wish, although not quite in the way they might have hoped.

Thousands of passengers got an experience they'll remember. Before the first night of the memorable experience was over, the beautiful ceiling designed by Lord Rogers had revealed its purpose: to entertain people who were lying on the floor, looking up at it. There was a shortage of chairs or benches, because why would they be needed, in a building that had been constructed for the effortless through-flow of multitudes moving almost as fast as their bags? But it was not only a memorable experience, like mumps, it was also terrific fun. The fun had definitely been put back into flying, or, in this case, not flying.

The most fun generated by the not-flying was had by those of us at home, who were watching the show on television or listening to it on the radio. It's the most fun I, personally, have ever had since the night the Millennium Dome opened, when the Director General of the BBC, who had been invited to the launch party of the biggest British marvel since the last marvel, turned up in order to pop his cork about being admitted late, whereas those of us who were actually watching or listening to the BBC were safe at home, sobbing with laughter and hugging each other while we passed the crisps. Whether or not we should enjoy such bungles is a question easily settled. If we're in them, we hate them, and if we aren't, we love them. Already too afraid of meeting Social Norm on any plane I might happen to catch, I was deep in a soft couch and ideally placed to relish the Terminal 5 spectacle, first of all in the broadcast media and then later on in the newspapers, where the headline act was about to appear.

I won't name her, because she is only twenty-nine years old, and when all this blows over there is still time for her to start a new career in some less-demanding field. But on the weekend in question, the weekend when things went terminal at Terminal 5, she held the position of BAA's Head of People and Change. The word 'change' bulks large in management speak, a tongue in which nobody ever asks what is being changed to what, but only whether or not change is happening, change being a good thing in itself, or else how could somebody be Head of Change, not to mention of People? The Head of Change and People said, with all the confident wisdom of her twenty-nine years, 'Our policy has been to create the context for change, then to apply changes within that context.'

Well, since that could mean anything it probably means something, and by now, after decades of people in management talking tripe, it is too late to expect that what someone in management says will happen will have any relation to what actually happens, even if it happens as it was supposed to, which in this case it didn't. We can only presume that at least a few of the people who speak this kind of high-flown abstract poetry have some awareness of the prose reality that lies beneath, and that the Head of People and Change will take her lessons with her when she moves smoothly on to her next position as a planning officer in atomic waste disposal, preparatory to her elevation to the peerage.

Can Britain still do what the French call *le grand projet*, the big project? But of course it can. Britain does almost the whole of Formula One, for example, one of the biggest big projects in the world. It's a matter of management, but that means real management, not management speak, which is a different thing: can-say instead of can-do. I'd be surprised if the standard of British planning didn't go up after this: it could hardly go down. All the planes will fly again, bearing the voice of Social Norm to every corner of the world, and I'll be glad enough to catch one next time I want to go somewhere. I'm going deaf anyway, and very soon Social Norm will be just a moving mouth.

And Britain should give itself credit for being hampered by civilized limitations. The people around Heathrow who protest at every new expansion of the airport would probably be outnumbered by the people who would protest if the airport went somewhere else. When the French planned their high-speed rail system, the arguments went on for years about how much land should be subject to compulsory purchase, but eventually the builders got their way. In Britain it would be harder, and finally there's something to be said for a country where anachronism still has a value. After all, what's so great about the opposite?

To the assembled minds of Ofcom, it seems obvious that the airlines should move with the times, and let mobile phones onto the planes, thus to remove one of the last vestiges of silence. But Ofcom doesn't rule the country yet. Neither does the Queen, really, but at least she's allowed to be old-fashioned. President Sarkozy and his ultra-chic wife looked pretty impressed with that when they sat down to dine at Windsor. No doubt the First Usher of the Mobile Telephone was lurking somewhere nearby, but they never saw him. They might have been lucky not to.

When they arrived in Britain for their state visit, the French royal couple landed at Heathrow. They were fortunate that they didn't arrive at Terminal 5 on the weekend, in which event Carla's suitcases might have been arriving in Windsor about now, and she would have had to do the whole visit in one frock. She would have looked fabulous even in jeans, but there are more important things than glamour. There are more important things than efficiency, although it's seldom wise to say that you're going to set new standards of know-how and then prove that you haven't got a clue. But Carla knows all about that. When the Duke of Edinburgh asked her how she could change outfits so often without losing track, she said, 'My policy is to create a context for change, then to apply changes within that context.' But she said it in a whisper, and hardly anybody heard it except him.

Postscript

When I wrote and recorded this broadcast I had not yet realized that it would be transmitted only once, instead of twice. It went out in the usual Friday night slot but the Sunday morning slot was cancelled because it was Easter Sunday. Thus I lost two million out of three million listeners, and was no better pleased than Adolf Hitler would have been if told that the speech scheduled for tomorrow night in the Sportspalast had been relocated to a kindergarten. I didn't precisely hit the roof, but I did a lot of skulking in dark corners. When I calmed down I realized that I had become spoiled. But I had better reasons for wishing that more people had heard me on this topic. As well as being a wonderfully amusing snafu in itself, the Terminal 5 debacle was a prime example of a peculiarly modern phenomenon. In days of old, the function of PR was to cover up the cock-up. Now, PR was causing the cock-up.

Nothing had really gone wrong with the new terminal except its marketing. Not very much later on, in what was really a surprisingly short time, Terminal 5 was working well. But almost no stories were written about that, and there was not a single television programme. One consequence of the modern vastness of the media is built-in vacuity: since the supply of talent is by miles overstretched, there are few journalists who can make any kind of story out of things going well, so there is no voice for normality, and everything is described in term of challenge, crisis and time running out, even the manufacture of a Persian rug. But a hack can improve with time, if he watches his own behaviour. When I was younger I might not have spared the feelings of the young lady carrying the title of Head of People and Change. It's not so much that you get nicer with age. It's that you begin to realize that common courtesy is your actual subject. If civilization is what a commentator is talking about, he should try to embody it in his style. It isn't easy, though, because history is made in the heat of the moment, and by the time it cools down there are fewer people to listen. Hence the tendency to go on banging away at a topic in the hope of keeping it alive. Terminal 5 cooperated long enough to spill over into my next broadcast.

RIGHT ON THE MONEY

Dates of show: 11 and 13 April 2008

Charlton Heston died last Saturday. He was a pillar of conservatism and there were many who despised him on that account, but before we get to that, let's consider some other news that broke about the same time. The Royal Mint, it was announced, has redesigned the coinage. The Royal Mint was suddenly a news story.

The first astonishing thing about the story was that the Royal Mint is still called the Royal Mint. You would think that by now it would have been rebranded as Mint™, in line with the way that the Royal Mail became Post Office™ so that it would be fully streamlined for its upcoming task of closing its own branches. But no, the Royal Mint is still called the Royal Mint. It now proves, however, to have other means of moving forward into the permanently transitional era that Post Office™ has already occupied.

The Royal Mint's mode of embracing the future is to take those old coin designs that did nothing except to tell you what they were worth and turn them into works of post-modern art. This raises the question of whether there are any limits to the extent to which art should influence everyday life. You might have thought that this question had already been answered by British Airways. Long before BA's participation in the recent and ongoing Terminal 5 launch happening – a multimedia event which has reinterpreted the connection between passengers and their luggage – BA turned the tailfins of its aircraft into display areas for modern paintings.

Though the BA PR brains who conceived the tailfin art initiative were convinced that their handiwork vouched for the nation's thrusting creativity, the travelling public made it clear that they felt safer in an aircraft that had no visible connection with an art gallery. There might be an art gallery in the city that the passengers left, and another art gallery in the city they were flying to, but they didn't want to be in an art gallery as they flew between art galleries. Correcting the error cost almost as much money as committing it, but eventually things were put back more or less the way they were. If turning the coinage into an art gallery similarly proves to be a mistake, it's going to be harder to find the money to correct it, because this mistake is being made *with* the money.

So far there is no mention of turning the banknotes into Picassos – a possibility that would certainly not have appealed to Picasso, who was a keen collector of banknotes in all denominations, but who preferred them to look as traditional as possible. The coins, however, will be turned into small works of art, and post-modern art at that. In other words, they will deconstruct traditional concepts of coin design. The Royal Shield of Arms will be broken up into pieces, one piece per coin across the range, thus providing us with a comment on the shield's previous unity, while releasing new possibilities of the asymmetrical and the unexpected. The young winner of the Royal Mint's design competition, one Matthew Dent, aged twenty-six, has himself put the purpose of his breakthrough into words: 'To intrigue, to entertain, and raise a smile.'

It's been argued that foreign visitors to Britain might have trouble with the denomination of coins that do not feature any numerals, only words. But as a foreign visitor who *can* read the words, I have to say that I'm having my troubles too. I have studied the designs closely, and so far I am intrigued only in the sense of wondering how on earth this latest case of the fidgets has been allowed to get so far, and I am entertained only in the sense that a previously dignified nation's ability to commit cultural self-mutilation is getting beyond a joke, and I am smiling only in the sense that if I laugh aloud it hurts.

Most of this adverse reaction will surely pass. When I get the actual coins in my hands I will no doubt be intrigued enough as I occupy some of my spare time in Terminal 5 trying to fit the bits of the Royal Shield of Arms together. Fitting round coins together so that they form the appropriate square picture sounds like a task for a particle physicist, but it could be intriguing to try. And it might be entertaining for my granddaughter when I explain to her that the various fragments of design add up to a decontextualized commentary on an obsolete symbol which has been simultaneously retained and rendered ironic, a bit like Thomas the Tank Engine. But I'm afraid my smile can be raised no further. It's becoming a fixture, and I've started seeing it on the faces of other people too. It's the smile worn by anybody who can't help wondering why there is such a passion for changing anything stable at a time when instability can be relied on to rise like an unstoppable tide. It's practically the only thing that *can* be relied on.

We might have predicted that Naomi Campbell would throw a luggage-related wobbly in or near Terminal 5. After all, almost everybody else did. But would you have predicted that some of the young men planning what they called 'martyrdom operations' designed to wipe out hundreds of people over the Atlantic wanted to invite their wives along for the ride? Neither would I. We might have predicted that Madonna would take her BlackBerry to bed so as not to miss the chance of making an important note about the mysteries of the Kabbalah, but would you have predicted that a sex worker in a Chelsea basement bordello would have captured the activities of one of her customers on a camera built into her bra? Would you have predicted the bra-cam? Neither would I. Yet after we read about these things, suddenly they seem normal.

They seem normal because abnormal happenings happen at such a rate that they cease to be differentiated. It remains true, of course, that if you weren't plugged into the news you would miss the full force of this tumult of innovation. But a lot of it would still get to you even if you boarded up your windows, and the same would be true if you could be magically transported to ancient Rome. In fact it would feel worse. That was why the ancient Romans had so many gods and temples. It was because the flux of the arbitrary was so overwhelming. What's new about us is not just that so many things alter, but that we give so much leeway, and even honour, to those who pride themselves on altering what doesn't even need to be altered.

America is the great land of permanent innovation but nobody tries to revamp the money, and indeed the Americans go on minting one-cent coins even though it costs more than a cent to make each one. Andy Warhol painted dollar bills but if he had been allowed to design a dollar bill it would have been an intrusion of art into reality that would have devalued art and reality, which are separate things, neither of which would be interesting if they *weren't* separate. When a chair features in a cubist painting by Picasso, it can intrigue, entertain and raise a smile. Look, there's one leg, and there's another, and there's the bit you sit on. Even my granddaughter will realize that it's brilliant, when she's old enough to grasp that the thing and the picture of the thing can be fascinatingly different.

But Picasso, though he painted cubist pictures of a chair, still wanted a non-cubist chair he could sit on, just as he wanted money that told him where it came from, and how much it was worth: money which, no matter how carefully designed it was, still left the actual art to him. Since his death there have been stamp issues in both France and Spain that carry reproductions of some of his most wonderful pictures, but never while he was alive did anyone dream of asking him to redesign the coinage, and if anyone had he would have packed his bags and left immediately for some country where the philistines were still in charge of the mint.

There are things that need to stay the same because everything else doesn't. This attitude is sometimes called conservatism, which finally brings us to Charlton Heston. In his later years he wanted to conserve the second amendment to the constitution, which supposedly guarantees the right of private citizens in the US to own guns. People who want that amendment changed thought he was dangerous. I myself sympathized much more with them than with him. There is such a thing as an institution that needs to be abolished, because it is no longer any good. But there are other institutions that need to be kept. Some of those are obviously vital, and even those that might seem not to be can still have the inestimable value of providing us with a hand-hold in the storm.

Earlier in his life, Heston was a radical who wanted another constitutional principle conserved: that all are created equal. One of the tallest white champions for civil rights, he marched for justice in the open air and could easily have been shot by one of the people whose right to bear arms he later strove to protect. His memory should be respected for trying to conserve a principle so important. He's more likely to be remembered for trying to conserve the gun laws, because he did that more recently, and only the recent counts. But that's the very reason for trying to conserve things that are neither plainly crucial nor obviously noxious: just recognized parts of a civilized existence, and not to be replaced without adding to the uncertainties of which we already have a surfeit. You could call them the small change of life. There was a case for decimalizing the coinage. But for turning it into a jigsaw puzzle? Save us.

Postscript

One of the things I love about the essay form is the chance to introduce a few examples of fax'n'info, as it was called in my boyhood. Ideally the item of fax'n'info should be illustrative but also open up another field of interest, thereby enriching the texture. (A good rule for prose is: the shorter the piece, the more it should seem to have in it.) Note, in the piece above, the cunningly timed appearance of Picasso. Perhaps I should have equipped him with white shorts, a horizontally striped matelot shirt, and three lightly clad odalisques dancing in the background, but what I wanted to emphasize was his deep and lasting interest in money. He not only died rich, he set about getting rich quite early in his life, and even when leading the apparently carefree existence of a young bohemian he was a diligent student of his prices and the state of the art market. It never hurts for the idealistic young – I fancied that there might be a few of these among my listeners – to hear that their pleasant dreams of justice can't be fully separated from the cash nexus. Or rather it *can* hurt, but the pain is salutary. Unless he makes a subject of his own early death, a genius needs money to keep going. The whole of civilization needs it, which means that one of the first things a civilization needs to produce is prosperity. Even an unusually canny mastermind like Picasso, however, can embody this principle in his own behaviour and yet still be clueless as to its truth.

I didn't have room to tell those same young idealists that Picasso had been one of their number. Although he was the kind of communist who disguised his limousine as a taxi in order not to arouse class resentment, a communist he was. The fact that his personal tastes were in utter and irreconcilable conflict with his professed beliefs never bothered him. Some men, even great men, need time to grow up, and there are cases when the very greatest never grow up at all. On the whole we forgive them if they are painters; forgive them less if they are musicians; and forgive them least if they are writers. That final reluctance to forgive is because the writers put the lie into words, where the young might believe it, as if the text were transmitting a particular truth instead of expressing a general view of life. In music or a painting there is nothing to believe, only something to hear or see.

LEGAL DILEMMAS

Dates of show: 18 and 21 April 2008

At a time when Iraqis who have risked their lives for Britain in Basra need a newspaper campaign to be allowed into this country, the radical cleric Abu Qatada apparently can't be allowed out. The case of Abu Qatada might have been designed as an extreme test for the principle that the rule of law must be put before our feelings. My own feelings on the matter are quite clear. I feel that Abu Qatada should be locked up in a suitably padded cell with a television set he can't turn off, the television set showing nothing except one episode after another of *Big Brother*.

So perhaps it's lucky that I am not in charge of enforcing the law. Undoubtedly my chosen method of dealing with Abu Qatada would be a form of torture. Since the law is against torture and I am too, another set of feelings enters the picture to confuse my first set of feelings, which turn out to be not as clear as I thought. My first feeling that Abu Qatada, clearly a menace to all Muslims as well as everybody else, should somehow be made to vanish, is complicated by my second feeling, which is that he should not be rendered up to a government whose promise to refrain from torturing him is compromised by the fact that officers of its prison system have tortured people before. That sounds like an untrustworthy promise.

So to my mind, increasingly feeble instrument though it is, there is a dilemma. Abu Qatada has a record of preaching the desirability of doing unlawful things. But there is no lawful way of getting him out of the country. There might not even be any way of withdrawing the considerable amount of money his extended stay here has so far cost us, through the benefits system that he didn't hesitate to invoke even while preaching death and destruction against all the workings of liberal democracy. So we are stuck for an answer, and, as people tend to do when they are stuck for an answer, we change the subject. If we can't deal with him, who *can* we deal with?

Well, we can deal with people who have done less, or done nothing. At this point, Sir Vidia Naipaul handily makes himself available. Getting in ahead of the biographies that will reveal all after his death, Sir Vidia has cooperated with a biography that reveals all while he is still alive. Thus we have it on his own authority that he behaved badly to the three women who have shared the greater part of his working life. It isn't a story that inclines me to share a drink with him, not that he is likely to ask me. But he has confessed to nothing unlawful and so far most of the reviewers of his biography have stressed the importance of separating the man from the work.

The *Independent*'s formidable journalist Yasmin Alibhai-Brown, however, was not minded to do so. She avowed her intention of not reading anything by Sir Vidia ever again. Like anyone who has ever taken tea with Yasmin Alibhai-Brown, I have a lot of respect for her powers of argument. Three rounds with Buffy the Vampire Slayer would be a more comfortable encounter for her opponent. Were we to take tea again, however, I would attempt to raise the same question about Leo Tolstoy, Ernest Hemingway and Bertolt Brecht, all of whom, when it came to their treatment of the women who loved them, left Sir Vidia looking like a therapist. Has she stopped reading them?

And in Sir Vidia's invidious case, the women could always have told the genius to go chase himself. None of them did, and it seems fair to assume that they put up with him because they thought he was an important man. Yasmin the Naipaul Slayer takes a lot on her shoulders when she declines to think the same. It's possible that she got carried away by the relief of being able to discuss a clear-cut issue. I don't think it is, quite, but it's certainly a lot more clear-cut than another issue that she has been facing lately with a bravery that must be a tax on the nerves.

Yasmin Alibhai-Brown hasn't given up on her warnings about the injustice of marginalizing Islamic citizens of Britain. Nor should she. But she has also continued warning Islamic citizens against extremists. The price she risks paying for this is to be called racist, even though racism is the very thing she is arguing against, because the extremists really *are* racists. But among her fellow journalists there are all too many who are ready to employ the word 'racist' against anybody, even a Muslim, who calls for the great majority of law-abiding Muslim citizens to explicitly condemn extremism, instead of just tacitly disapproving of it.

Non-Muslims who agree with her, of whom I am one, can only help to earn her the title of traitor from some Muslims, even though we vocally believe in religious freedom, cultural pluralism and every other fruitful complication that makes for a living society. It takes equality before the law to ensure all that, but you can be called a racist for saying so. And of course there are non-Muslims who don't believe in religious freedom one bit and yet they might be keen to give her their unwanted endorsement as a convert to their intolerant cause. Clearly she has the courage to face these possibilities, or she would not have spoken. But she is stuck with a dilemma.

It must be a whole lot easier to recommend that the books of Sir Vidia Naipaul should not be read. There is a dilemma in that too, however. It's just not so easy to spot. But if we embark on a course of not reading books written by all the people we don't approve of, we risk missing out on valuable knowledge about the world. Not just in his great novel *A House for Mr Biswas*, but in his subsequent volumes of non-fiction, Naipaul told a lot of awkward truth about the backwardness of the culture he came from, and the new creative energy in Bangalore today partly depends on the awareness – an awareness he helped to encourage – that there is such a thing as an historical dead weight that only creativity can overcome.

It's only a few years since the British poet Philip Larkin got the Naipaul treatment. It happened after his death instead of before, but there were similar calls for his books not to be read. In his collected letters he had revealed himself to be a racist, a misogynist, and a lot of other kinds of 'ist' that nobody sensible could admire. But in real life he would rather have drunk water than be discourteous to anyone of any race or gender, and he also wrote dozens of the most magnificent poems to have graced our literature in modern times. They're magnificent not just because they are lyrical even in their despair, but because they register the real world, in all its complexity. Poetry like Larkin's, and prose like Sir Vidia's, is still the best safeguard we've got against the rage for simplicity, the total view that wants to achieve a false peace by silencing everyone who might contradict us.

Or it would be the best safeguard, if the law wasn't even more important. Without a structure of reasonable law, art can do little to shape opinion. And there are no laws, however reasonable, that do not produce dilemmas. I don't think China should ever have been awarded the Olympic Games. That having happened, I don't think the British section of the torch relay should have been allowed any scope beyond a single lap around the Millennium Dome while the Chinese security heavies were locked up for re-education in Raymond's Revue Bar. But that's just what I think. Less than that, it's merely what I feel. The law allowed a torch relay. Luckily it also allowed demonstrations in protest. The reason that protests should not be violent is that the law disallows violence, not that it disallows protests. You can't help wondering, though, whether some of the young people all over the world who think they are helping the oppressed people of Tibet by embarrassing China really have any idea of what China has been doing to Tibet over the last half-century.

When China intensified what it called the peaceful liberation of Tibet, the world hardly cared. Anyone who knew about it also knew that there was nothing they could do. The Dalai Lama persuaded the United Nations to make some resolutions but China ignored them. The Dalai Lama got a better hearing from Richard Gere. Tibet's fate was news outside China but the news made few waves. Inside China, Tibet's fate was never news at all. Inside China there was no news except news controlled by the state, and there was no law that applied, so there were no dilemmas. If the Chinese leadership had ever been faced with their own equivalent of Abu Qatada they would been in no doubt about what to do with him.

Our best hope for China now is that it is has entered a new stage where dilemmas will be possible. A dilemma is the surest sign that the rule of law exists. By that measure, China started coming back from the dark in 1978 when the Chinese people were invited to read wall posters about the Four Modernizations that would make China an advanced society. A student called Wei Jingsheng wrote on the poster that none of these four modernizations would mean a thing without a fifth modernization, democracy. He was thrown into jail more or less for ever, but they didn't kill him. Occasionally he was even allowed out, until he said something untoward and they threw him back in again. His first short break from jail happened in 1993, when China was bidding for the 2000 Olympics. In 1997 he was deported to the US. Perhaps this year the Chinese will ask him back, to carry the torch into the stadium.

Postscript

Since I didn't see any prospect of sweeping away a whole religion, and didn't even think that a very good idea, I stuck with my argument that the real task, with regard to the Islamic minority in Britain, was to protect it from its own extremists, if necessary by encouraging the mass of law-abiding Islamic people to separate themselves from any of their religious leaders who had trouble understanding the general implications of the message that Allah is merciful. Esteemed contemporaries such as Richard Dawkins and Christopher Hitchens preferred to believe that religious extremism is a product of religion, and will be a menace as long as religions exist. I didn't believe it. Religious extremism is a product of extremism. It's a disposition. Systems of belief can undoubtedly exacerbate that disposition but no amount of rationalism can entirely eliminate it. The kind of man who wants to deal with an insubordinate daughter by cutting her to pieces would want to do that whatever form of worship he favoured, and would still want to do it if he worshipped nothing at all except the knife in his hand. Multiculturalists who, in order not to offend the Islamic culture, wished to soft-pedal any criticism of repressive behaviour by Islamic men towards their women – the perverted concept of 'honour crime' was the most conspicuous example – were thus making what the philosophers used to call a category mistake.

But it was easy for me, speaking from the bleachers, to push that line. For Yasmin Alibhai-Brown it was more difficult, so I tried to give her credit for her courage. Nobody should ever underestimate the sheer amount of physical danger waiting to be unleashed. In 2010, in Blackburn, some young Muslim male dimwit recruited three other young Muslim male dimwits to help him in the task of firebombing his sister, who had 'dishonoured' the family by breaking free of a husband she had not chosen and falling in love with someone who more closely resembled a mentally functional human being. The four dimwits firebombed the wrong house, wiping out a couple who were entirely innocent: not that the daughter had ever been guilty of any crime under British law. Despite all the usual protestations put up by the local 'community' about the supposed requirements of honour, the four dimwits were tracked down, tried and found guilty. The trial lasted six weeks; keeping them in jail will cost more than sending them to Eton; and the total expense will probably end up exceeding the annual bill for running a Trident submarine. One thinks automatically of a deterrent, but of course there is none: except, that is, the law of the land, strictly applied. To do them credit, Lancashire Constabulary were unequivocal on the subject, pursuing the miscreants without fear or favour and never employing the word 'honour' without qualifying it with the compound adjective 'so-called'. If only the media could do the same.

Those of us who have managed to grow out of our religious faith might think that we are left with the question of whether we want the same outcome for everyone. But we are getting ahead of ourselves, because the capacity, if not the need, to have faith of some kind tends to linger. I myself am well aware that I am professing faith when I assume that prosperity will bring justice. It might not. Under Hitler, the German population recovered its lost prosperity but a hideous injustice was part of the price. It still seems fair, however, to call anyone a dreamer who thinks that there is a natural justice to be found in poverty. Wealth has to be created before it is shared. That puts Bangalore ahead of most of the subcontinent when it comes to the potential for, if not yet the actuality of, social fairness. It was instructive that the Bangalore IT tycoons instantly saw the desirability of investing wealth by giving it away. It took Bill Gates a large part of his lifetime to reach that conclusion. Early on he was too busy.

INSTRUCTIONS TO THE SEA

Dates of show: 25 and 27 April 2008

Kevin Rudd, the Prime Minister of my homeland, Australia, covered himself with glory early this month by telling the Chinese leadership that China's behaviour in Tibet raised human-rights issues. He said that Australia recognized China's sovereignty over Tibet, which you might think was still an issue in itself for some Tibetans, but at least he had said something. He said it in Mandarin so that the Chinese couldn't mistake his meaning. He sent another message, in English this time, by means of British journalists to whom he entrusted the warning that Australia would not tolerate the idea of the blue-suited Chinese security heavies who accompany the Olympic torch actually doing anything about security when the torch passed through Australia. They could model their blue suits, and that would be it.

Put these two messages together and they added up to something the Chinese could understand, even if they didn't like it. Liberal in the best sense, this clarity of voice was especially welcome at a time when, back in Australia, Mr Rudd's celebrated Summit, with a capital 's', was producing at least one suggestion that didn't sound very liberal at all. Mr Rudd's Summit is billed as a meeting of all the best minds in the country to decide what policies Australia should adopt next, Mr Rudd's own party apparatus having apparently neglected to think of any during their eleven years out of power.

It seems that at least one of these minds has decided that any Australians who are deemed insufficiently eco-friendly should have their citizenship withdrawn. Speaking as one who might very well fail to meet the criteria of eco-friendliness – I used power tools to build my windmill – I could be a candidate for withdrawn citizenship. The proponents of this initiative have not yet said what will happen to those whose citizenship gets withdrawn, but in the event of a resolution that they be deported, I am rather glad to have deported myself already.

Mr Rudd has not bound himself to any proposals that might be agreed on by his Summit talking-shop beyond a promise to take them under advisement. But the possibility that at least some of the best minds might be talking illiberal tripe must have struck him already, so it's a relief to find that he has talked turkey to the Chinese. Not all of the turkey, perhaps, but as much of the turkey as can usefully be talked without a threat to intervene in some way against Chinese government policies, which would be a task beyond even the combined ingenuity of Australia's best minds.

When we come to the question of Zimbabwe, things get harder, and precisely because in Zimbabwe's case an effective intervention looks a bit less impossible than giving instructions to the sea. Economic sanctions, for example, might work, even in the face of Mr Mugabe's time-tested capacity to pass any imposed hardships along to his increasingly impoverished people. In September last year Mr Gordon Brown published an article in the *Independent* in which he indicated that Britain was the second biggest donor to Zimbabwe's relief funds but might not continue to be so if Mr Mugabe did not relinquish power. Mr Brown also said that as far as he was concerned, if Mr Mugabe was present at the upcoming EU–Africa summit then he, Mr Brown, might have to be absent. Mr Brown's feelings were clear enough, but as a call to action they have been somewhat clouded by his later exhortations that the world must do something.

By the world he apparently means all the nations that have condemned Mr Mugabe's reluctance to let go. In this case, however, it isn't at all clear that the world can be said to exist. The world only partly includes South Africa, for example. To their credit, the South African courts have put a stop to the Chinese ship-load of small arms heading for Zimbabwe, small arms which Mr Mugabe might well have employed to influence those who have voted against him already and thus ensure that they would be less ready to do so next time. But the President of South Africa, Mr Mbeki, has still not told Mr Mugabe that it's all over.

This reluctance can only encourage Mr Mugabe's apparent conviction that it isn't all over. Similarly, alas, the UN has so far offered little beyond an assurance that it will supply observers and helpers for a new election, or a run-off for the old one, or whatever the event might be called. But everybody knows that there has already been an election and everybody suspects that Mr Mugabe lost it. If that were not so, Mr Mugabe would have announced the result.

So we are in a condition where everybody suspects but not everybody says. That still gives Mr Mugabe room to believe that the time has not yet arrived when he must deport himself to somewhere else in the world and end his life in poverty. For indeed there are people abroad who think that Mr Mugabe never stole anything and that it is racism to say that he did. According to them, Mr Smith's white government stole everything, and then the white farmers who stayed on in Zimbabwe stole everything again, and all that Mr Mugabe ever did was take it back, stealing from the rich to give to the poor. They are rather stuck, though, with the question of how he contrived to make the poor even poorer.

Still, even while waiting for the world to unite on this issue, Mr Brown comes out looking determined. It hasn't been an easy fortnight for him, because the best minds on his staff decided that it would be a wise move for him to visit America at the same time as the Pope. The Pope arrived in a large aircraft supplied by Alitalia and Britain's Prime Minister should have arrived in a large aircraft supplied by BA. But BA had no spare aircraft, only a mountain of spare luggage left over from the Terminal 5 triumph. So Mr Brown arrived in America in a charter aircraft and cut the kind of figure the British press strangely most likes to report on: the British leader being outshone by any other leader.

It's true that Tony Blair used to be harder to outshine. But Mr Brown also faced the problem that the Americans not only agreed with him about Zimbabwe, they had already spoken out even more roundly. Secretary of State Condoleezza Rice had called Mugabe's regime a disgrace, and even Mr Bush, putting two and two together and getting the right result for once, had concluded that his chosen honest broker, Mr Mbeki, had not done enough brokering. From that, you would think that Mr Mugabe would have had the tactical sense to identify the US as the No. 1 enemy of his regime. After all, everybody else blames America for everything. But Mr Mugabe – and this is almost a source of pride – continues to blame Britain. The awkward thing, however, about Britain being placed first on the dictator's list of villains is that it also places on Britain the onus of action.

What should the action be? I wish I knew. This week my website got a letter from a citizen of Zimbabwe who no longer lives there but would clearly like to live there again. He said some nice things about an article I had written in favour of the Palestinians' desire for their own state, and how a policy of indiscriminate suicide-bombing could only ensure that they would never get it. On the strength of my analysis, which he agreed with although he had never been to the Middle East, he asked me to write something about Zimbabwe before it was too late. Well, I've never been to Zimbabwe, and even if I had, I doubt I could write anything that would affect the course of events to even the smallest degree. But I feel obliged to have an opinion, as we all do. Just imagine the kind of courage that it would take to vote against Mr Mugabe all over again, and try not having an opinion about that.

My opinion about Zimbabwe, far from being original, is pretty much the same as Mr Brown's opinion. I have been following Mr Brown's statements of policy with care, not as if my life depended on them, but as if the life of my desperate correspondent from Zimbabwe would depend on them if he were still there. I think I can see what Mr Brown is after. He is trying to send a message to anyone in the political class in Zimbabwe who is fearless enough to realize that there is a better chance of the aid money being sent in if Mr Mugabe is sent out.

In the absence of a united world, which can only mean the armed force that the UN has conspicuously not yet mentioned, there is no other kind of intervention available except a promise of hard currency to supplant a currency which inflation has turned to liquid mud. To promise that, and to promise that Zimbabwe can't have the aid money until Mr Mugabe takes off.

Where he goes to is a separate question, and less important. Where do we go, we deported ones who have been stripped of our citizenship for capital crimes, eco-negligence in my case, the wilful destruction of his own nation in the case of Mr Mugabe? There's always somewhere. Idi Amin, now a mere memory, never faced justice in Uganda. He faced it in a hospital in Jeddah, Saudi Arabia, not far from the Sands Hotel, where he had spent the last years of his life finding out that no matter how much money you steal from your people, it can't buy you immortality. Omnipotence, yes, but only for a time, and Robert Mugabe's time has come. All we have to do is get him to agree. Hence my message to my correspondent from Zimbabwe, whose friends are still there to face whatever happens next: good luck to them, and I only wish that they could depend on us.

Postscript

For Westerners to dismiss Africa's problems as insoluble is a bit glib, when you consider the extent to which the West caused the problems. Even today, with Western liberal sensitivity at its height – the sensitivity and the knowledge tend to be inversely related, but let that pass – few among even the most appalled foreign commentators on Africa's colonial history are fully aware of what Belgian colonialism was like in the Congo at the time of Leopold II. If they were, they would have a much less condemnatory attitude towards British colonialism. But when all the allowances are made, we are left with the depressing fact that few of the sub-Saharan countries have done well since their exploiters went away. The new leaders, the *wabenzi*, have often done well out of exploiting their own populations, but that's a different thing, and a very different kind of wealth. An economy whose fruits are embezzled by the government and exported to Western banks will very soon be no economy at all, and the same might be said for any African country whose finances depend on aid. But no matter how blatant the present corruption, the departed oppressor still gets the blame. Honour among thieves makes it mandatory to support the perpetrator and accuse the phantom. At the time of writing, Robert Mugabe still bulks large in Zimbabwe. There is a tacit worldwide conspiracy among the *bien pensant* to suppose that his wings have been clipped, but it might be wiser to suppose that, if he has retained only some of his power, the power that he has retained is the power to wreck the lives of his people. He has a taste for doing so, and always has had. In his quest for unchallenged power, white people were not the first people he murdered.

What to do about Africa's disaster? The first answer, surely, is that there might be nothing we can do. The assumption that one's emotional concern might be valuable in itself was the assumption that drove Mrs Jellyby to her charitable absurdities. With that first answer firmly given, the second answer can be better understood: we can give money. But we need to be certain about where the money is going. Michael Moore, at one point, was loudly giving forth the opinion that Africa could have clean water overnight if only the criminally negligent West willed the means. The truth was that even for something as apparently simple as clean water the means must begin with double-entry book-keeping, otherwise all the money will be stolen. In many of the stricken nations, the government is the last organization you should give money to, and you have a better chance with some faith-based outfit whose prayers you would rather not hear but whose immediate pastoral aims you approve. My own course of action – the reader has a right to ask – was to give a few pounds for the education of women in Ethiopia. The project was in the hands of Catholic missionaries whose sense of dedication seemed to chime with my own conviction that Africa would get nowhere until its women were treated justly. I was assured that girls, and girls only, would be going to the school I backed. Then it turned out that boys were going there too: yet another illustration of the abiding truth that Africa isn't there to fulfil your dreams. It just sometimes looks as if it is.

Australia, on the other hand, really is dreamland: a democracy with proper elections. But the properly elected Kevin Rudd was already showing signs of a Hugo Chavez-like belief in his own supreme mental powers. Marking the start of his reign, like a jamboree for egos on the rampage, his personally convened Summit was one of the signs. It wasn't so much that most of the proposals advanced by the thousand delegates were fatuous where they were not insane. It was the fact that Rudd, joining in the discussion, sat on the floor, so that the press could catch him looking involved. For the discerning, here was clear evidence that Australia had elected, for its Prime Minister, an incorrigible poseur. Well before the end of his one and only term, everybody knew. But to know it early on, you had to be able to assess what was before your eyes. Remarkably few could. Even more disturbing than what the journalists couldn't see was what they couldn't hear. Rudd's use of language, hyperbolic from the jump, should have tipped them off that he didn't really mean what he was saying. He spent three years saying that man-made global warming was the biggest moral threat to face mankind. Speaking like that, he could have been the *Guardian*'s science correspondent. Everything depended, said Rudd, on an agreement being reached in Copenhagen in October 2009. When it wasn't, he came back to Australia and never mentioned the matter again. The electorate caught on and his support in the polls dropped into the basement. Finally even the media realized what his silence signified: he had never really meant any of that stuff. It was an unsolicited oratorical display, from a man devoid of reticence or judgement.

SNOOP AND AMY

Dates of show: 2 and 4 May 2008

When the American rap star Snoop Dogg gets into trouble, he goes from strength to strength. When the British singer-songwriter Amy Winehouse gets into trouble, she goes from weakness to weakness. This is especially sad because, whereas you might think that Snoop Dogg has a talent from hell, Amy Winehouse clearly has a talent from heaven. Already it has earned her millions of pounds, so you might say that her worries are working in her favour. But even the press is by now realizing that it's callous to say so.

Last weekend a voluntary visit to the police turned into an overnight stay and the story was instantly in all the papers, but there was a new note detectable, as of a farce finally being recognized as an incipient tragedy. If there was ever any fun to be had from reading about her troubles, the point has been reached where there is no fun left even in writing about them. Probably the best we can all do for her is not to mention her name except when buying one of her albums, so perhaps I am making a bad start. But I remember too well the first time I heard her sing and was so moved that my heart hurt.

And I also remember the first time that I saw her in real life. It was last year, in downtown New York. We happened to be staying in the same hotel, and I passed her in the foyer. She looked so frail that my heart hurt again, but in a different way. When that young woman sings, it's the revelation of a divine gift. But when she behaves as if the gift were hers to destroy if she feels like it, you can't help thinking of divine wrath. Can't the same force that made her so brilliant give her strength?

Which brings us to the aforementioned Snoop Dogg, who has all the strength in the world. Whether he is brilliant is another question, which I don't presume to answer. As a lyricist who has made no more than a few hundred pounds over the course of a whole career, I try not to speak ill of any lyricist who makes thousands of pounds a week, even when I can't understand what he is talking about. In Snoop Dogg's case I'm not sure that I'm meant to. At about the same time that Amy Winehouse was emerging from a police station again to be greeted by demands from her own father that she be sectioned as soon as possible, Snoop Dogg was being cleared by a British judge from a no-visa order imposed on him in 2006 when there was a dust-up at Heathrow, that venue where so many memorable performances take place.

You will notice that I continue to refer to him as Snoop Dogg. It's easier than calling him by his real name, Cordozar Calvin Broadus. I hope I have pronounced it correctly. I'm not one to point the finger, because I myself found it convenient to abandon my unpronounceable original name, Balthazar Wickerwork Bruce-Barrymore. Nor do I hold against him his self-confessed earlier career as a pimp. As any female sex worker will tell you when she has a knife to her throat, pimps perform a useful function.

Anyway, he grew out of it, and became famous as a rap star. You can see, however, that the rapper's reputation might have been against him when he and his entourage were told that they were to be demoted from the Heathrow VIP lounge to life among the ordinary people, whereupon a fracas ensued and Snoop Dogg found himself face down on the carpet, an audience unresponsive to his charm. Subsequently he was denied a visa, despite his assurances that his purpose in this country would be to warn against private firearms, and not to glorify them. The rapper took the rap.

But recently a senior immigration judge overturned the decision, after viewing a tape of the incident. Those of us who don't like to be videotaped wherever we go might reflect that in this case a videotape served justice. Upon close inspection, the tape revealed, according to the court, that some of the staff involved might have been at fault. One can't help feeling that a rapper's reputation for condoning violence might recently have been overtaken, on the scale of notoriety, by the reputation of Heathrow staff for doing the wrong thing on a massive scale at every opportunity.

Nevertheless, Snoop Dogg deserved a hearing for his contention that one of his reasons for wanting to be free to enter Britain would be to counsel this country's disaffected youth against guns. Snoop Dogg's argument is that he has seen a lot of people blown away and that the use of guns by ordinary citizens should therefore be discouraged. There is no reason for thinking that he does not feel this now just because some of his lyrics previously seemed to say the opposite. When I listen carefully to one of his songs – a lot more carefully than I would like to, if the truth be told – I seem to hear him say that he's from the streets and he hangs with killers, by which I think that he means that he hangs out with killers, not that he suffers capital punishment in their company.

In the next line he seems to be saying that if he and his killer friends got problems then they're gon' bust them triggers. I think that means that they are going to fire so many shots that they wear their guns out, but it could just mean that they intend to voluntarily decommission their weapons. Or it could mean anything, it's hard to tell. I'd be surprised if it meant anything conspicuously non-violent, but we must remember the artist's right to invent a character. It might be just the narrator talking, while the man who invented the narrator is a philanthropist. Charles Dickens, after all, invented Bill Sykes. Dickens wasn't himself a psychopath, and Snoop Dogg could easily argue that he is fundamentally a businessman.

He's certainly got the money to prove it, and if people are going to be shut out of this country for once having seemed to condone violence, I can think of a long list of candidates that I would put ahead of Snoop Dogg. Whatever his street-smart origins, he has become a prosperous taxpayer manufacturing a legitimate product people want. It isn't a product I want. Watching someone making gang-signs at me with his fingers while his snarling mouth confuses loquacity with eloquence was tough enough when Ice T did it. But Ice T turned into one of the best actors on television, and Snoop Dogg, if he manages to dodge all the drive-by shooters who were stupid enough to take his lyrics literally, will probably end up with his face on Mount Rushmore.

And then there's Amy Winehouse, whose best songs really are works of art, no question. And she can actually sing them to you, in a way you would rather remember than forget. And yet she looks as if she can't wait until it's all over. Billie Holiday, by the end, had reasons to feel like that. But at the start, she guarded her gift. And Ella Fitzgerald sang on into old age as if her gift belonged to the world, which indeed it did. Amy Winehouse, if she wished, might build up an achievement that could be mentioned in the same breath as those two: perhaps not as varied, perhaps not as abundant, but just as unmistakably individual, and even more so because some of the songs would be composed by her, and not just handed to her on a piece of paper.

It could be that she does wish to fulfil her vast potential, but she has another wish that conflicts: the wish for oblivion. It's hard to speak against that wish without sounding like an advertisement for a package holiday. As this world goes, there are ample reasons for wanting to be out of it even if your personal history is a comfort, and I imagine hers has been the opposite. But she knows all this. The proof is in some of her songs. The proof is in her voice. You don't get to sing like that unless you can give a shape to grief.

Not long before he died last week, Humphrey Lyttelton said that he admired the way Amy Winehouse sang and would have liked to meet her. Some commentators have wondered what he would have said. There's no telling. He was the prince of joy, and he might have told her that he was glad to have lived out a long life in music. The Old Etonian would surely have admitted that he had begun his career in conditions of privilege, as she had not, and that he had always had the gift of happiness, which she plainly hasn't, or anyway does not have yet.

But he could have added that he only had to listen to a few bars of her singing to realize that she had been given the greatest gift a musician of any kind can have, and that a gift on that scale is not possessed by its owner, but does all the possessing. Maybe that's what she's afraid of. When people say that you have a duty to your talent, they all too often mean that you have a duty to them. But they're misstating the case. The duty of the greatly talented is to life itself, because what they do is the consecration of life. I could end with something that Pavarotti once told me in his dressing room before I interviewed him. He wouldn't say it on air, for fear of sounding immodest. He said he knew his gift was from God. But perhaps a better ending would be what Philip Larkin said to the ghost of Sidney Bechet. 'On me your voice falls as they say love should, like an enormous yes.' Come on, kiddo. Give us a song.

Postscript

Snoop never did get round to writing a lyric on the theme that anyone who would kill for 'respect' had the brains of an amoeba. But he was already too busy graduating to the status of film star, a rank which any rap artist was eager to attain, for the obvious reason that rap music could last just so long as a fashion before the market realized that it had only novelty value, like the hula hoop or bits of string with coloured light in them. Amy Winehouse, one need hardly say, was on a different track. A greatly gifted singer bound for glory if she wished it, she could be stopped only by her inner demons. Unfortunately they were very resourceful. For a while they could depend on the press for an ally, but it must be said that the British press coverage showed signs of restraint when it became clear just how sick she was. In fact she got less coverage than Lindsay Lohan. Perhaps (and I don't really believe this, I just hope) there was a general realization even among the press hacks that Amy was carrying a precious cargo, which might still be saved. Finally, with the popular singers, what matters is their ability to convince you that they sing the way you would like to speak. That strangely familiar quality – strange because it seems to be already inside your head – can survive anything except physical damage. Matt Monroe's voice, as purely conversational as Frank Sinatra's but with even better control of overtone, could hold your undivided attention even when he was wearing a brown safari suit. Similarly, Amy would be able to thrill you if she had to sing through the window of an isolation cell. But not if a poisoned blood-stream ruins her throat.

*

Amy Winehouse died while this book was in the final stages of preparation, but I could have rewritten the postscript had I wished. Somehow it seemed wiser not to. Left as it was, it was at least a record of how one of her admirers had felt about the danger she was putting herself in, and of how much we all stood to lose. Brought up to date, it would have been a claim to prescience. The truth is that I thought she could still be talked out of it, if enough people could combine to persuade her that there were rewards waiting for her even more satisfactory than those offered by intoxicants and narcotics. Alas, she was short of ambition. So I left what I had written as it was, as a kind of wreath. Several times in my own lifetime I have seen people with great talent destroy themselves, and on top of my professions of regret I have always asked their retreating shades the same silent question: couldn't you have left me some on the way out? Poets, you sad young men, what you have to ask yourself is how you can make your voice as thrilling as hers.

GAFFES

Dates of show: 9 and 11 May 2008

Step forward anyone who has never made a gaffe. But that very instruction would be a gaffe if you delivered it to an audience of people in wheelchairs. You would be in the same verbal slide-area as President Bush, who instructed a press correspondent to stop hiding behind his dark glasses, and it turned out that the correspondent was clinically blind. But really President Bush is in the same verbal slide-area as us. We all make gaffes when speaking impromptu, and the only remarkable thing is that we don't do it more often.

The American presidential election is still six months away and judging from the current coverage you would think that the outcome was going to be decided by gaffes. In the mini-election still being fought out between the Democrat contenders Hillary Clinton and Barack Obama, most of the news between contests in the individual states is provided by whether or not either candidate has made a gaffe lately.

As they were bound to, because both the contenders are human beings, the gaffes keep coming, although with nothing like the copiousness of the press attention which is devoted to them. Admittedly some of the gaffes sound revealing. Hillary Clinton really shouldn't have said that she once landed in Bosnia under sniper fire when she didn't. Nor should Barack Obama have said that ten thousand people died in a Kansas tornado when the real number of deaths was ten. The most that these supposedly revealing gaffes revealed, however, was that either of these two senators can get carried away, just like you and me, although you and I will never be called upon to stay cool in the Situation Room.

Senator Clinton apologized for her gaffe later and Senator Obama corrected himself almost immediately. And really most of their gaffes are on that comparatively small scale. Obama has got himself in a real tangle with his ties to a preacher who proclaims that AIDS was an invention of the US government to victimize African-Americans. Obama's repudiation of those ties came late, but that wasn't a gaffe, it was a strategic error, probably arising out of loyalty. In declining order of importance, a true gaffe reveals an unfortunate underlying belief, or ignorance, or an inability to choose words. That last kind of gaffe is normally the most frequent, but even by so trivial a measure there have been remarkably few gaffes from the main players in this fearfully long run-up to the presidential election. Perhaps they have all learned a lesson from the reigning world-champion gaffe-maker, who is still in the White House.

President Bush was thinking on his feet when he composed the poetic masterpiece 'Families is where our nation finds hope, where wings take dream.' But President Bush already had a solid track record of talking like that before he got anywhere near the White House. Clearly those who voted for him thought it didn't matter, because they approved of what they took to be his underlying beliefs. There are whole books of Bushisms available and I won't indulge myself now by picking the plums. The most radiant examples have been routinely quoted in the newspapers for years on end, yet few of them are totally impenetrable. You can usually tell what he set out to mean before the English language got its remorseless hands on his throat.

If you don't like what he set out to mean, of course, it's easy to argue that his twisted language is the expression of a twisted soul. Either way, his gaffes long ago ceased to tell us anything we didn't know. What they continue to do is tell us what *he* doesn't know. The general impression, to put it as politely as one can, is of a lack of historical awareness that ranks President Bush several rungs below President Reagan. With the help of his busy staff, Reagan made a gaffe in Germany in 1985, when he wished a peaceful rest to the German soldiers buried at Bitburg. Despite repeated warnings, somebody had neglected to note the significance of the fact that a contingent of the buried soldiers had once belonged to the SS.

Reagan's detractors ran a mile with the story, but in fact it was inconceivable that Reagan had a morally neutral attitude towards Nazism, and he visited the Bergen-Belsen memorial shortly afterwards, making his feelings clear. His feelings always had been clear: it was just his language that wasn't. He subsequently made a much more important, because much more revealing, gaffe, when he assured Israeli leaders that he had never forgotten the scenes he witnessed when the extermination camps were liberated. But he forgot to say that he wasn't there. He was in Hollywood at the time, where he must have seen the footage, but the effect of his statement was to give a false impression, like Hillary saying that she had landed under sniper fire. Those, if you like, are the gaffes that count. But Bush has made few of those. And he is not even the all-time American champion of verbal inadequacy. The standards were set for ever by a name now remembered for nothing else, T. Danforth Quayle.

Younger listeners might need telling that Dan Quayle was Vice-President of the United States during the administration of the current President Bush's father, George H. W. Bush. George H. W. himself was no master of cogent speech. When his writers gave him a word like 'vision' he would go on television and start talking about 'the vision thing'. Luckily for him, Dan Quayle took most of the heat by never wavering in his capacity to reduce the English language to a heap of twitching wreckage. Sometimes there were complete sentences. One of them was: 'If we do not succeed then we run the risk of failure.' Another was: 'We're going to have the best-educated American people in the world.' And then there was: 'The future will be better tomorrow.'

In all those cases, you could tell roughly what he must have meant. But he went beyond that, and especially when talking about America's future in space. Something about space excited Dan Quayle. 'It's time,' he said, 'for the human race to enter the solar system.' There were scientists listening and they couldn't figure it out. It was still some kind of sentence, though. Quayle was at his most creative when he got beyond the structure of a single sentence and embarked on a free-form excursion that sometimes ended where it started but facing in the wrong direction. As I hold on to my temples with both hands, let me quote you an example. 'My friends, no matter how rough the road may be, we can and we will never, never, surrender to what is right.'

And yet, and yet. Even with Quayle at his John Coltrane-like heights of dissonant improvisation, you could hazard a guess as to what he roughly might have meant. What we were listening to, with emotions ranging from disgust to sheer delight, was the sound of democracy. If you have a choice between speakers, some of them will speak better than others, but it isn't always the elegant speaker who has the competence for office, and quite often the best-qualified candidate is at a loss for words. If verbal bumbling seems to be more prevalent all the time, it is mainly because the newspapers now miss nothing. Until the end of World War II, when tape recorders arrived, reporters would neaten up what they heard when they wrote it down in shorthand. But President Eisenhower was already a victim of press precision when he was not yet even a candidate. He was still commander of Allied Forces in Europe when he addressed his troops thus: 'Do not needlessly endanger your lives until I give you the signal.'

With his verbal handicap already widely recognized, he went on to become a President whose fitness for office was never in real doubt. Inevitably he was mocked for some of his decisions, but nobody thought that his tangled syntax proved him a fool. And indeed all the evidence suggests that Churchillian phrase-making has never been an advantage in American politics. JFK was meant to be the exception, but I never much liked a too well-balanced rhetorical exhortation like 'Ask not what your country can do for you: ask what you can do for your country.' It sounded manufactured, and in fact it was, by a speechwriter.

Borrowed or not, JFK's eloquence didn't stop him foolishly invading Cuba, or ignoring the CIA's advice and putting US military personnel on the ground in Vietnam. I preferred the bumblers. When Nixon temporarily forgot his own wife's name and said 'America can't stand pat', at least it was a human moment, proved by the depth to which he blushed as soon as he said it. If Nixon had really been the perfectly calculating Machiavellian, he would have made no gaffes at all.

The threat now isn't from the public figure who makes gaffes, but from the pumped-up media coverage that gives the gaffes disproportionate attention, or even manufactures the gaffe. President Bush's real achievement in the gaffe area is so mountainous that you would think it unnecessary to add anything artificial, but it happened when he appeared to say that he thought Nelson Mandela was dead. That wasn't what he meant. He only meant that there were no Nelson

Mandela figures left alive in Iraq because Saddam Hussein had killed them all.

What Senator Obama really thinks about race relations in America can be deduced from a thoughtful speech which can be read in its entirety on the web, which is already proving a valuable supplement to the press. When we can read the whole speech we will be less likely to be swayed by the soundbite. That even goes for President Bush, who wasn't being entirely foolish, just sounding like it as usual, when he said, 'You never know what your history is going to be like until long after you're gone.'

Postscript

I might have gone a bit easy on Hillary Clinton, whose gaffe about landing under sniper fire really amounted to a lie. She should have caught herself in the process of editing the truth to boost the effect. It's something that almost everybody does, at least on a small scale, and if only to make themselves momentarily less boring. Tony Blair, before he became Prime Minister of Britain, told stories of how he had been some kind of irrepressible runaway rebel in his childhood. Later on he was stuck with the stories, and had to pay the price in embarrassment when reporters checked timetables and found out that he hadn't run anywhere. Luckily he was not the kind of man who could be much slowed down by embarrassment. Nor was Ronald Reagan, whose mind worked like the successive drafts of a movie script, always looking for the most dramatic presentation of a scene. But he was rarely trying to inflate his own importance: he was just trying to be entertaining. There is a clear difference between that mild degree of elaborating the truth and the utterly fantastic self-promotion gone in for by the supposedly distinguished British current-affairs anchorman – dead now, for a mercy – who claimed to have flown in the Battle of Britain, when he would have had to do so in short trousers. Most of us get over the *Billy Liar* kind of lying when we are caught at it once too often in the school playground, but there is always the danger of a relapse, and there are people who base their lives on promoting a fiction. The old man with the chest full of unearned medals is a familiar figure at the memorial service. He might even, if put to the test, have proved quite brave in real life, but for some reason real life was never good enough. Hemingway, who was at least as brave as any lion but could never stop proving it, wore military decorations to which he was not entitled. He was not as canny as William Faulkner, who, when people assumed that he had flown in combat, kept modestly silent, instead of vocally proclaiming the truth, which was that he had not. Those who improve on the truth are always role-players, and are therefore most at home in showbusiness, a field in which scarcely anyone on the creative side is genuine for long. But role-playing in politics is as dangerous as role-playing in a hospital, where the doctor who claims to have a degree in anaesthesiology had really better have one.

2008 – SERIES TWO

HOW RICH IS RICH?

Dates of show: 31 October and 2 November 2008

I hope I'm not stepping on Daniel Craig's toes if I let it slip that I'm being considered to play the starring role in the next James Bond film. It's going to be called *Parabola of Solicitude* and the script is on my desk in front of me now. I have no problem with the action sequences. At one point Bond has to run up the side of the Washington Monument before punching a fatal hole in a helicopter full of Chinese assassins but the stunt double can handle that, just as he will have to handle the bit on page three where Bond is described as getting up out of an armchair suddenly. I don't do 'suddenly' any more but I think the producers know that. Nor do I have any problem with the sex scenes. Bond has been slower off the mark in that area lately and I know just how he feels.

In fact the script seems to contain no sex at all except a mention in the last scene of an old woman who applies for a job cleaning Bond's flat and she turns out to be the granddaughter of a hotel receptionist he knew quite well in Havana during the Spanish–American war in 1898. No, my problem with *Parabola of Solicitude* starts with the villain. He's a Russian oligarch called Oleg Garkov and he couldn't be more boring. It's not just that his plan to destroy civilization is boring. The plans of Bond villains to destroy civilization have always been boring: the stolen atomic bombs, the microwave satellite, I mean, save us, but don't hurry. Now that we know that within ten years there'll be nothing left of the inhabited world except a few hundred thousand windmills sticking out of the ocean, where's the threat in diverting the water supply of South America? Every Sunday night at home before the bins are collected on Monday morning I get accused, by my assembled family, of destroying civilization by not paying enough attention to separating potato peelings from excess plastic packaging. Who *isn't* threatening to destroy civilization?

According to the script, Oleg Garkov's plan is to hack into the command console of the world's central recycling centre and un-recycle the whole globe's garbage with a program of advanced software devised by the Graeco-Croat body-building computer genius Spyros Virus, a part which I understand has already been offered to Madonna, who might well be available. But the boring thing about Oleg Garkov isn't his plan. The boring thing about Oleg Garkov is his character. He's a super-rich Russian, and the whole world has at last realized that nothing could be more boring than that. I don't mean that being Russian is boring. What I mean is that being super-rich is boring.

By excitable journalists, being super-rich could be made to look glamorous until recently, but when the global financial crisis got under way the penny dropped. Or to put it another way, the entire world economy dropped, leaving us all facing the question of how much is enough. A closely related question is how much is too much, and not even those journalists who were previously fascinated by people with big yachts are any longer quite convinced.

It was a wonder they ever were. Nobody with any brains has ever stayed on a yacht an hour longer than necessary. Even the owners of yachts, if they have sufficient money, are careful to purchase yachts big enough to carry helicopters and submarines, accessories with no other purpose but to enable them to get off the yacht as often as possible, leaving their guests imprisoned. There is nothing to talk about on a yacht except the last meal or the next, and one rule is inflexible: the bigger the yacht, the smaller the library, until you reach the point where the yacht is too big for any harbour but has no books on it at all. Quite often there are paintings of great value, but they are only there so that they can slide upwards for the screening of the latest Bond movie. Finally the owners of yachts believe that there is a level of luxury where the life of the mind becomes irrelevant. But for anyone who values the life of the mind, the life of the senses has its limits, and anyone who believes otherwise will be the worst company in the world. On a yacht, you're stuck with them unless you can book a seat on the helicopter or the submarine.

When we cluck disapprovingly at politicians who are keen to be the guests of people who own yachts the size of battleships, our objection shouldn't be to the possibilities of corruption. David Cameron is impressed by Rupert Murdoch's influence, and why not? After all, Tony Blair was, and there will always be a reason for a politician to sit down beside a media magnate. But what's alarming is that David Cameron seems also to be impressed by Rupert Murdoch's yacht. A politician is in a desperate position if he is attracted by the way the rich live, especially when they decide to live afloat. If the Russian oligarchs have managed to hold on to some of their money even in current conditions, maybe our politicians can find out how to do the same on behalf of the rest of us, so George Osborne of the Tory Party and Lord Mandelson of the Labour Party might have had good strategic reasons to brave the mild Mediterranean waves on the teak deck of a Russian host. But heaven help both of them if they get the urge to live like that.

Not that anybody's asking them, as they lie back in their deck-chairs, to reject the idea of a refined life furnished with goods of high quality. After World War II, the best of the Labour politicians knew what the gentry had but wanted the working class to have it too, and they were right. Any state that tries to eliminate the idea of gracious living will eventually impoverish everyone except pirates. That's where the Russian oligarchs came from: the ruins of a social structure. Here in the West, in the old order which democratic politics made more just but sensibly did not destroy, the aristocracy and the middle class shared the belief that the things to own should be well made in order to wear well. That belief survived as a principle: good shoes are expensive, but they last longer, so they cost you less. It was a principle that could be abused, mainly through snobbery. Julian Fellowes, who wrote the brilliant script for *Gosford Park*, got the whole attitude into a jam-pot when he gave Maggie Smith, playing a grand guest in a grand house, her snarling drawl of disdain at discovering that the marmalade on her breakfast tray had been bought instead of home made.

By those standards, which are really an assertion of unearned superiority, belonging is such a hard test that ostentation can seem like an escape from it, a blazing act of defiance. But the trouble with ostentation is that it looks awful. Somebody who wants a gold bathroom suite is probably helping to keep a lot of gold-miners employed, and he might even be enjoying an exalted bathroom experience, but he looks ridiculous, like King Midas with his pants down. Saddam Hussein had gold bathroom suites in all his palaces, most of which he rarely visited, and now the Iraqi government has put his yacht on the market. Apparently it needs to be redecorated, but the gold bathroom fittings are still in place.

Simplicity can be overdone. Warren Buffet, one of the richest men in America, washes his burgers down with cherry cola. Try not to be there when he belches. But there is such a thing as a reasonable sufficiency, a concept which depends on the realization that although it's good to be well off, there's more to life than just wanting to be better off than everyone else. And anyway, you can't win. The Russian oligarchs are nowhere beside the kind of Arab prince who has a Boeing 747 all to himself. One of them has just ordered an Airbus A380. What's he going to do on that thing, play polo? Even the President of the United States has to share Air Force One with the press. He, or it might be she, isn't allowed to get rich in office, and presumably wouldn't want to. Whether Democrat or Republican, the next President will serve the people, and we are right to find the upcoming election infinitely more interesting than even the most extravagant display of personal wealth.

It will be a contest between two views of society, but they are not views of two different societies, they are two views of the one society. The Democrats want more distribution and the Republicans think that if there is too much distribution there won't be enough to distribute. Both parties, I think, are correct, and that's exactly what makes the conflict so fascinating. The election will probably turn on the question of which candidate is thought more likely to restore the American economy, on which so much of the world's material welfare still depends. That's why we all behave as if we had a vote. I speak as someone who is comparatively well off, or at least I think I am. Never having had the desire to buy a yacht, I still have some money in the bank. What I'm not absolutely sure of is whether the money is worth anything. That's why I'm considering going back to work. The best James Bond ever was George Lazenby, and maybe it's time for another Australian in the role. But the script needs a more formidable villain. Couldn't he be a British Labour peer with a sinister smile and uncanny powers of resurrection? And we need a new title: *The Man Who Resigned Twice.*

Postscript

Somebody wrote in with the information that George Lazenby wasn't the best James Bond at all, and that I could say so only because I, too, was an Australian. Well, yes: that was supposed to be the joke. (Radio has the same limitation as the telephone: the tongue in your cheek is invisible.) The Russian oligarchs, despite my admonitions, continued to dominate the scene, making steadily more extravagant gestures such as buying the *Independent*. One of them eventually bought the London *Evening Standard* and turned it into a free-sheet. When the economic crisis came it was remarkable how few of the rich had to pull in their horns. I was pleased to have an excuse for mentioning *Gosford Park*, whose script by Julian Fellowes was a little miracle of precise social notation. As his novels reveal, he grew up in the stratified atmosphere of grand houses and carefully graded snobbery. The world is different now, and many notes are missing from the music. But sometimes we long to hear it, especially when depressed by the extent to which vulgarity has taken over. Vulgarity, like the mob, is the detritus of every class. Gold bathroom fittings are on the same social level as *Big Brother*, whose heroines, lost in their foam-bath dream of luxury, always purr least raucously when the tap they turn with their painted toes is made of gold, or seems to be. But Saddam Hussein's aureate palaces were not just glaring evidence that he had no taste. They were also glaring evidence that he had been stealing the oil-for-food money, and that those countless children who had supposedly been deprived of medical aid by the ruthless sanctions of the West had really been deprived of it by him. The case being so clear, it was instantly forgotten by the Western media, lest the public conclude that Saddam had deserved to be toppled by force.

CHANGING THE GOVERNMENT

Dates of show: 7 and 9 November 2008

Hands up if you can remember the year in which Hu Jintao was elected. Don't worry, there are more than a billion Chinese whose hands aren't up either, because Hu Jintao wasn't elected, or anyway he wasn't elected by them. He just emerged, by a mysterious process taking place somewhere within the only Chinese political party that counts. Nevertheless the fiction of elections is maintained, even when the reality doesn't exist. It's a kind of lip service, a tribute that un-limited power pays to justice, just as hypocrisy is the tribute that vice pays to virtue.

As we begin the long process of absorbing the news that Barack Obama has just been elected to the presidency of the United States, we might reflect on the importance of the word 'election' itself, and what it signifies. In China it signifies little so far. In the United States the word 'election' signifies so much that President George W. Bush had to serve out the whole of his first term under the shadow of the accusation that he might have won office only because the Supreme Court put a stop to a recount in Florida. A great deal of what President Bush did, or didn't do, in office will eventually be forgotten. The world might even forget what he did, or didn't do, in Iraq, if, as now seems likely, that country turns into one that has regular elections of its own. But few Americans will ever forget the hanging chads of Florida. They sound like weird flowers in the Everglades but they were in fact tiny bits of cardboard that might or might not have deprived Al Gore of the presidency and handed it to George W. Bush. No American will ever forget the hanging chads. In America, an election is as important as that.

Much of the twentieth century was turned into a nightmare by countries where elections didn't exist, or were rigged if they did. In the old Soviet Union there were elections of a kind, but every member of the Politburo was always elected unanimously, after which those very same members unanimously elected Stalin, or any of his successors until the regime fell apart. Hitler was democratically elected, but he made it his first business to ensure that the electorate could never choose again. If only all that was all over. But now take a country like Zimbabwe, where Mr Mugabe called an election only after attempting to terrorize everyone who might vote for someone else. A lot of brave people voted for someone else anyway, so he ignored the result and proposed another election. By maintaining the fiction, he was saying the fact was important.

Any election that can actually depose a government fulfils the minimum requirement of democracy, by which no oligarchy can count on maintaining itself in power, because the electorate might decide otherwise. Being replaceable won't automatically guarantee that a government will behave well. It might try to restrict freedom. But if it isn't replaceable it will always try to restrict freedom. A government should be certain that it has been elected, but never certain that it will be elected again. All kinds of benefits flow from that uncertainty. The next government might review the behaviour of its predecessor. With a free press on the case, it is harder to act in secret. This relative openness might not seem much of an advantage until you remember what its absence is like. Since the clamorous defeat of its militarist regime in World War II, Japan has been a democracy, at least to the extent that its Prime Minister is no longer appointed by the armed forces. The armed forces, in fact, must now answer to the government.

Last week we saw an example of that, when the air force chief of staff got the sack after going public with his private opinion that Japan was tricked into World War II by the United States. The same opinion is held by the great American essayist Gore Vidal, to whom I defer for his prose style and general brilliance; but I have always thought that in this matter he was out to lunch. More important here, the Japanese government also thinks that such an opinion is a dangerous denial of Japan's imperial history. There have been several Japanese Prime Ministers, including the current one, who have been personally slow to condemn Japan's military adventure in Asia. But not even a Prime Minister is free to say what the air force chief of staff said. There is an official policy which can't be unilaterally contravened by anyone. This official policy came about through democratic discussion, which sets a limit to how far people in office can impose their private opinions on everybody else.

The same is true in Israel, the only democracy in its region if you don't count Iraq. In 1995 a young right-wing zealot called Yigal Amir murdered the Prime Minister, Yitzhak Rabin. Many liberals both inside and outside Israel thought that Rabin was the most important Israeli alive, because he might have brought a peaceful settlement of the Palestinian issue. Unfortunately that was exactly what Yigal Amir was afraid of. In a non-democratic country he would have been quickly dealt with, but in democratic Israel he is still alive. Last week some enthusiasts from a couple of the Israeli television companies tried to fix it so that Yigal Amir could broadcast from his cell. The mere attempt drew a predictably mixed reaction from the Israeli public. Whatever you think of his right to be heard, you have to concede that there is something to be said for a system in which such a controversy can take place. Only a democracy would put up with the embarrassment.

In the long eye of history, the outgoing American administration will have to answer for what it did to hide the embarrassments that might have been better examined in the open. I speak as one who would like to see if Dick Cheney, who said that waterboarding might occasionally have something to be said for it as a form of persuasion, could have stood the treatment any longer than my friend Christopher Hitchens, who at least volunteered for it. But that's a personal dislike on my part. On a public scale, among Americans, there is wide preference for plain dealing, where all that matters can be seen happening. Only democracy can even begin to provide this. Let's take, finally, the story of the Three Men of Colour, a title I just made up. But I didn't make up the characters. In my own country, Australia, an Aborigine leader called Noel Pearson has emerged as one of our most acute political commentators, whose opinions on how justice can best be delivered for Aborigine people are required reading in Canberra. It could only have happened in a democracy. Born and raised in Britain, Lewis Hamilton last weekend became the Formula One motor-racing champion of the world, an achievement which will bring such financial rewards that he will probably decide to go on living in Switzerland. But his rise to supremacy against all odds could only have happened in a democracy.

And in the United States, Barack Obama, long before his election, said that his story could have happened only in America. You might say that something like it could have happened in any free country where so gifted a man grew up with the chance to exercise his brains and charm, but he was right to remind us that black people in America had a long way to come since the days of slavery. Without democracy, it never would have happened. President Truman routinely used the 'n' word in private, but he struck the biggest blow for black emancipation since Lincoln. Truman was told about the black soldiers who had come back from World War II only to face violence from white thugs, and Truman felt compelled to say that it could not go on. And so the long process towards justice took a further step.

Precisely how justice can be achieved in a democracy is a big issue. But we can be certain that there is never much justice without democracy. It gives the people a chance to tell the government what to do as well as vice versa. After Truman, the much mocked drawling cracker Lyndon Johnson did a good deal more than JFK for black voter registration in the South. But what really counted was what the black heroes did. And in the week of Barack Obama's triumph we should remember, as he has always remembered, not only Martin Luther King but the black women who moved out of the back seats on the bus, the seats that were reserved for second-class citizens, and took their seats in the front of the bus, the seats that had been traditionally reserved for the white folks. It was only a few short yards from the back of the bus to the front, but there were white people who wanted to kill those women for travelling the distance. Their courage was boundless, but now the new reality they created seems so normal that their names are not much remembered.

Yet their spirit was there in Barack Obama's speech of acceptance. And what was almost equally inspiring, it was also there in John McCain's speech of concession. McCain is a man with a sense of history. He would have been a worthy successor to a man who spoke as if he didn't know that history had ever happened. But perhaps President Bush could think what he couldn't say. McCain, however, knew how to say it. He quit the stage not just with personal dignity, but in a style that gave dignity back again to the democratic process, which is the true wealth of America, and much more important than the economic wealth that will undoubtedly return. When the speeches of the winner and the loser equal each other in their magnificent generosity, you can only bless the moment. The euphoria won't last. If it could, it wouldn't be euphoria. But democracy will always be democracy, as long as the leader who takes power knows that one day it must be given back.

Postscript

In the communist world, lip service to elections first became conspicuous after World War II, when the Party apparatus in the satellite countries of Eastern Europe had developed the means to ensure the same 100 per cent results that prevailed in the Soviet Union. In the early days of each satellite country, it was customary for the Communist Party to make a show of tolerating other parties, claiming for itself only the Ministry of the Interior. But the Ministry of the Interior controlled the police, and in the brief course of time the police controlled public opinion. My fleeting mention of Iraq's new status as a democracy still passed for provocative boldness at the time. Although the likelihood of civil war had begun to retreat early in 2007, almost two years later much of the supposedly progressive media in the West would still have preferred it if Iraq had torn itself apart. Until at least a year too late in the day, the *Independent* had the headline IRAQ SLIDES INTO CIVIL WAR set up and ready for use. Whatever you had thought of the legitimacy or otherwise of going to war with Saddam's regime, it seemed a daunting aberration for Western intellectuals to be either claiming that Iraq had not become more free or else, if they conceded that it had, wishing that it had not.

Later on, in 2009, the admirable Noel Pearson published a little book called *Radical Hope*, a treatise written in his characteristically transparent, rhythmic and evocative prose which goes to the heart of the argument about the position of Aborigines in the country that once was all theirs. For reasons that defy logical analysis, but can only be ascribed to a collective obtuseness on the part of the editorial board, all writings by Pearson were left out of the gargantuan anthology *The Literature of Australia* (2009), whereas every uninspired polemic by any other Aborigine at all was put in. Political advance can take a long time to work its way through a culture. The advance of liberal opinion on civil rights from Truman through Kennedy and Johnson to the measure of equality that America knows today was a slow process, but at least it happened. Had there been no democracy, there would have been no advance. It should be obvious. Unfortunately it isn't. An American resident in the UK wrote in to remind me, correctly, that Johnson was no cracker: he was a good ol' boy. I have left the mistake in the text to remind myself that one should always be careful of American idioms, just as American writers should always check to be reminded that the Albert Hall is the place, whereas Albert Hall is just a chap.

ROBIN THE HOOD

Dates of show: 14 and 16 November 2008

Britain's most successful director of Hollywood films, Ridley Scott, has plans to give us a new version of *Robin Hood*. In earlier news about this project, it was suggested that Robin Hood would be the bad guy and the Sheriff of Nottingham would be a fair-minded administrator whose central role would be reflected in the revised title, *Nottingham*. This prospect was greeted with derision in some quarters. But I, for one, welcomed the news. In these broadcasts I have been stressing the importance of lawful institutions and here was a sign that the message was sinking in. At the very least, I had caught a mood. People are learning to distrust the image of the rebel and have begun to favour the ideal of the responsible official.

Later news from Hollywood, alas, reveals that Ridley Scott might already be starting to equivocate. The wobbling Ridley is now outlining a scenario in which the Sheriff is indeed a responsible official who invents the first equitable tax system, but Robin may not be a mere hoodlum, Robin the Hood, out to wreck a good man's plans. Robin will be a social democrat who contributes a critical overview in a responsible manner. But he will still do so in a raised voice. The antagonism of old will still apply, even if Russell Crowe, as has been rumoured, plays both roles. For Ridley's latest blockbuster, *Body of Lies*, now in the cinemas, Russell Crowe put on a lot of weight in a hurry. I myself possess the same talent but I've always admired how quickly Russell can do it. He should certainly be in shape not only to play both Robin and the Sheriff, but both of them on screen together when the scene requires.

I just hope he doesn't have to resort to violence against himself just because a few armchair critics have been attacking the new concept. What we want up there on the screen is reasoned discussion. We want Maid Marian to make a rational choice. Stay with an adventurer of no fixed income and have a baby on the floor of the forest, or bring up a family in a secure castle with a sheriff who does his share of the washing-up? Let all this be laid out in the form of dialogue uninterrupted by action. If we have to retain the scene where Robin is almost defeated by the Sheriff's champion whose arrow hits the bull's-eye, let Robin's arrow not split the champion's arrow, but end up where it belongs, in the chest of a spectator, thus to illustrate the danger of lethal weapons in private hands. I've also got ideas for a Friar Tuck who eats sensibly and a Little John of average height.

Having laid out these ideas in script form under the provisional title of *Conflict Resolution in the Nottingham Area*, I've already sent a message to Ridley Scott that I'm willing to help with the project, and I got an e-mail straight back. It was labelled Out of Office Reply but I have high hopes that he'll be in touch. Meanwhile I continue to work on the tricky scene where Robin and his band of reasonably merry men confront Guy of Gisborne in the forest and persuade him by force of argument that there should be no relief on capital gains tax without a concomitant lowering of the basic rate. Guy of Gisborne, I think, should be played by Hugh Grant in his terribly nice chap mode. 'Well, Robin, I, and I say this advisedly, I think that, that there's something to be said for your views, judging by that sword you're holding, and I'll tell Nottingham, or Nottie as we call him, that you . . .' But you know the sort of thing.

A previous collaboration between Ridley Scott and Russell Crowe, *Gladiator*, was a worldwide hit. Russell was of normal size for that occasion. It was fitting, because there was very little fast food in ancient Rome that you didn't have to hunt on foot first. Though born in New Zealand, where he first learned to throw telephones at a moving target, Russell, like Nicole Kidman, is one of those Australian citizens who look good in a skirt. But think how much more inspiring *Gladiator* would have been if Maximus Musculis could have subdued the wild animals with his powers of logic and reached an accommodation with the Emperor on an intellectual level. Instead, the action got in the way.

In Hollywood, it always has, until now. And there tended to be too much action even in the Tudor theatre. Shakespeare tried to break away from all that when he made Hamlet think things through instead of just going mad with the muscle, but sure enough, Act Five was ruined with poison, sword fights, poisoned sword fights, and all the standard high-concept mayhem, the early sixteenth-century equivalent of Go! Go! Go!, 5 4 3 2 1, the car chase in the tunnel and the hero somersaulting towards you propelled by the flames of the exploding building. If Shakespeare were alive now, he would follow Ridley Scott's example and make the whole thing more nuanced. Hamlet and Claudius, after taking counselling together, would sign a peace treaty drafted by Polonius. Prime Minister Laertes would solve the economic crisis by raising the bank rate, or lowering the bank rate, or whatever it is you do with the bank rate, and Ophelia would take over as the new presenter of *Countdown*. Parties of foreign tourists being conducted around Elsinore, instead of stepping over bodies in the corridor, would hardly know that the royal family was in residence except when Hamlet's voice came over the public address system. 'Oh what a rogue and peasant slave I was, before I got in touch with my inner child.'

What we're talking about here is the duty of mass entertainment to transmit constructive values. One evening last week I accidentally sat on the remote control, tuned in to cable channel 67 and was face to face with a re-run of *Mr and Mrs Smith*, starring Brad Pitt and Angelina Jolie respectively. You may not have seen this movie. If you are a clinically sane person, you will almost certainly not have seen this movie. But a lot of susceptible people have seen this movie, and you fear for what they might do under its influence. Brad and Angelina play a married couple neither of whom is aware that the other is a professional assassin. Each of them keeps an arsenal in the house unknown to the other. It's true that most wives could keep the complete equipment of a panzer division in the house without the husband ever finding out, but husbands who can keep even a pop gun in the house without being rumbled by their wives are surely very few. Brad, however, works the trick, and needs every gun in his collection when it turns out that each of the married assassins has been assigned to assassinate the other.

As Mr and Mrs Smith exchange bursts of machine-gun fire with underlying affection, the plot expands instantly into a whirlwind of Go! Go! Go!, 5 4 3 2 1, cars through the window and body-surfing on a wave of flame. Never once are younger viewers warned: Don't try this at home. The accumulating two-way spouse abuse adds up to a story boring beyond belief. Think how much better it would have been if the two assassins could have just sat down and discussed the matter, or, even better, taken counselling together. The counsellor, Billy Crystal, could have told them that they would get even greater job satisfaction out of just behaving like a normal Hollywood married couple, the husband a standard leading man with his head on upside down pursuing a big career while his wife, a lush beauty with a mouth the size of a paddling pool who adopts every stray child in the world, pursues an even bigger career. The real excitement is in realism, not fantasy.

Sometimes the unrelenting action of a blockbuster movie makes sense. By now I have seen *Armageddon* five times. I find it hard to explain why. It isn't just for Bruce Willis, although the way he can maintain a wry smirk while being blown backwards through plate glass is an inspiration to any man who spends his life doing nothing more challenging than face a computer screen that says: 'There has been an error. Do you wish to report it?' What makes the level of violence in *Armageddon* legitimate, I think, is that there really is no other way of dealing with an asteroid approaching Earth except to send Bruce Willis to drill a hole in it and blow it up with a nuke. His crew have to be tough characters of frightening aspect. But why do Bruce and his band of unreasonably merry men have to hit each other all the time? Couldn't they save all the aggression for the asteroid? Nevertheless, you can see how things might get rough when the Earth has been left behind yet nothing else but a concerted effort by a group of dysfunctional half-wits can save it from destruction.

Back on our planet, however, the age of mindless action is surely over, and Hollywood knows it. There is a whole new climate. Reason has prevailed even in America, which has just elected a President who gives evidence of mental activity in everything he says, whereas his predecessor spoke as if he had just rammed his head through a wall for the third time shouting 5 4 2 3 1. There is no going back now to when Robin Hood could be played by Errol Flynn. Let's leave Kevin Costner out of this, because we know that Kevin Costner was born to play a postman. But Errol Flynn was born to play Robin Hood in the old style. In an earlier programme I drew mockery for suggesting that the Australian George Lazenby was the only James Bond who looked the part, but surely the Australian Errol Flynn was the Robin Hood best fitted to wear tights. He just couldn't understand that the Sheriff of Nottingham had a point of view meriting respect. Peace.

Postscript

Luckily Ridley Scott's *Robin Hood* project was postponed and revised, so that in the end Russell Crowe played only the title role, instead of climbing into drag and playing Maid Marian as well. Persuading a bankable male film star to throttle back on his power is never an easy matter, but somehow it was managed. Right up to the point where they get too capricious to be employable, however, it is common for the male film stars to hog the screen even when they are playing only one role at a time. The most common way of hogging the screen is to look about a lot while talking and indeed while anybody else is talking. Run a DVD of *Body of Lies* and watch what Crowe does with his head. It's everywhere, like a hungry pigeon's. Almost all male film actors will do this unless stopped. Ben Kingsley is practically the world champion. (See him in *Species*. Who needs an alien?) For a director like Ridley Scott, the downside of recognition in the industry, and in all the media, as the man in total control of his latest picture, is that he must bear the responsibility when it tanks, even if the damage has been done by a lacklustre central performance. *Kingdom of Heaven* might have been as exciting as Eva Green's eyes or Jeremy Irons's voice if only Orlando Bloom could command the screen like ... well, like Russell Crowe. But Ridley Scott chose his cast, so he must take the rap. The matter concerns me because my gratitude is eternal for what he did with *Blade Runner*, a supreme example of how a director fully equipped with a producer's powers and responsibilities can bring disparate and even antagonistic elements together in a poetic unity. Just because *Blade Runner* was no fun to make, and a comparative dud at the box office, Harrison Ford still doesn't mention it among his triumphs. Yes, the leading actor was as dumb as that.

A career of directing movies on the scale Ridley Scott likes to make them requires such powers of generalship that megalomania is only ever a step away, but he seems always to have avoided it, except when, very occasionally, he falls prey to the illusion that he can make a comedy. But soon he is safely back into space, the future, ancient

Rome or Sherwood Forest, where the concept is high, the budget huge, the technical demands are infinite, the dialogue doesn't matter very much, and the leading male actor, though bonkers enough to suck on his own cell phone like a lollipop in order to strengthen his facial muscles, has the wherewithal to command the central space around which, with prodigies of organizational prowess, the director knows just how to arrange everything. Only a few people can do it, and if they weren't doing it they'd be invading Russia, so we should count ourselves lucky. Nobody I subsequently met or heard from, incidentally, admitted to having been gulled even for a moment by my concept of an action-free action movie: but they all knew someone who had.

BAD LANGUAGE

Dates of show: 21 and 23 November 2008

Early this week I was in a supermarket stocking up on light bulbs, which I seldom replace until they all fail and I have to find my way out of my office by feeling the furniture, swearing all the way. But I wouldn't swear if children were present. Perhaps I should. Swear words are only words, and a case can be made for children hearing as early as possible the language of the world they will grow up in. I wonder, though, if that case is very good. The young mother who was checking out in the next aisle to mine seemed to have no doubts on the matter.

She was no harridan. In fact she looked like a fashion model. But she had a trolley piled high with stuff, her two attendant children were behaving like children, and she told them off in roughly the following terms. 'Stop something about or I'll something leave you at home next time.' The word 'something' was delivered several times with tremendous force, so that the light bulbs rattled in my trolley. I use the word 'something' instead of the word she used. The BBC has rules about using that word and I wouldn't want to use it anyway if I didn't know who was listening.

In private, when I do know who's listening, I use it frequently, possibly too frequently: a question I'll get to. But I can't imagine myself using it in the presence of children. The young mother with the trolley couldn't imagine anything else. It was clear that she used it all the time because the children didn't bat an eye. You would think their lack of response might have tipped her off to a salient fact. The word can't have any shock effect if you use it all the time. It is indeed only a word, but it isn't even that if it's done to death. Bad language can energize normal language, but bad language used all the time is no language at all. The only signal that it sends is that the user is in the grip of anger, or is nervous, or is a member of the male television cooking profession, or perhaps all three.

Or the constant user might be a comedian. Almost all stage comedians of the present day use swear words constantly. The comedian Frank Skinner, however, has just told us that for purposes of experiment, for a single night on his latest tour, he tried doing his stand-up act without any of his usual swear words, and that the act went surprisingly well. He didn't say how much shorter it was, but apparently nobody complained. Nobody came up to him afterwards and said, 'Your something act was twenty something minutes shorter than something usual and I'm really something disappointed.' Everybody thought he was just as funny as ever.

Having made this discovery, Frank Skinner has transmitted it to us via the press, with the proviso that he still thought some parts of his act really needed the swear words, so he put them back in the next night. On the whole, though, he was amazed by the results of his bold venture. He had left most of the swear words out, and the audience had still laughed. He didn't draw the conclusion that all the other comedians should follow his example and leave most of the swear words out, but he seemed to be asking for someone else to draw it for him, so let me be the one to try.

At this point I should hasten to say I made a big mistake last week when I conjured a fantasy of Hollywood action movies that left all the violence out in favour of reasoned discussion, and a version of *Hamlet* in which everyone took counselling instead of fighting with swords. I was joking, but some of the people who wrote in to the BBC website didn't realize it. Perhaps I didn't swear enough. Swearing has become the mark of comedy, but I really do think that comedians who swear a lot are hardly ever funny, and this time I'm not joking. People with a talent for comedy should watch their language, and people who can't watch their language should cook food. There, I've something said it.

Stage comedy was already filthy well before the time of Shakespeare, and the Puritans who tried to clean it up were always more frightening than the poor clowns dishing out the verbal offal. When it comes to the stage, where nobody is exposed to the spectacle except people who buy a ticket, better the most depraved comedian than any censor. But on stage, the filth that works the trick has always depended more on the dirty idea than the dirty words. Max Miller, who dominated the music halls from the 1930s to the 1950s, dealt in a line of innuendo scurrilous beyond belief, but he never swore, he just conveyed insalubrious ideas. In fact he sometimes never even completed the idea. He let the audience complete it in their minds, and then accused *them* of being filthy.

Delighted, they agreed. They were all adults and they were on a night out away from the kids. The BBC banned him for a good reason: some of the kids might still be awake. In modern times, Lenny Bruce pushed comedy into forbidden areas, and those who thought that he was shining a necessary light on darkness were right to praise him. Later on Richard Pryor took it further, and people were right to praise him too. But always these liberating advances into a less squeamish awareness – a true and necessary breaking down of barriers – depended more on the picture conjured up than on the words employed, and trouble began to arrive when there were suddenly thousands of comedians who had no pictures to conjure up, but only bad language to distract the listener from their paucity of invention.

For a long while, television would not do what the stage did, but finally the argument began to win out that comedy has to have 'edge'. Victoria Wood was the first comedian I ever heard who was brave enough to wonder aloud if 'edge' was a good thing in itself, but by now, I think, most comedians who actually know how to raise a genuine laugh are wondering seriously if their profession hasn't been invaded by people who either aren't working hard enough or have very little to work with. With no boundaries left to push, with no edge left unexposed, those comedians devoid of any real ideas will have no resort except to join all the swear words together, putting in nothing except what Frank Skinner left out.

Suppose they did so, would any grown-up get hurt? Well, probably not, even if they did it on television. Only words, swear words are barely words at all without an idea behind them. Mainly they're just punctuation, and when we get a message that's all punctuation we either wait for a real message, or, more likely, shut down the computer. The test is, can you say something interesting without the swear words? If you can, then you can always bung a few in to make what you say more effective in the right company. You might be trying to entertain your friends. If you're a man you might be trying to impress a woman – very dangerous, that: she might be well brought up. Or you might just be telling someone to go away. But in that case, the person you are telling to something off had better be smaller than you are. Not so small, however, as to be a child.

Which is where we really come to the crunch. A child who grows up not knowing the difference between swearing and ordinary language will not be employed by anyone who does know the difference, and there are still quite a lot of people like that, although their number might be declining. And a child who grows up listening to swearing adults, and who in turn becomes an habitually swearing adult, has been deprived of one of the most precious features of the English language.

The English language has many levels, stretching from the mundane, the everyday, to the divine, the level of love, worship and poetry. Used with point and a sense of pace, the profane can reinforce all of them, but it is not a language level in itself, and anyone confined to using nothing else has effectively been deprived of speech. Luckily nobody has to stay that way. Anyone with any brains at all will eventually notice that most people are getting more said with fewer expletives, and will try to copy them, if only to land a job.

It's a counsel of despair to say that we can't get back to decent speech. Almost everybody gets back to it for at least part of the day. I myself swear too much in private company, and swear far too much when I am alone and the last light bulb goes out. But when I watch my words, I realize that I have fallen back on a swear word for effect only because I ran out of ideas for saying the same thing better. No, I don't mean that all comedians should clean up their act. I just want them to be something funnier.

I don't think Frank Skinner would have made his historic statement on this subject if he hadn't been aware that the tide is on the turn. I hope the puritans aren't trying to regain their lost ground, and if they are, I hope I'm not one of them. But I do think the time might have come to listen to the laughs more carefully. Comedians always listen to the laughs. Quite often they count them. But a wise comedian listens to the quality of the laugh. Is it that thin laugh that he gets when people are determined to have a good time and will laugh at anything flagged as funny? Or is it the solid laugh that they grant to something really funny? There's all the something difference in the something world.

Postscript

Perhaps I overdid my pitch. Now, listening to the broadcast, I sound peevishly out of date even to myself. Years before, I delivered a lecture to a television conference in which I contended that bad language would have a corrosive effect on comedy. Some of the executives present kindly looked concerned, as if I might have a point, but they went on doing nothing about it. Listening to the talent was their business, not listening to a critic, and the screen comedy writers went on writing it the way they wanted. The way got dirtier, but eventually it arrived at a masterpiece. I had to admit that *The Thick of It* made me laugh right along with my well-behaved family. We were creased. And the foul language was fundamental to the effect. But I noticed that in the episodes that worked best, the leading actor – the wonderful Peter Capaldi – had a monopoly of the putrescent talk. When another character was allowed a share of the scatology, the impact dropped away, sometimes to nothing.

The lesson was plain. Foul language needs a context in fair language. If foul language is all there is, the possibilities of expression are restricted rather than expanded. In private, if we are wise, we use dirty words only to add texture. Using them too often is a sign of self-assertion, which an astute interlocutor will quickly detect as weakness. The trouble with the foul-mouthed yob is that he's asserting the only self he's got. Sometimes I think I see that happening on screen. But had there been room, I would have admitted in the broadcast that there is such a thing as failing to keep up. It's not the content that one fails to keep up with, so much as the style. I find Sara Silverman brilliantly funny, but I have listened for several hours on end to Russell Brand, watching his face carefully, and I have to say that I just don't get it. Not that he swears a lot. But he does carry on as if uninterrupted insolence were the purpose of life.

If it were, it would be as boring as uninterrupted reverence. In the days when the mass media were censored, we could take comfort from the obvious signs that the censors were at least trying to throw us a bone. In my treasured early copy of Norman Mailer's *The Naked and the Dead*, the word 'fugg' occurred frequently. I was so young that I took a while to figure it out. Even today, the American TV networks still demand clean language. But in *Battlestar*

Galactica the word 'frak' still gets through. I find it touching, as if something were being protected. The universe in which anything can be said is only a jump away from the universe in which nothing is worth hearing.

GLAMORIZING TERROR

Dates of show: 28 and 30 November 2008

In the growing category of German movies shining light on the murky past, *The Baader Meinhof Complex*, a movie about the core group of the Red Army Faction that was infamously active in Germany for almost thirty years, is currently making an international hit. Since I like to keep up even in my years of retirement, I suppose I'll have to see it, but I'm not looking forward to it. Part of my trepidation comes from the possibility that the film will be full of exciting action, that I'll get caught up with the characters, and that I'll start to find them attractive. The producers of the movie say that they were intent on avoiding chic glamour, but there are people who say that Elvis is still alive.

At my age I can easily recall what was happening in the 1970s, and I can assure anyone too young to remember that the Baader Meinhof bunch weren't attractive at all. Some of them were quite good-looking, and the actors playing them in the movie are even better looking, which is already a worry. Because even if the originals were easy on the eye, the attraction soon faded if you were getting the news of what they were up to, which mainly consisted of murdering law-abiding citizens to make a point.

The gangsters claimed to be rebelling against a repressive state. Too young to have had much direct experience of what a genuinely repressive Germany had been like, they thought that the Germany they were living in was authoritarian. There was some evidence for that, and the evidence grew as the authorities panicked under pressure. But when the gang's founder members were finally arrested, the repressive state kept them alive to face trial. They were held in what was called maximum security, but anything they wanted was smuggled in, usually by their defence lawyers. When they wanted guns, those were smuggled in as well.

On the outside, Red Army Faction members still at large tried to spring their friends. The most prominent businessman they took hostage undoubtedly had a Nazi background. But in order to kidnap him they shot his driver, his bodyguard and two cops. No doubt they thought the cops had it coming, being uniformed representatives of a repressive state, and as for the bodyguard, stopping a bullet was his job, was it not? But the driver was just driving the car. Perhaps he was driving it in a repressive manner. Anyway, all rescue attempts having failed, the prisoners committed suicide, two of them using the smuggled guns.

Once again, they had their pictures in the papers, and now, what with the movie coming out, they've got their pictures in the papers all over again, along with the pictures of the actors playing them. The actor playing the driver is only an extra, so I haven't seen that actor's picture in the papers yet. Come to think of it, the original driver's picture wasn't very often featured in the papers either, even in Germany. He was only a driver. Let's forget him while we talk about more important people: Hitler, for example.

One of the previous German movies shining light on the murky past had the same director. It was *Downfall*, concerned with the last moments of Hitler's life. That one I did see as soon as it came out, and I admired it very much while hating every minute of it. How, you might ask, were two such contrary reactions possible? Well, it was easy. On the one hand, the movie was wonderfully well made. On the other hand, it had a thumping lie right in the centre of it. When Hitler violently expressed his anti-Semitism, the good-looking personal secretary was stunned, as if she had no idea.

The original girl was good-looking but she couldn't have been stunned. The one thing that everybody in Germany could be sure of was that Hitler was a violent anti-Semite. He told them often enough. But he hadn't told them often enough for this girl to hear about it. When I first saw her beautiful eyes widening with shock I asked myself, are we meant to believe this? And then it struck me: we were meant to be her.

We were meant to believe that we, too, could have total horror going on all around us and not spot it until the roof fell in. To that extent, and it's almost the whole extent, *Downfall* is a dream world.

It's a story without a context. It's been glamorized. That might seem a paradoxical thing to say about a story which dares to feature Himmler's horrible haircut and people blowing their brains out all over the place, but it's true. When you take the historical context out of a story, what you are left with is glamour.

When we move to Hollywood movies shining light on the murky past, we get the glamour principle operating at full steam. Steven Spielberg's *Munich* was a case in point. Spielberg had done his best with *Schindler's List*, but his best left some of us wondering just how useful a contribution it was, to make a movie about how some of the Jews had survived, when the real story was about all the Jews who hadn't. Spielberg tried to cover that aspect with his brilliant device of the little girl in the red dress. She was doomed, and we felt for her. But what we were mainly left with was a story about how one kind man could make a difference. And the real story was about how it took whole armies to make a difference. But to tell that story, you have to give a history lesson, and in a movie there is never time.

Munich was so short of time that there was almost nothing left in the plot except secret agent derring-do and John Woo-style gunfight face-offs. The tip-off scene was the conference in which the Israeli leaders planned their retaliation against the terrorists who had killed the athletes in Munich. That conference should have been the key scene, as it was in real life. There were pluses and minuses to be debated, dilemmas that took in the whole of modern history. The scene went for nothing, to make room for more action.

I was only kidding a couple of weeks ago when I said that the action in action movies should be replaced by reasoned discussion, but in *Munich* the movie would actually have been more exciting if the underlying issues had been explained. They weren't, because movies have their own logic: the logic of glamour.

Glamour nearly always shapes the movies and it took over completely when Carlos got famous. His real name was Ilich Ramirez Sanchez but he called himself Carlos as a code-name. It was already a bad sign when the press agreed to call him Carlos too, and an even worse sign when they started calling him Carlos the Jackal, apparently on the grounds that a copy of Frederick Forsyth's novel *The Jackal* had been found among his kit: but perhaps it would have been less catchy to call him Carlos the Casually Lethal Reader of Second-rate Fiction.

The original Carlos was a psychopath whose idea of a political gesture was to roll a grenade into a crowded Paris cafe. But he believed himself to be a glamorous figure. The press went along with it and the movies went mad with it. Movies with a charmingly ruthless central figure based on Carlos proliferated. There might have been something to the idea that he was charming, if you can be charmed by a puff adder with a nice smile. One of his French defence lawyers was, and she married him while he was in jail.

He's still in jail but I prefer to speak of him in the past tense. I hope he never gets out. Why do I hope that? Because I could have been in the cafe, and so could you. No, of course we weren't. But we should be able to imagine it. We should be able to imagine being the unglamorous figure, the one that gets blown away. But the movies will always try to make us imagine we're the glamorous figure, the one in the close-up.

Defending themselves with passion in the middle of a shouting match that has split German opinion in a big way, the makers of the Baader Meinhof epic are keen to point out that they have shot their action sequences from the viewpoint of the victims. They probably have. I'm sure it's an accomplished movie, and I'll be sure to see it before I judge it. The trailer looks to me like a cross-section through a pile of tripe, but judging things unseen is a habit that needs to be resisted.

I'll see it, though, because I want to find out what the movies are doing, not because I need the history lesson. If you already know something about the history behind its nominal subject, you can judge a movie against its context. But the thought that people might be learning about history from the movies is enough to drain the brain. It's already bad enough when it takes the release of a new movie for the press to get interested again in the events it purports to treat. But at least the press has the resources to recall the events in some measure of their complexity. For the moviegoers, unless they are reading all the newspapers and magazines at once, the movie might replace the event.

Almost always it will replace the event with a glamorous fiction, because there just isn't room in the frame for the people who don't matter. I'm sure that when the businessman gets kidnapped I'll see the driver getting shot, but I doubt if we'll hear anything else about him. Yet he's the one we should think about as us. The one who doesn't matter. I know it would be a different movie if it was all about him. In fact it wouldn't be a movie at all, because it would just be the story of an ordinary life, which finished at that moment. I'll be keen to look at the cast list at the end, and see if he's been given a name, or just called Driver. His name, incidentally, was Heinz Marcicz. I think that's how it's pronounced. I've never heard it said. And now, let's talk about Mumbai.

Postscript

A few days later I saw the movie and it was even worse than I had expected. The driver vanished from the screen as soon as he was killed, but that was no surprise. All the terrorists were beautiful young people but that was no surprise either. What was truly astonishing was the poverty of the film's historical imagination. It made *Downfall* look profound. The special squad of policemen assigned to track down the terrorists featured an extra-special grand old man (played by none other than Bruno Ganz, fresh from his role as Hitler) to provide gravitas, guidance and wisdom. The wisdom was apparently designed to sound wise to anyone who knew nothing at all about modern history. The penalty for knowing anything was to sit there open-mouthed as the grand old man opined that the terrorists would be less active if the Middle East crisis could be solved. Such a view, already wrong now even though widely accepted, is simply incongruous when projected decades into the past, when scarcely anyone proposed it. To hear it turning up as a piece of received wisdom in the movie was to fear that the world had been taken over by high-school students, and not very bright ones at that. Thus the essential point – that the Red Army Faction, like the Brigati Rossi in Italy, needed nothing more to drive them crazy than to have been brought up in a free country – was allowed to vanish by default. Whether it was the director who had no sense of history, or whether, possessing that sense, he had prudently decided that his audience didn't, was a nice question. Keen to put him in the best light, I prefer to believe that he is a confident ignoramus of the type that currently sets the tone for the progressive intelligentsia throughout the West. To say that he perpetrates his distortions knowingly would be to accuse him of iniquity.

Still, it was an exciting movie. Whether exciting movies about politics do much good for those who have no other source of political knowledge is a larger question. One tries to be optimistic and believe that seeing a movie might count as making a start, no matter how empty the movie is. I knew very little about post-war politics in Poland when I first saw *Ashes and Diamonds*, or about Algeria when I first saw *The Battle of Algiers*. But subsequently, when I read up on their subjects, I found that both movies had been reasonably true to the complex facts. No young person who reads up on the background of *The Baader Meinhof Complex* is going to reach a similar conclusion. In that regard, there has been a precipitous decline over the last half-century, with the movies becoming more brainless as their resources increase. The best we can hope for is that the low point has already been reached. It's hard to think of anything emptier than the way the Albert Speer character, in *Downfall*, just stood around in his leather overcoat looking deeply concerned. Nowhere to go but up. Or so I thought, until, in late 2010, an epic movie about Carlos was announced, with a running time longer than *Parsifal*. I saw the short version, took due note of the hero's infinite supply of cigarettes and beautiful young women, and briefly wondered why I had never gone in for terrorism myself. One trusts that this was not the desired effect.

WRITER'S ROOM

Dates of show: 5 and 7 December 2008

The great thing about speaking in this slot is that I can pontificate. But a wise pontificator should always remember that he won't solve a global problem in ten minutes, or even do much more than usefully touch on it in ten hours. There are two main reasons for that. One reason is that the global problems are, by their nature, devilishly complicated. But everyone knows, or should know, that.

The other reason is less obvious, because it lies within the nature of the pontificator. He, or she – in my case he – speaks with a special pontificating voice: integrated, judicious even in its doubts, purporting to contain the distilled wisdom of a lifetime's experience. Almost always, I suspect, this voice is at odds with the personality from which it emerges, and in my case the discrepancy is so glaring that even I can spot it.

As I prepare this script, tapping away at the keyboard as Socrates might have done if he had owned a PC, it seems to me that my brain is at my fingertips, with all its scope and knowledge. But then, after looking up at the screen and noticing that the last two sentences are all in capitals and include various chemical formulae for substances unknown to science, I bounce my forehead off the desk and make the supreme mistake of looking around my room.

It's in chaos. The pontificator with plans for fixing the world can't organize his own desk, and as for what lies beyond the desk, forget about it. The evidence that I've spent years forgetting about it is all out there. Piles of old newspapers and magazines. Stacks of box files containing folders containing memos about the necessity to buy more folders and box files. Hundreds of books uselessly hidden behind hundreds of other books. A small statue of a Sumo wrestler, or else a life-sized statue of a small Sumo wrestler. A bag of random receipts that my accountant might have found quite useful in their year of origin, 1998. But let's start with the desk.

Or rather, let's not. The desk is too much. Little of its surface is visible through piled notebooks and shuffled papers. But observe this vertically striped earthenware mug full of ball-point pens. If the phone rings with information I must take down, I reach for one of these pens and find that it does not work. In the same vertically striped mug there are fifteen other pens that do not work either. Vaguely I remember the day when I planned to sort through these pens and retain only those that did work. But I got distracted. What else is in the same mug? Jelly beans, several of which have grown fur.

And that's just the mug. What about this desk drawer over here on the right? Ah, there's a touch of organization here. Every year I put a new set of vital names and addresses in the designated section of my appointments diary. But I never get round to transferring vital names and addresses from previous diaries into the current one. So there are ten years of diaries in this drawer alone, to supplement the line-up of twenty years of diaries standing over there in the corner of the room behind that valuable stack of obsolete phone books. Or, as I have just typed, obsotel nophe kobos.

All over again I count my blessings that I have not been chosen as one of the subjects for Eamonn McCabe's series of photographs called 'Writers' Rooms'. In London, an exhibition of these photographs has just opened. The photographs have been running as a series in one of the upmarket newspapers. When I looked at the early photos in that series I was envious. Would I be chosen? Then I started praying that I wouldn't be, a prayer which has mercifully been answered.

There are some prizes I would like. I would quite like the Nobel Prize, if the money could be delivered tomorrow in a suitcase, clearly marked 'Nobel Prize money: bank immediately or it will burst into flames'. I would quite like the Booker Prize, the Whitbread Prize, the Forward Prize and the UNICEF prize for the chronically disorganized. I can hear myself pontificating while accepting any or all of those awards. But what I don't want is to be photographed in this room, because any shred of credibility I had as a pontificator would evaporate instantly.

I noted with shame that even the most shambolic of the writers' rooms in the photographs was better organized than mine, and the majority of them might have been deliberately arranged to remind me that I myself was working in a skip. These paragons had got it all together without it getting on top of them. You could tell that everything was there for a reason. If a woman writer had the propeller of a Sopwith Camel mounted on the wall, it was because her great-grandfather shot down Baron von Richthofen's second cousin in 1917. Writers had their books arranged by category, in alphabetical order. I moved into this office ten years ago, the books came out of their tea chests in any old order, and any old order is still the only order they maintain on my shelves. There are books I know I own but I have to buy them again because I can't find them. Let me add that everything is well dusted. A cleaner comes in once a week and she does a good job. But she is under instructions not to move anything, in case I need it. So she has learned just to polish the whole lot as if it were an installation at Tate Modern.

Other writers clearly find it easier to get their act together, and no doubt most non-writers do too. But judging from my own admittedly extreme experience, they can only get things under control by striving mightily against a force of nature that wants things to be disorganized rather than not. Scientists call it entropy. Back in the early nineteenth century, Carl von Clausewitz, in his great work about military strategy *On War*, called it Friction. Clausewitz said that you have to have a plan for the battle but the plan had better include plenty of room for the absolute certainty that the plan will start growing fur from the first moment of its execution.

I have just been checking up in my copy of Clausewitz – I had to buy another copy, because my original copy is somewhere in my bookshelves, which means that it might as well be on Mars – and I can tell from every sentence that he was writing with the insight conferred by self-knowledge. I'll bet all the money in my foreign coin collection – it's over there in the fruit bowl, and some of those hundreds of obsolete francs and Deutschmarks are sure to be worth something to collectors a hundred years from now – I'll bet all that money in the fruit bowl – and if you're asking where the fruit is, I gathered up all my powers of organization and threw it out only a month after I forgot to eat it – I'll bet all that money that Clausewitz, when he was working on his magnum opus in his last years, was sitting at a desk that looked like the morning after the Battle of Waterloo.

His name for the accumulated effect of Friction was the Fog of War. When I read that, I could tell straight away that here was a man who, like me, couldn't toast a slice of bread without filling his apartment with smoke. When his widow prepared his manuscript for posthumous publication, she probably found sandwiches in it.

When DVDs came in, I rarely played my VHS tapes again, but the VHS tapes did not move out. There are several hundred of them here, stacked on the floor. My first copy of Clausewitz might be somewhere behind them. I know there is a squash racket behind them because I can see the edge of its frame sticking up. Will I ever play squash again? Of course not, so why is the racket still there? Perhaps it's trying to remind me that the best-equipped pontificator is the one who is aware of his own propensities towards chaos. Unable to organize his own breakfast, he will be less ready to condemn officials who can't organize an efficient system for sending out student grants, or collecting private information onto a CD-ROM that won't be left on a train.

But even the most self-aware pontificator is still likely to expect too much of the world. Rarely will he be sufficiently amazed that society functions at all, considering some of the human material it has to work with. In ancient Greece, the philosopher Diogenes, wedded to simplicity, lived in a tub. But he still roamed the streets of Athens by daylight while carrying a lamp. He said that he was look-ing for an honest man, and everybody wrote it down, saying that Diogenes the cynic was a piercing analyst of the human condition. But maybe he just didn't know how to turn the lamp off.

Sitting at this computer, on whose keyboard I have just typed the word 'lamp' and actually written the word 'lump', I am face to face with an item of technology that Diogenes would not have known how to switch on. I barely know how to switch it on either, have often failed to switch it off – why does it ask me, 'Do you wish to report the error?' when I don't know what the error is? – and yet I do know that its mere presence in the pile of rubble I call my desk is sending me a dangerous signal.

This miracle of machinery is telling me that order can emerge from chaos after all. Well, yes, it can, but only against heavy odds, because chaos is inherent even in the minds of those who make the miracles. And it is certainly inherent within the pontificator. I can pontificate about that with some certainty, even as I type the last words of this sprict, scirpt, script, reach for my mug of coffee, and get a mouthful of ball-point pens.

Postscript

I can promise that this broadcast was not a sly signal that I should be considered for the honour of having my room photographed by Eamonn McCabe. Shortly afterwards, however, the phone rang and the date was made. Heroically I did not neaten the room up before he photographed it – apparently almost everybody gets the builders in – but I was impressed to notice that in the published picture it looked neater anyway. Just as a film camera makes even grunge look premeditated, a still camera squares things up. Or perhaps the messes we make don't look as bad as we feel they do. Malcolm Gladwell, early in his career, published an article explaining that the jumble on your desk is really a filing system in which an elaborate operational set of priorities is being observed. Instantly I felt a lot better about my heaps of paper. On a grander scale, Beethoven, had he been told that his personal chaos was really a form of organization, might have convinced himself that he would never have composed the *Hammerklavier* sonata if half a cold chicken had not got lost in his piano.

Years ago the Library of New South Wales kindly invited me to hand over my papers *pari passu*, and as the years go by I burden the library's basement with more and more used notebooks. I have to be careful, though, not to hand over any notebook until I have searched through it to extract vital marginal thoughts so that I can transfer them to yet another notebook which at the moment I can't find.

If that's the way you are, that's the way you'd better stay. My friend Bruce Beresford, whose job as a film director entails the ability to run an efficient office, was the first in my generation to transfer all of his vital addresses and information to one of the new hand-held electronic devices. Not long after being loaded with the last scrap of crucial data, the device went missing, thereby sending him back to square one. Square one, in his case, was easily found. For most of the rest of us, square one is like the Lost City of the Jungle. But at least I know that all my stuff is somewhere, even if I can't say exactly where. Somewhere in that fuzzy concept of putative retrieval is my capacity to concentrate on what I consider important. With few exceptions, most of the writers I know who do smooth work are scruffs in real life. They just haven't got the time to neaten everything else up. There is an economy to winning effort. It knows what to concentrate on. Quite soon after the invading German army was fought to a halt before Moscow, German engineers examining a captured Russian T-34 tank noticed that it was well finished only where it needed to be, and as rough as guts everywhere else. They realized to their horror that their own tanks were too well machined, and that the discrepancy could very well cost them the war.

NATIONAL IDENTITY

Dates of show: 12 and 14 December 2008

In my homeland, Australia, the question of national identity is once again in the news as the assembled brains of the entire country wonder whether the new film about Australia, called *Australia*, will finally establish the national identity of our neglected island in the eyes of the world. Let me start out by saying that I have always found this supposedly nagging question of Australia's national identity to be a mare's nest. Everyone in the world knows that Nicole Kidman, the leading lady of the film *Australia*, comes from Australia, so how much more national identity does one nation need? But I'll get to that later because I want to start out with another question: the national identity of Lapland.

Lapland's national identity in the eyes of the world took a bit of a hammering this week when a Lapland theme park in the New Forest closed down in response to universal lack of enthusiasm. Ticket buyers were promised snow, cabins, elves and appropriate animals. The snow was sparse, the cabins closely resembled the kind of bolt-together huts you get on a building site, some of the elves behaved in a non-elf-like manner, and at least one of the appropriate animals was made of plastic. I won't go into further detail because the newspapers were full of it, but let's just say that, except from people who had been optimistic enough to actually buy tickets, a great laugh went up.

The great laugh told you two things. The first thing is that the British enjoy a bungle. They have come to see a bungle as part of their national identity: a tilting train that tilts too much or doesn't tilt at all, a Millennium Dome with not much in it, a Heathrow terminal that separates passengers from their luggage on a long-term basis, a

Lapland theme park with snow-deficiency syndrome. How very British. One might even say that the nicest aspect of the British national identity is that the British can laugh at themselves.

But the other thing that the great laugh told you was that Lapland really does have an identity problem, because apart from its status as the official domicile of Santa Claus it would have had very few things notably Laplandish to offer for a thirty-quid ticket even if the theme park had been a big-budget number. Cabins and reindeer, is that it? The expectations of Lapp culture are low. Not even a British stand-up comedian would expect to get away with the suggestion that Lapland is where the Lapp dancers come from, because everyone knows that almost nothing comes from Lapland. On the international scale of celebrity, Lapland scores low unless you are deeply interested in hearing the one and only real Santa perform in a Lapp accent, hoeh hoeh hoeh. And very few Americans even know where Lapland is. Right there we get to the heart of this supposedly vital question about national identity. Small countries want America to have heard of them.

Britain counts as a big small country because it has a lot of people in it, but even the British are apt to waste time caring about whether the Americans have heard of them. Not all their time, however: for which I bless their sanity. For smaller small countries – and I mean smaller by population – it can be a continuing obsession. The clearest case is Canada, which is large in area even by comparison with the United States but is short of people. Crucially, Canada is right next to the US, and speaks the same language. Everyone knows that Mexicans are Mexicans but few of us can tell a Canadian from an American unless the Canadian is speaking French. The Canadians are forever bothered by a sense of being dominated by their famous neighbour to the south.

The Canadians try to laugh, however. There was a Canadian best-selling book recently called *Coping with Back Pain*. It did so well that the Americans printed their own edition. But the Americans called it *Conquering Back Pain* because America is a can-do nation that conquers, it doesn't cope. A friend of mine who told me about this had already worked out her own jokes, which I gladly borrow. The Canadian version of Julius Caesar's memoirs? *I Came, I Saw, I Coped.* Get ready for *She Stoops to Cope* and *Hail the Coping Hero Comes.* But the nice thing about the Canadians is that they can come up with jokes like that at the drop of a Mountie's hat. They know they're stuck and they've learned to enjoy it.

Long-time commander of the Starship *Enterprise*, the Canadian-born William Shatner, one of the funniest men I ever met, is full of jokes about Canadian star-fleet admirals. Canada has been supplying stars to Hollywood for a century but everyone thinks they're American. The best the Canadians can do is laugh about it and they always have. Finally the national sense of humour is a vital factor. National identity and a sense of humour: there are two themes trying to get together here.

I should say at this point that for all I know the Lapps are as funny as a circus on the subject of their minimal international standing. Perhaps they are even now rolling around in the snow, yelling with laughter at the reports of how the lavishly appointed Lapland New Forest theme park project went belly-up. But we don't know, because we never hear from them on the subject. This seems to me a wise attitude, for reasons I will discuss.

But not, alas, until I have discussed the national identity of Australia. It's a duty that there's no getting out of. As an Australian who lives in Britain, I spend a lot of time fielding calls from the media in my homeland wanting to know what Britain is thinking. These calls have been coming in every few hours in recent weeks, because the film *Australia* will soon open here and perhaps I might have seen it at a press screening. As it happens, I have seen it at a press screening, so I'm in a position to say that although I have no idea what the British will think when it goes on general release, I have an exact idea of what I think.

About the film's merits I prefer to be silent at this stage, except to say that it seemed quite long, in the same sense that the Thirty Years War probably seemed quite long to anyone who had been expecting it to be over sooner. But I have a definite opinion about what the film *Australia* will do for Australia's national identity. It will do nothing, because nothing needs to be done.

Unlike Lapland, Australia is world famous. Australian actors and film makers and writers and arts people have been colonizing the planet for years and all the jokes about Australia's deficiency of culture are old hat, like all the jokes about Australians knowing nothing about wine. Australia killed the wine jokes by producing supertankers full of wine that the whole world wanted to drink and it killed the culture jokes by flooding the world with an outburst of quality remarkable for a country that looks big on the map but has fewer people in it than Mexico City.

Most important, Australia has even more great stuff at home than it sends abroad. Unfortunately it also has a whole army of commentators who are permanently anxious that the world hasn't heard of them. Well, there's a reason for that. It's because they are talking nonsense. There is no Australian national identity crisis and never has been. Indeed Australia after World War II was a desirable destination for people from countries that really did have an identity crisis: Poland, for example. When Nazi Germany and the Soviet Union have ruined your country from two different directions, that's an identity crisis.

Australia's only problem was that it felt itself to be a bit of a backwater, and that is obviously no longer true. But it isn't obvious to the people who draw a salary for saying Australia must do something to put itself on the map of the world. Just such anxious minds are behind the notion that the film *Australia* will make all the world's tourists aware of Australia. They hope the film will work like the Paul Hogan commercial in which he threw another shrimp on the barbie. They think an epic film like *Australia* can act like an advertisement.

If these tireless promoters think that people will come to visit Australia after they have seen the film *Australia*, I can only say that those people will be very old when they arrive. But I also have to say, with reluctance, that the movie has plainly also been made in order to impress the Yanks. Australia, says the film *Australia*, is even bigger than Texas. Any Americans who make the trans-Pacific trip on the strength of this movie are going to be disappointed not to find Hugh Jackman, who plays the drover, droving a herd of cattle down one of the main streets of Sydney. They stand a better chance of bumping into Nicole Kidman, who is now once again living in her home town, and probably for two main reasons. One reason could be that she finds the relative obscurity a nice change after all the Hollywood hoo-hah: rarely, in Sydney, is she trailed by more than two car-loads of paparazzi at once.

Another reason could be that Australia has got its own sense of humour, which not even the Americans can take away, re-package, and sell back. Finally, it doesn't have to care about national identity.

All that a nation needs is national pride, and it only needs that if it's a nation. At which point it might be time to reveal that there is no such nation as Lapland. It's just an area, some of which is in Finland. But judging from the advertisements it puts on the web, Lapland is probably the best place to meet Santa in his grotto, with proper elves. Better, anyway, than in the New Forest, where the remains of the Lapland theme park are even now being loaded onto a skip. Hoeh hoeh hoeh.

Postscript

Having admired Baz Luhrmann's *Strictly Ballroom* so much, but his *Romeo + Juliet* and *La Bohème* a good deal less, I admired his *Australia* so little that I declared open season on it, and in my stage solo act I would spend a full fifteen minutes evoking its leitmotif of a hundred and fifty thousand head of cattle crossing Australia very slowly, each animal being awarded an individual close-up. The house, I felt, was with me, but later on, when I was signing books, there would be people who protested, thereby reflecting, on a small scale, the undoubted fact that, out there in the world, a lot of people, not all of them Aussies, thought that the film was marvellous. I suspect them of being the type of people who once bought sets of plastic-bound encyclopaedias on the instalment plan, but there is no point doubting the genuineness of vociferous enthusiasm. If people dance up and down when they disagree with you, they always have a belief, if not a point; and there was something about the film *Australia* that inspired belief. Especially among British people who had never been south of Benidorm, the movie evidently stirred dreams of mankind returning to simplicity through contact with the wide open spaces.

But the dreams that mattered were stirred in Australia itself, where some quite bright people took it for granted that the movie had played a noble part in the necessary task of establishing Australia's identity on the international stage. The argument that there is nothing necessary at all about this task is still thought treasonable in my homeland. In the script I make fleeting reference to an example which in other forms of writing I am usually careful to elaborate much further: the example of Poland. In the period up to, during and after World War II, Poland's national identity was deliberately torn apart from two different directions, and the chaos never really took shape again except as a totalitarian regime so repressive that the Pope, when he came to visit, was hailed as a freedom-fighter. Some of those lucky enough to survive the earlier phases of this catastrophe ended up in Australia, where they were bewildered to discover that there was a whole chorus of locally reared intellectuals bewailing Australia's fate as an immature nation. Hailing from a nation whose maturity had killed off a large number of its inhabitants, the refugees were stunned, but usually too polite to comment.

As for the intellectuals, no amount of international recognition for Australian arts, sciences, sports and industries is enough to satisfy them, and they persist in cherishing an inferiority complex so at odds with the facts that it amounts to a psychosis. Prime Minister Kevin Rudd's evident determination to cut a figure on the global stage – God help him, he thought that the United Nations was where the global stage might be situated – was one of the earliest signs that he was unfit for his post. John Howard, so despised by Rudd's admirers, had always made it clear that he thought Australia's ranking among nations to be sufficiently important and its Prime Ministership a sufficient honour. While he was in power, such evidence of realism was regarded by his enemies as a mere tactical distraction from his tyrannical aims. Later on, under the rule of Rudd, Howard's enemies were obliged to think again on the topic – an obligation that only made them angrier, because, even though Howard's faults were numerous, they preferred to believe he had been without any virtues at all.

WRAP IT UP

Dates of show: 19 and 21 December 2008

For some of us, the hardest part of Christmas now looms, which is wrapping presents. In our house, jobs for the festive season are allocated according to intelligence, which leaves me at the bottom end of the roster, doing simple tasks that involve physical strength. There are bags of coal to be heaved into the shed from the back of the car, and then, one at a time, to be heaved back out again to the step outside the back door, with the usual pause for recovery after I crease my head on the door-frame of the shed.

The step outside the back door is the transfer point for the coal in the bag to be loaded into the brass coal bucket, which then has to be hauled upstairs and lowered into position beside the fireplace before I go back downstairs to pick up the coal that missed the bucket and then clean my hands in the kitchen sink, which then has to be cleaned in its turn.

Since there will be other people including my granddaughter for Christmas dinner, extra leaves for the extendable dining-room table in the extended kitchen will need to be hauled out of the utility cupboard, which has never been extended, except by the accumulated impact of what happens every time I go into it. The sloping roof of the utility cupboard is waiting for me to bang my already tender head against it, provoking a reaction from me which is a recognized part of the festive season. The extra-table-leaves hauling ceremony has to be completed well before my granddaughter arrives after church on Christmas morning, lest she hear my language. Above all she must not hear my language when I am lying on the floor under the table trying to fasten the metal clips which hold the table leaves in position. Nobody must hear that.

Extra chairs have to be brought down from various rooms and assembled round the table. Intelligent people might be able to do this, but why should they, when I am available? Bags of potatoes and new potatoes have to be hauled from the back of the car into the kitchen. For years I have harboured the forlorn hope that my low IQ would excuse me from the comparatively finicky task of peeling these potatoes and new potatoes, but not so. Peeling counts as a physical task. Add all these physical tasks together and you would have thought, or at any rate I would have thought, that I was on the limits of what I could be expected to accomplish. But all these public physical tasks are as nothing beside the task that awaits me in private on Christmas Eve. It is yet another physical task, but there is a mental element. Yet this I am allowed to do. Indeed it is made clear by all that I have to do it. Wrapping presents.

There is no way out of it. Nor should there be. Presents have to be wrapped. I accept that. I once tried giving my elder daughter the collected poems of Philip Larkin without wrapping it and it was made clear to me that it didn't matter how good the poetry was, the effect had been spoiled, perhaps for ever, by the fact that there was no wrapping to be removed first in order to reveal what the present was. I already knew all that, but I hoped to get away with it for once. You can't get away with it even once. In that respect, our house is like Japan, where the wrapping of the gift is at least as important as the gift. Many years ago, on my first trip to Japan, I rewarded my official guide with a bottle of high-grade Scotch. But I handed it to him in a plastic bag. He received it politely but later on I was told I might as well have hit him over the head with it.

Wrapping the presents shows that you have not only employed your credit card for a few seconds, you have taken care. I can see the force of that argument. As W. B. Yeats once put it, while wrapping a piano for his wife, 'For how but in custom and in ceremony / Are innocence and beauty born?' Unfortunately I wrap to a low standard. All presents given to me will be wrapped impeccably. All presents given by me will be immediately identifiable by the clumsiness of their wrapping. It shouldn't be like that, because one of my vacation jobs when I was in high school in Sydney more than fifty years ago was in the wrapping department of one of the big department stores.

I learned the principles of how to lay out the paper and tie the initial slip-knot, but the day came when I had to wrap a tricycle and after a couple of hours there was a crowd of other workers gathered around me laughing and laying bets. My spirit was broken for ever, and now I can't get much further than laying out the paper without everything going wrong. I cheat by using plenty of sticky tape but I can't get a piece of sticky tape off the tape dispenser without the piece going in the wrong place, usually nowhere near the present.

And there is always too little paper to be folded at one end of the present and at the other end too much. And then the length of ribbon that is meant to tie the whole thing up is always exactly not long enough, so that the bow is very small, or else a tight little reef knot which I can't cover with a fluffed rosette without masses of sticky tape radiating in all directions and . . . but why go on?

Which is my sentiment in a nutshell, but it has to be done. So I'll get it done and get it done badly, finishing the job on Christmas morning not long before dawn, with Santa's sleigh already getting set to touch down on the roof. There was a time when my younger daughter could be hired at piece-work rates to wrap presents for me, but when she grew old enough to work a calculator she declined to renew the contract. And I gave her the calculator, reasonably well wrapped. Now, there is no way out.

Or is there? And here we come to the biggest news of the week for any man in my position. Apparently you can now contact, via the web, an organization which will wrap your presents badly at only £3.96 per item. A spokesman for this organization says that, quote, 'It takes a high degree of skill to deliberately wrap presents this badly.' Actually all it takes is a man like me, but there is no denying that the service provided by this outfit is worth every penny they are asking. They will wrap my presents to make it look as if I wrapped them, which is what my family wants to see. The drawback when my daughter wrapped them was that everyone could tell that I hadn't. This way, it will look as if I care. And I do. I just don't want to go mad proving it.

The bad-wrap merchants have identified a gap in the market, and I'm sure they will flourish. I would put money into their enterprise, if I had any. In view of the magnitude of the current world economic crisis, I still haven't dared ring the bank to find out if I'm still solvent, but the mere urge to invest in such a bright idea is a sure sign that free enterprise is still alive. As I understand it, which is to the minimum extent compatible with earning a living, there is nothing inherently wrong with a market economy. As long as people make money by making things, and then invest the profit in making more things, an economy can boom for ever. Trouble starts when people start making money out of money itself. Then the whole deal comes tumbling down and finally lands on the less well off, which at this rate might effectively mean everybody less well off than the Sultan of Brunei.

But the source of recovery is still there, in the creative imagination it takes to realize that an offer to wrap presents badly could be a money-spinner, because some poor klutz might need it. That kind of creative imagination has its well-spring in human sympathy, in the spirit of charity. And if we have not charity, we are nothing. In a commendably charitable move, a High Court ruling has just opened the way for those asylum-seekers who really can't go home – but haven't been allowed to earn a living either – to work their way out of a financial limbo that beats anything the rest of us are likely to be faced with.

A fair day's wage for a fair day's work is at the basis of all dignity. In my homeland, Australia, it used to be called the Fair Go. When I was very young, after World War II, there was an Australian film called *The Sons of Matthew*. Any Australian film was big news in those days and we all went to see it, even those of us in short pants. It was about a poor family living in the bush who faced a bleak pre-war Christmas, and the older brothers made toys in secret for the younger ones. I remember a close-up of one of the older brothers as he fought sleep after midnight. He was still working on the details of a little toy train carved from wood.

I was from a poor family myself, but I knew that the presents I would get would be more lavish than that, even though they had cost my mother just as much in labour. Times had changed in Australia since the depression era evoked in the film. I think it was probably that same year that I unwrapped the box containing my Hornby 'O'-gauge train set imported from Britain. It was a delightful surprise, and would have been less so if it hadn't been wrapped up. I'll try to remember that when I'm fighting the sticky-tape dispenser, even though wrapping isn't among my gifts, if you get what I mean. Merry Christmas, and wrap up well.

Postscript

For the truly bad-ass wrapper, there is another way out that I didn't have room to cover. You can buy gifts in the kind of shop that will gift-wrap them to be picked up later. The shop is already draining your credit card so it might as well do a bit more for you. The trouble is, though, that the recipient of the gift might still find reason to wrinkle the nose. When I give a present that has been purchased at Liberty's and wrapped by the store's expert wrappers in the store's unfeasibly luxurious paper, I have noticed that I am still looked upon as having taken the easy way out. What Liberty's needs is a bad-wrapping department. In the overture to this broadcast I gave a pretty thorough survey of the simple muscle-intensive tasks that I was then allowed to do. I found my identity, akin to the elusive national identity of Australia, in my ability to carry them out. Little did I suspect that in the first month of 2010, not really a very long time later, I would be felled by various ailments and have to spend more than half the year forbidden to lift anything. The period of enforced leisure passed no more quickly than eternity, and at the time of writing I have only just regained the classification by which I am allowed to carry my share of the shopping bags on Saturday morning. It was a savage reminder that people really do define themselves by their jobs, even when the job is humble. That's why the lady behind one of the many counters of the department store proclaims her ownership of the goods you wish to purchase from her. ('I've only got it in these two colours at the moment but I should have the complete range in again by Saturday morning.') At the supermarket, the person on the cash desk will ask you to enter your pin number even after you have already begun to enter it. ('Can you enter your pin number for me?') The person is really telling you that he or she is an indispensable part of the process. We should try not to smile knowingly: in the same position we would do it too. And in any kind of cooperative venture, to make light of somebody's job is the quickest way of making an enemy.

JESUS

Dates of show: 26 and 28 December 2008

In the first scene of Shakespeare's *Hamlet*, on the battlements of Elsinore, just before dawn, Marcellus speaks. Marcellus is a walk-on part who gets only a few lines, but it was typical of Shakespeare to give even the pizza-delivery man something fabulous to say. Marcellus says that in the season wherein our saviour's birth is celebrated, the bird of morning singeth all night long. And Horatio says, 'So have I heard, and do in part believe it.' It's by no means certain whether Shakespeare believed that his own soul could be saved by Christ or any other saviour, but it is certain that there were all kinds of things about the Christian religion that Shakespeare believed at least in part.

Well before the arrival on earth of our greatest writer, the process of ceasing to believe in a life beyond the grave had already begun. The question was already in existence of how much of the Christian religion would be left if it were deprived of the certainty that anyone who had faith would join the exalted Christ in the next life. And the answer was already in existence too. There would be a lot left. Shakespeare's plays and poetry were saturated with Christian ceremony, Christian symbolism, the seasons of the Christian year. The soul of Hamlet flew to heaven with an escort of singing angels.

Living his life a hundred years before Shakespeare, Leonardo da Vinci was quite possibly no believer in a life to come. All the evidence suggests, or at any rate little of it does not suggest, that he was a scientific empiricist whose atheism would have satisfied the requirements of Richard Dawkins. If Dawkins had been alive at the time and wearing the appropriate Renaissance clothes, in which he would have looked quite good, he might have paid a visit to Leonardo when the genius was at work in the dining hall of Santa Marie delle Grazie in

Milan. Richard of Oxford could have asked Leonardo of Vinci if he really believed in all that supernatural stuff and Leonardo would probably have said no.

The conversation would have been brief, however, since Leonardo was hard at work painting *The Last Supper*, which is still there, although only the ghost of what it was, because he painted it not as a fresco, but directly onto the wall, thereby multiplying the chances that his new masterpiece would deteriorate with time. Almost certainly he knew that, but he was in the grip of inspiration, so he got on with the job anyway.

What kind of inspiration, if he didn't believe in how the story ended? But he did believe in the story's hero. The picture was already a ruin by the time Shakespeare was born, but even today, when you look at the many-times restored remains, you can see that the figure who occupies the vanishing point of all its perspectives is a concentration of everything that Leonardo knew about the force of human personality. And the same was true even when he painted Christ as a child. The infant Jesus always looks like an athlete in the making.

Michelangelo, who was twenty years younger than Leonardo and outlived him by forty-five years, made Jesus heroic at any age and in all media. In Michelangelo's sculpture of the Madonna and child now in a church in Bruges, the boy Jesus is already a little tower of strength, and in the famous drawings of the dead Christ rising from the tomb, the figure that floats upwards is no wraith, but the sublime expression of a warrior. In the most famous Michelangelo Pietà, when the dead son lies across the knees of his mother, he is indeed the wreck of man, but it is a man who has been wrecked. Again, it's a matter for argument whether Michelangelo believed in the heaven he painted around the body of God at the centre of the ceiling of the Sistine Chapel, but there can be no doubt that the personal force of Jesus was the focus of all his attention.

The supernatural visitor had been humanized. It was one of the things that humanism did. When the early painters of the Renaissance began painting religious figures as people instead of icons, a new kind of belief had begun. The centre of attention was switching from the next world to this one, according to the revolutionary conviction that the life that really matters happens between birth and death. The Churches, both Catholic and Protestant, did all they could to fight back, and they were especially fierce on art. The Catholic counter-reformation was partly an attempt to pull the artists back into the service of dogma, and in England the Protestant image-breakers weren't just out to nail idolatry. They wanted to wipe out all suggestions that religion could be reduced to the level of mere humanity.

The Churches survived, they are still here, and there are many people who still believe, in the old sense. But everything the Churches had ever taught came in for half a millennium of questioning, until finally only one thing was left unquestioned. Paradoxically, the humanists, who had begun the process of undermining Christian belief, had reinforced the importance of the personality at its centre.

I know that my redeemer liveth. Well, I doubt if he can redeem me. I wish he could. But I do have faith that he lives on, as an ideal. All the Christian religions are lucky to have him, and those of us who have ceased to be Christians in the old way are lucky to have him too. In these weeks, in all the days of Advent until Christmas Day and from then on until Twelfth Night – the season wherein his birth is celebrated – have been giving him, and will yet give him, much thought. For me, he didn't need to be crucified in order to prove his capacity for sacrifice. He proved that when he faced the crowd who wanted to stone to death the woman taken in adultery.

It was a turning point in history, because nothing quite like that had ever been recorded before. Since the same crowd of fanatics might very well have stoned him for interrupting their dreadful ceremony, clearly he was brave beyond the imagination of most of us. But it was the generosity of his intervention that set a new mark. He met the same mark again when he promised a place near him in heaven to the whore who had washed his feet. Imagine the whispering abuse he earned for that. Imagine the shouted abuse.

I first heard about these things in Bible class when I was very young, and I can't think of how the same permanently necessary message about tolerance could have been transmitted in any other way. No matter how intolerant the Churches got in all their years of power, not even when they were burning people by the thousand, they never managed to wipe out the impression of his understanding spirit. Those moments in the Gospel would alone be enough to prove the importance of keeping alive all we can about his story.

We can debate the difficult points of interpretation, hit each other over the head about the truth of what he said here and what he did there, but the essence of his personality still deserves to be cherished as a salvation, a redemption. It won't, I think, redeem our sins or save our souls for heaven. But it will give us a measure for how we should lead our lives on earth, even if we are bound to fail. I notice that even my friend Christopher Hitchens, who has lately become famous all over again for declaring that religious belief is inimical to human reason and a threat to justice, would still rather like to maintain some of the traditions. Writing beautifully himself, he knows that much of the beauty of the English language has the Bible as its fountain, and that an education without a Bible education is no education.

How the traditions can be maintained without the religious institutions being maintained as well is a question he will no doubt tackle in the course of time, but for now it surely can be said that we should cherish any of the Christian remnants that do not conflict with the merciful and all-comprehending nature of the man whose life on earth was the beginning of it all. Some of the remnants are in ruins, but still too beautiful to lose, like Leonardo's *Last Supper*, still being restored even though there is almost nothing left of it to restore except restorations. Other remnants are trying to be ruins, and it takes money to repair them. Ely Cathedral would still be a miracle even if it were to be reduced to the condition of Tintern Abbey, with grass growing in the nave and the sky for a roof. But we would lose the magnificent ceiling, and how can we not find the money to protect that, if we can find the money to lay more runways for more airports to take more people in search of a paradise on earth?

Other remnants are trivial, but vital all the same. During the days of Advent, when our granddaughter came to visit, she would search for a chocolate in one of the pockets of Tommasina, our Advent doll. Made of rag, Tommasina is a lot taller than our granddaughter and has many pockets. For now, the hidden chocolate that somehow always got into one of the many pockets of Tommasina is a sufficient mystery. But the Christmas will come when our granddaughter will want to know more about just whose birthday Christmas is, and an important part of her upbringing will begin. Her parents are both believers in the classic sense, but it might be that their daughter will one day become an unbeliever, as I did. She might not believe that Jesus is still alive, in heaven. But there is one important thing that even I will be able to tell her, which is that Jesus, the first great man to be a champion of women, believed in her, and that alone would be sufficient cause to bless every night and day of the season wherein his birth is celebrated. The bird of morning will never sing all night long, but nor, if we are wise, will the memory of that man ever die.

Postscript

Greatly daring, the BBC still allowed the odd mention of Jesus during the Christmas period, although there was always the chance that somebody, if sufficiently provoked, would put in a planning application to turn the lobby of Broadcasting House into a mosque. There is no religion that I believe in, but I have a different way of not believing in Christianity than of not believing in, say, Islam. This doesn't mean that I am a Christian agnostic, but it does mean that I am not an atheist along the lines of Richard Dawkins and Christopher Hitchens. That I am an atheist goes without saying, and on the whole I would rather not say it, because as a position it holds scarcely any interest in itself. More interesting, to me at any rate, is that I am an ex-Christian atheist whose unbelief is consciously informed by the Christian heritage. So really the question of proselytizing for my irreligious convictions never comes up, because I would rather that other people, should they arrive at the same state, did so under their own steam. It's a case of self-persuasion being the only kind of persuasion that matters.

When Dr Johnson said that it was not the act of a gentleman to shake someone in his faith, he missed the opportunity to say that it was the act of a bore. Via YouTube I watched my friend Hitchens preaching his godless creed many times, and it was the only theme on which he was ever less than thrilling. As for Dawkins, it is remarkable how a man so brilliant can be content to sound so trite. The contention that a God who might intervene in human affairs does not exist is so manifestly irrefutable that it scarcely bears saying even once. But sometimes clever people get bitten by a bug. They become worried that a truth which has come to them like a revelation might not have struck you with sufficient force, even though you, too, profess to agree with it. Thus I once spent a delightful hour at the dinner table with David Hockney. The dessert was finished but the coffee was still being brought around for unlimited refills, and in those days smoking at the table was still permitted. A world-champion smoker, Hockney was pleased to meet a contender for the title. Nothing could injure the easy conviviality, but I'm bound to say that it would have been even more perfect if Hockney had accepted my agreement to his proposition that Picasso was a great painter. Yes, I assured him, I knew that. 'No,' said Hockney, in a kind of evangelistic desperation, 'Picasso was a *great* painter.' He thought I didn't really get it.

In the same way, the otherwise scintillating Dawkins is likely to suspect that we have not really taken in the news about the non-existence of God. Dawkins should be given credit, though, for his integrity. Once, in conversation with him on stage in Edinburgh, I argued that the mass of believers in the various religions might conceivably behave worse if they were deprived of a deity to believe in. Dawkins pointed out that he didn't proclaim the non-existence of God in order to make the world better. He proclaimed it because it was true. Hard to argue with that, except to say that it might be where the argument starts. I hasten to add that it was he, and not I, who wrote *The Blind Watchmaker*, and that we should be slow to award ourselves prizes when we detect a quirk in the head of a genius. Newton was utterly batty on the subject of chronology, but on the whole it's wiser to note that he said useful things about celestial mechanics.

NEW YEAR PREDICTION

Dates of show: 2 and 4 January 2009

This is my last broadcast until my next spell and I'm in a summing-up mood. I have no New Year resolutions apart from the usual one about tidying my office in case the body of my missing cleaner is lying mummified under that pile of magazines. But I do feel like making a New Year prediction. I want to put down a marker that proves I have a grip on world events. The best way to prove this is to make a prediction that everybody knows has already come true, but that few people are yet ready to admit.

I hereby predict that from now on, starting today, nobody will look good who gets rich quick. I can predict more than that, in fact. Even getting rich slowly is going to look silly, if getting rich is the only aim in mind. Getting rich for its own sake will look as stupid as bodybuilding does at that point when the neck gets thicker than the head and the thighs and biceps look like four plastic kit-bags full of tofu. And on the men it looks even worse.

Just before Christmas, as if the collapse of some of the world's relatively honest financial institutions had not already been unsettling enough, a hustler called Bernard Madoff was caught swindling the world's smartest investors out of a grand total of fifty billion dollars. How, it was asked, could the world's smartest investors have fallen for this character? The answer, surely, is that they were all like him. They thought they had found a way of making money out of nothing. Unfortunately for them, the ineffable Madoff *knew* he had found a way of making money out of nothing. All he had to do was tell them he had invented something called 'a split-conversion strategy' and they handed him their money.

But most of them had got their money the same way, by promising vast returns on money from other people who were trying to make money out of nothing. Many profound articles were written by the financial experts to explain how the whole mad Madoff cycle had been generated, but the question that was never asked is the one that bears most closely on my theme. What was he going to *do* with fifty billion dollars?

Back at the start of this series I raised the issue of what the multibillionaires who owned yachts were hoping to achieve. At best, their ridiculous unarmed battleships, permanently parked in the teeming marina of the sort of city where the world's well-dressed dimwits gather to gamble at the casino, were described as floating palaces. What kind of numbskull wants a palace that floats, when he could just have a palace, out of whose front door he could stride with some confidence that he would not plunge face-first into the harbour? I was really asking a question about what you can do with too much money, and the answer was obvious: never enough.

How much money is too much? It's too much when you've already got all you could possibly need, and there's nothing to do with any more except count it. There have been some encouraging signs that this elementary realization has at last begun to dawn. Bill Gates saw the light early. Bill Gates, who invented the software which has just given me a picture of Donatella Versace after I pressed the wrong button – wait a second, I certainly don't want to see any more of that – Bill Gates got to the point where he started to look for useful ways of giving some of his money away.

It was good news for Africa, which needs the kind of well-researched, well-targeted and well-protected money that will go into things like roads and seed, and not the kind of money that will go into the bank accounts of black leaders even more greedily aimless than the kind of white dolts who buy yachts as big as the USS *Nimitz*. If there is a tragedy anywhere in the uproarious comedy of the Madoff madness, it lies in the fact that some people who were trying to do what Gates did – assemble a fund that would help the world's poor – handed the fund to someone who promised to make the fund bigger by handing it to Madoff, so that he could apply his magic split-conversion double downdraft fiscal disappearance strategy.

So good money vanished that could have helped to build a road that would have carried the equipment to the right spot to build a well that would have watered a field that might have grown the grain that might feed the sort of people who are currently eating their own carpets in Zimbabwe. The first thing Zimbabwe will need, of course, after Mr Mugabe finally gets sent off into exile to live in a suite at the top of some nut-job Gulf hotel with an uninterrupted view of ten thousand square miles of desert, is honest government, which is based not only on real elections, but on double-entry bookkeeping.

Worldwide, the mundane but crucial concept of balancing the account books with earned income against genuine expenditure is more likely to become implanted now that all the split-conversion doubletalk is suddenly no longer fashionable. The upmarket weekend papers have been full of canvassed opinions about what good might come out of the recession but the right answer is already in. The recession isn't just a wake-up call telling us to get real. We've got real. The *Good Housekeeping* seal of approval has returned to power. It's the end of an era of silly money.

The actor George Clooney gives some of his time to good causes. He's famous for it. You could say that all the publicity he gets for doing it helps to make him even more famous than he is already and that therefore charity is to his advantage, but it would be a mean view. He couldn't make all those interesting little movies we admire him for so much if he didn't make all those uninteresting big movies for which we admire him a little less, so we should forgive him the huge salary.

But already, because of the new mood, it's getting harder to forgive him for advertising coffee. If the coffee commercials make him the extra money that he gives away, that must leave the huge salary intact. Well, yes, he might say, but he has a lot of people on his payroll. Ladies, I like him too, so I want to believe that it all checks out. But one thing doesn't. He isn't credible when he tries to sell me coffee. I just don't believe that a brand of coffee tastes better because George Clooney drinks it. He looks silly.

I advertised something myself once. I made a set of commercials for an Australian telephone company. The commercials were beautifully shot but the campaign was a total failure, because the competing telephone company was selling a better product cheaper, so nobody believed what I was saying. I could still use that kind of money even now, but if I tried to get it that way I would expect to be told that I looked silly.

Matthew McConaughey is doing commercials for a certain

fragrance. I'm sure the extra money he is making is going to a good cause but there are two questions that I ask automatically whenever I see those commercials. The first question is: who wants to smell like Matthew McConaughey? And the second question is, doesn't he look silly?

Life is harder and shorter for female film stars than it is for male film stars and I'm sure there are good reasons for Charlize Theron to be the face of a certain fragrance. She might even sincerely believe in the stuff if it gives her the confidence to wear nothing else except a pair of high heels as she sways away down the corridor into the bedroom, the bare behind of a certain fragrance trailing a subtle cloud of bliss, but I can only ask: couldn't she have just sold her Oscar? And doesn't she look silly?

For Nicole Kidman, also, life might be tougher than we think. A beautiful woman reduced to starring in a film like *Australia* when she could have negotiated a year's work painting the Sydney Harbour Bridge with a nailbrush and made a greater dramatic impact might well need extra income, but her commercials for another certain fragrance ask us to believe that it must smell good because she's wearing it. If I could be assured that the certain fragrance doesn't make Nicole Kidman smell different, but instead smells exactly like Nicole Kidman, I would buy a bottle and drink it. But otherwise I'm convinced of nothing except that she looks exactly as if she's hustling for a buck she doesn't need. Even if she does, is this the way to get it? Doesn't she look silly?

In the old days, the actors did commercials offshore. Harrison Ford advertised products in Japan on the understanding that the commercials would never be screened in the US. He was following the example of Laurence Olivier, who advertised cameras in the US on the understanding that the commercials would never be screened in the UK. It was agreed, back in the day, that serious artists should not look like hucksters. Now it is assumed that serious artists look even more serious if they do look like hucksters. They look bigger, more corporate, more influential. Or they did until yesterday. But now it's today, and it suddenly looks like a fast buck. It looks off. Madoff off. And it looks silly.

We've reached a turning point. A madness has gone out of fashion: the madness of behaving as if only too much can be enough. There will always be another madness, but not that one. From now on a man will have to be as dumb as a petrodollar potentate to think that anyone will respect him for sitting on a gold toilet in a private jumbo jet. Excess wealth is gone like the codpiece. The free market will continue, but any respect for the idea of free money is all over. If you've got it, flaunt it by all means, but if you haven't earned it, forget about it. There isn't going to be a change of consciousness, there's already been one, which is why I can be so confident when I predict it. Until next time.

Postscript

I was going to say, 'If only I'd been right,' but in fact I was more right than not: after 2008, the big money never did look quite so respectable again – not, at any rate, when men without principles were using it to buy themselves a background. I was wrong, though, to suppose that the bankers and executives would get the point. After the Western governments bailed out the financial institutions with public money, the first thing the financial institutions did was to revive the bonus system, on the principle that arbitrageurs or whatever their French name was would never try hard unless they were overpaid. To put it briefly, the banks gave even more of our money to the very breed of grifter who had been busy losing it. But who knows, there might be something to the idea that nobody will knock himself out playing electronic percentages unless he is rewarded with enough cash to buy a Lamborghini and rebuild his girlfriend. We can be sure, however, that the oft-stated assumption behind huge salaries in the public corporations – that those same executives would be able to earn even more in the open market – was moonshine. The BBC was already a bad example and later on the bad example became blatant. Once there had been a whole romance attached to the idea of working devotedly for small reward. The romance depended on the ability of the system to pay a public servant in prestige, honour and perhaps, upon his retirement, a small sandstone bolt-hole in an Oxbridge college. The cash nexus had put an end to that, and it would have been hypocritical for a performer to complain: we, after all, were keen enough to get the market price. But there were limits.

They were set higher, but they had always been there, just as there had always been wide boys who thought it smart to break them. For anyone who had been alive long enough, Bernie Madoff was very familiar. Once he had been called Bernie Kornfeld, and back in the sixties he'd had television programmes made about him – the BBC was especially respectful, as it too often is in the early stages of a scam. Bernie Kornfeld's scheme for doubling your money was an early form of Bernie Madoff's split-conversion strategy. Journalists and TV front-men who flew to Switzerland to catch the pearls of wisdom as they fell from Kornfeld's lips would have done better to stay home and do an elementary cash-flow analysis of how his companies were set up. But scepticism was in short supply even then, and lately it has been in retreat, overwhelmed by a millenarian urge to believe.

Scepticism got a bad name after climate change acquired religious status, but really scepticism is not the enemy of science, it is just the opposite of gullibility. Old enough to remember that the global warming scare had been preceded in the 1970s by the global cooling scare – some of global warming's star figures, such as Jim Hansen, had been in on the earlier boondoggle – I also noticed something familiar about the mechanism by which a putative menace was to be warded off with government money. The putative menace might or might not be a phantom, but the government money definitely came from the taxpayer, and there were whole regiments of Bernie Madoff types on the alert to take their cut for handling it as it flowed out of the public coffers and into oblivion.

2009 – SERIES ONE

THE SPEEDING JUDGE

Dates of show: 27 and 29 March 2009

In a case which has deep resonance for Britain and the entire civilized world, the whole of Australia has been glued to the media in recent weeks, following the story of an eminent judge who has ruined his reputation because he tried to lie his way out of a speeding fine that would have cost him about £36 sterling. At the age of seventy, he is about to go to jail for a minimum of two years because he failed to cough up thirty-six quid at the right moment. On the face of it, you can't call his disaster a tragedy. A tragedy, according to classical principles, is a fall from high degree because of some great flaw. Marcus Einfeld, the judge in question, was certainly of high enough degree: none higher. Queen's Counsel since 1977, Australian Living Treasure 1997, United Nations Peace Award 2002, the list goes on. He retired a few years ago but he has continually been brought back to judge important cases about refugees because the Australian legal system can't do without his experience and prestige.

Or anyway it couldn't. In 2006 a speed camera in Sydney caught his silver Lexus doing 6 mph over the limit. At this point we have to forget about the dizzy speed of the car and try to slow down the thought processes going on in his head. There he is, at the top of his profession, with a national, indeed international, reputation for wisdom. This is the man who was the founding President of Australia's Human Rights and Equal Opportunities Commission. In 1987 he headed the Commission's inquiry into the living conditions of Aborigines in the border area of New South Wales and Queensland and he wept openly at evidence that a young Aborigine boy who had been denied a proper rugby ball had played instead with an old shoe.

Those were famous tears, and there is every reason to think that they were sincerely felt. As a judge of great matters of justice, Marcus Einfeld had deservedly been revered for many years. He had a right to think of himself as the very incarnation of the law. Now here he was, with a speeding ticket in his hand, facing a fine of a paltry £36 for having exceeded the speed limit by a lousy 6 mph. And right there the fatal error begins to take form. It wasn't so much the £36 fine. He could afford that. It was that the penalty points would bring him closer to losing his licence. Somehow the top judge and national treasure didn't see himself in a position where he was not allowed to drive.

Unusual, that. Many seventy-year-old men of his exalted rank are very content to be driven, rather than having to do the driving. They have a man with a cap to drive them, so they can say, from the back seat: watch out for the speed cameras, Bruce. Perhaps Marcus Einfeld is one of those strange men – there are thousands of them in every country and they are nearly always men – who need to have a driving licence just so that they can get points on it, who think that the whole purpose of driving is to drive as far over the limit as they can and still get away with it, and still keep going for as long as the licence lasts even if they don't get away with it.

But the judge was only 6 mph over the limit, which scarcely made him a boy racer. He must have thought the prospect of getting yet more points on an already point-scarred licence was an awful lot of inconvenience for practically nothing, and he must also have thought – and here the other half of the fateful mental pattern comes into play – he must also have thought of how easy it would be to get out of it. All he had to do was say that someone else was driving the silver Lexus that day. So he said he had lent the car to an American friend, Professor Theresa Brennan. Satisfied, the magistrate dismissed the case, and the judge walked free. In just such a way, King Oedipus believed himself to be in the clear when he left Corinth.

If he – I mean the judge, not King Oedipus – had said that he had lent the car to an Australian government secret agent whom he could not name without rendering him vulnerable to attack by terrorists, Marcus Einfeld might still be enjoying his place at the top of the heap, admired by all. But Professor Theresa Brennan was an actual figure, who could be traced. When a newspaper did trace her, it turned out that she was no longer in existence. At the time of the speeding incident she had already been dead for three years.

It was probably already too late for Marcus Einfeld to save his career. Yet he might conceivably have climbed relatively unbesmirched out of the hole he was occupying, and even drawn some sympathy for the depth to which he had dug himself in by telling one of those little fibs that almost everyone tells over small matters. But like President Nixon in the Watergate scandal, the judge, although trying to cover up an infinitely smaller crime – dodging a £36 fine instead of okaying acts of black-bag espionage against a rival party in clear defiance of the Constitution of the United States – the judge chose to go on digging himself further towards the centre of the earth.

He said he didn't mean *that* Theresa Brennan. He meant *another* Theresa Brennan. A Greek chorus at this point might have said that the judge was anything but a natural liar, because he lied so very badly, just like most of us. Further proofs of his amateur status followed in quick succession. Finally, in a skein of inventions that we needn't bother to unravel, he managed to implicate his own mother, aged ninety-four, when he claimed to have been using her Toyota Corolla that day, so he couldn't have been at the wheel of his silver Lexus.

Alas, there was security camera footage to prove that his mother's Toyota Corolla had not emerged from the garage of her apartment block between daylight and dusk. We were left with the thought-picture of a team of trained investigators examining a whole day's worth of CCTV footage to establish that a Toyota Corolla had remained stationary throughout. With that thought-picture, and with the thought-picture of a man of true stature with his life in ruins.

Did any of this really matter? Well, obviously the original offence didn't matter much. At 6 mph over the limit, the judge wasn't going to hurt anyone. And the first lie shouldn't have mattered much either. People really do lie all the time. Often they lie to protect themselves, sometimes they lie to protect their loved ones, and there is even such a thing as a saving lie, a lie that wards off the dreadful consequences of the truth. Ibsen wrote a play about that, called *The Wild Duck*. None of this means that lying is a virtue. Almost always, it's a vice, to be avoided. But it's a universal vice, and its prevalence is the very reason why any properly functioning legal system has a harsh law against perjury, because a court is where the lies have to stop, or there can be no justice.

And what the judge did was knowingly to put himself on the road to perjury. He was on the road at only 6 mph over the limit and he could have stopped himself by coughing up thirty-six quid, but there was an inner momentum. Just why that should have been so is a question he'll be occupying himself with for the next two years at least. Everyone else will be thinking about it too, but his will be easily the finest mind concerned with the subject. He doesn't need me or anyone else to tell him that a judge who commits perjury, over no matter how trivial a matter, has sinned against the spirit of his profession.

That's why his case really is a tragedy, and not just a farce. It's a tragedy because he not only fell from high degree, there really *was* a tragic flaw: a capacity to forget, at the critical moment, the central ethical precept of the calling to which he had given his life. Suddenly, belatedly, and for almost no reason, he put himself in the position of a doctor who is arraigned for selling body parts, and, because he was selling only fingernails, defends himself by saying it hadn't been him that sold the fingernails, it was Professor Theresa Brennan, or another Theresa Brennan, or his mother at the wheel of a Toyota Corolla. The doctor wasn't supposed to be selling anything, so he should have owned up.

But the judge doesn't need to hear that from me, or from any other of the thousands of Australian experts – editorial writers, television commentators and philosophers of all descriptions – who are now picking this matter over. The judge is already hearing about it from himself. He's hearing about the fatal road that led from the speed camera to the truly tragic climax, which wasn't the moment when one of his fellow judges had to send him down for three years, two of them without parole. The tragic climax came when the distinguished Judge Marcus Einfeld found himself on the telephone to his mother saying: 'Mum, remember how you lent me your Toyota that day?' and she said, 'Marcus, what have you got yourself into?' And suddenly he was a little boy again, as all men are when the truth they must face is about a mess of their own making.

Postscript

Though Caesar never got around to explaining exactly why his wife had to be above suspicion, we generally take the maxim to be true. Caesar stole money to pay bribes but he was clean compared with

Pompey and very clean compared with, say, Lucullus. Tyrants do better when not hampered by greed. Hitler is an arch example. He knew exactly how to corrupt others (a little-known aspect of his control over the Wehrmacht generals is that he bribed them with land grants) but he was not interested himself in amassing wealth or even in living well: he left that to Göring. More keen year by year to fulfil his role as a grasping clown, Göring carried on almost as if Hitler had written the script in order to profit from the contrast. Similarly, Robespierre had an advantage over Danton in being less concerned with money. Danton's penchant for embezzlement not only gave Robespierre useful evidence with which to destroy him, it took time that he might have spent preparing his defences well in advance, had he been so minded. Take enough examples like Hitler and Robespierre and you start wondering if personal integrity might not be a public danger.

But of course it isn't: not in itself. Whereas corruption probably is, to the body politic if not the individual. One says 'probably' because a state entirely without corruption is hard to find. Australia, despite its history of 'bottom of the harbour' scandals and the occasional instance of an entire police force on the take, comes close to being clean. We can guess that might be so because in Australia a case of a corrupt judge is always even more surprising than it would be in America. But in comparing the liberal democracies with one another, it is always important to remember that even the most corrupt of them doesn't begin to approach what the old Soviet Union used to be like. Concentrated use of the state's immense powers of judicial violence allowed for some areas of business that were relatively free of corruption – the state could, after all, build a space station – but in everyday life, for anyone not a member of the *nomenklatura*, the only way to get anything done was to break the law. In such an atmosphere, scruples sound like principles, as I suppose they always should. A correspondent pointed out that 6 mph extra in a 30 mph zone mattered. Thinking about it, I had to agree.

HIGH-PRICED PORN

Dates of show: 3 and 5 April 2009

Very few voices have dared to speak up in defence of the Home Secretary's husband, but let mine be one of them. The Home Secretary, Jacqui Smith, is in an invidious position. Before I start defending her husband, Richard Timney, let me be blunt about just how invidious that position is. It always looked unduly cosy that the Home Secretary should claim forty thousand pounds a year of public funds to pay Richard Timney to run her constituency office.

Though it is common practice for parliamentarians to employ their spouses, the Home Secretary's employment of her husband was bound to draw scrutiny to her broad interpretation of what constitutes a legitimate expense. A bedroom counted as a primary home. It looked even more unduly cosy when her husband started claiming his expenses, including the purchase of a bath plug and a home entertainment system. Some might have thought, the modern world being what it is, that although the bath plug might be morally neutral if used responsibly, the same might not apply to the home entertainment system: and so, indeed, it proved.

While the Home Secretary was away on official business, on the evening of 1 April 2008 at 11.18 her husband watched an adult entertainment movie and on the evening of 6 April at 11.19 he watched another adult entertainment movie. Since these movies were available only on subscription, he had to pay for them. He charged the payment to the public. The fact that the Home Secretary's husband watched pay-for-view pornography in her absence, and the further fact that he then charged the payment to the taxpayer: these facts were made public by a tabloid newspaper which can be said to have some expertise in the matter, since the fortunes of its proprietor were largely made in this very business of adult entertainment.

It is doubtful if the Home Secretary was entertained at all when she found out that this story was going to be made public at the very time in her career when she has legislation going through parliament to regulate such adult-entertainment matters as businessmen putting visits to pole-dancing clubs on expenses as if they'd just been to the pub. Tough on pole-dancing, tough on the causes of pole-dancing: it's a New Labour policy in the grand modern tradition, which takes a moral view that includes the economics, or, if you like, an economic view that includes the morality. Either way, when you hold the position of Home Secretary and have been so outspoken on the topic of adult entertainment on expenses, it isn't the best moment for headlines to be telling the world that your husband has not only been watching porno movies, he has been off-loading the cost of doing so on to the tax-paying public.

Her husband has dropped her in it. Some would say that she was already in it, because she has patently never been able to judge the effect of an expenses claim in which a principal item is a salary for her husband's efforts in running her constituency office, a salary with an expense allowance down to and including bath plugs. But he has dropped her further in it, as if that were possible. If she was already in it up to her lower eyelids, he has now stood on top of her head. From where her fringe was previously visible, bubbles are coming up, and it's all his fault. Is there no one to speak for him?

Let me be the one, because it just so happens that I know the truth about pornographic movies. As a professional critic of the media I have always felt it was incumbent on me, as a public duty, to keep up with developments in all the means of expression however disreputable, so for purposes of research I began checking out the adult-entertainment channels in hotel rooms all over the world. If I was filming in Hawaii or Tokyo or Berlin I would switch on the adult-entertainment channels late at night to see what was on offer and make notes.

One of the first things I noted was that although there were hundreds and even thousands of pornographic movies they all had the same few half-witted story structures and almost without exception they were manufactured in Los Angeles, with a cast of characters that soon became recognizable no matter where in the world you were watching. Indeed that was the chief comfort they offered. If you were lonely in a hotel room in Sydney or Amsterdam, there on the screen were the same old familiar few faces from the San Fernando Valley, the men with their improbably low foreheads and permanently puzzled expressions, the women with their enhanced lips and strangely rigid chests, as if wearing a tungsten basque internally.

For a student of bad acting, there could be no richer field. It's not as if the porno stars merely lack dramatic talent. They have the opposite of dramatic talent. Yet touchingly they are more interested in the challenges offered by the roles they play than in the sex part. The man pretending to be the scientist whose job is to check the sexual sensitivity of the female astronaut just back from space keeps adjusting the collar of the white coat which proves that he is a scientist. He holds his clipboard in a scientific manner. Meanwhile the woman playing the astronaut delivers her line of dialogue. 'I don't know, Doctor. I guess something happened to me out there.'

None of them can act because none of them really has a personality: a fact which is only further emphasized when they attempt to effervesce. As a result, they are no more erotic when they disrobe than plaster casts of roughly the same size and weight. I hasten to add that not all of the women are low rent in their physical attributes. All the men look stupid beyond belief, but some of the women would be almost personable in the right light, which this definitely isn't. The lighting is harsh for the same reason that there is so little pubic hair in evidence. The aim is to make the whole thing look clinical.

From the erotic angle, adult entertainment movies are made for men whose idea of the adult barely gets beyond the babyish. For anyone with a brain, there is not only no question of being aroused, there is a detectable shrivelling effect on the libido. In time, a connoisseur of the form learns to trust it as a sure-fire means of getting the mind off sex.

Is your partner away in Brussels making a speech? Get your mind off sex by watching a porn video. Just don't watch too many of them, or you might burn out your circuits permanently. Plenty of men have done this. They watched *Barely Legal Teenage Terminators* once too often, and now nothing stirs even when they eat blue pills like peanuts.

Yes, men, you can watch the stuff in perfect safety any time you want to quell that urge. But it might, on the whole, be safer not to expect the public to nod with understanding if you charge the expense to them. I'm quite confident that Jacqui Smith's husband was doing her a service, as it were, when he switched on the purportedly hot movies. He was doing it to cool himself down while he counted the hours until her return. But then he made the mistake of claiming the cost as a legitimate expense. You could say that it was, in a way. If his job of running her office is legitimate, then keeping himself sane in the absence of his partner is plainly part of his duty, and the attendant costs shouldn't have to come out of his pocket, especially in view of the fact that her position as Home Secretary must infinitely multiply her effect as an object of desire. I can remember very well when I felt that way about Sir Geoffrey Howe.

But Richard Timney should have realized that the mass of the British public is still convinced that there is such a thing as sauciness. They are not yet living in the modern age. They are still living in a Carry On movie. Only a comparatively small proportion of the public have as many channels as Mr Timney had in his home entertainment centre and have seen what a cable channel programme like *Sexcetera* is actually like. The presenters of *Sexcetera*, when they aren't hearty young American females with breasts bigger than their behinds, are hearty young American males with grins bigger than their heads, screaming in a stage whisper about the secrets behind the silver-studded black-leather-quilted door. There are never any secrets worth bothering about behind the silver-studded black-leather-quilted door. There are people of repellent aspect doing ridiculous things to each other with clinical-looking equipment, but there are never any secrets.

Because there is only one secret about sex, and that is that it's a feeling, and you can't see feeling. Some of the greatest artists who ever lived did their best to register the look on a woman's face when she is in ecstasy. Bernini almost did it, Gustav Klimt almost did it, and if you're a man dying for lack of love you could start with them. But looking at porno movies will get you so far in the opposite direction that you might as well watch a programme about stock-car racing.

The real story in this matter, however, isn't about a man watching images. It's about a man leaving a paper trail. In that respect, it was he who hadn't caught up with the modern age. In a hotel, they promise you that the name of the porno movie you watched won't show up on your bill. But if somebody else is paying your bill, they

can easily figure out that you watched it. If you had resigned yourself
at the time to paying for those two stupid movies with your own
money, Richard, Jacqui wouldn't be paying now.

Postscript

I was only just exaggerating about the tedium of pornographic videos.
If the weeping pink caverns and the torrential money shots are what
you're after, you (I take it that 'you' are a bloke) doubtless already
know that the Web is the place to cruise. On the Web, just checking
out the free samples and without handing over a single credit-card
detail, you can click from one mind-rotting spectacle to another until
one day you wake up and realize you have turned into a puddle of
grease. Off the Web, in the videos available for rent or purchase, what
you mainly get is the acting in between the bits you're after, and the
acting is invariably in full keeping with the intelligence and talents of
the participants. The porn videos attract much solemn sociological
comment but none of it should be trusted, because the subject is too
funny for anyone except the occasional gifted writer like Martin Amis
to do it justice. The discrepancy between intention and effect, between
self-importance and actual importance, is so great that only a comic
imagination can see the tragedy.

Any writer planning a novel about porn who does research on the
Web had better have plans prepared for getting his hard-drive crushed
at a moment's notice, in case the police break in. On the prevailing
scale of public condemnation, 'research' into adult porn rates comfortably lower than 'research' into paedophilia, but it would still make
a good story in the press. For now at least: I suppose the day will
come when there will be a market even among six-year-olds for
pictures of five-year-olds being violated. In no other area of everyday
life do the Latin tags *tempus fugit* and *o tempora, o mores* apply with
quite such force. For those of us who once thought that *Deep Throat*
and *The Devil in Miss Jones* were hot stuff, the computer now on our
desk might as well be a window on the underworld. Don't even think
of poking your finger in there.

On the subject of time passing, I should note that Jacqui Smith
lost her seat at the next election and duly took the path to oblivion,
which can happen to famous politicians as it happens to their ideas.

My gag about New Labour being tough on pole-dancing depended upon the slogan 'Tough on crime, tough on the causes of crime', a catch-phrase now forgotten like most of Tony Blair's other promises. Generally one likes to future-proof one's prose but not at the cost of leaving out the commonly quoted current verbal trivia. And anyway, some of it stays current: *o tempora, o mores*, for example. Nice one, Cicero. One in the eye for Catiline.

BRIGHT SIDE OF THE CANE TOAD

Dates of show: 10 and 12 April 2009

People who despair for the future of life on earth should take heart from the capacity of living creatures to adapt when threatened. In the last few days there has been news about an inspiring instance of this capacity. Once again the focus of international media interest is on my homeland, Australia. I speak of the cane toad. The size of a cheap handbag and covered in warts, the cane toad can be found in many parts of Australia. Indeed the cane toad can be found in so many parts of Australia that experts predict there will be soon no part of Australia in which at least one cane toad, or more likely several thousand cane toads, cannot be found.

No matter what the degree of force and ingenuity employed, there has so far been no getting rid of the cane toad. We are invited to worry about this, but I prefer to be encouraged, and to worry just that little bit less about Iranian atomic bombs, North Korean multi-stage rockets, and the imminent immersion of the inhabited world under a rising ocean dotted with the charred corpses of polar bears. Earthly life-forms are tough, and the career of the cane toad shows just how tough they can be.

You probably know most of the cane-toad story already because my country of origin, in order to ensure that its high standard of living should not be threatened by a population of excessive size, has a kind of anti-tourist board dedicated to making Australia look less attractive than it might be in the eyes of the world. After World War II, the anti-tourist board spread stories through overseas outlets about Australia's teeming range of poisonous spiders and snakes. There were stories of the red-back spider that hides under the toilet seat to avoid publicity, and the taipan snake that was so poisonous it could kill a man on a horse after killing the horse, and would do both these things unprovoked, because it liked publicity. The anti-tourist board was scarcely obliged to exaggerate. Australian spiders and snakes are really like that. So you're a prospective migrant and you're afraid of getting bitten a little bit? What are you, a man or a mouse? If you're a mouse, you've got no business going near a taipan anyway.

More recently, the anti-tourist board positioned its enormous influence behind a film called *Australia*, which was plainly designed to put immigrants off going to Australia by presenting, at enormous length, a prospect of a country where nothing happened except a hundred and fifty thousand cattle moving slowly across the parched landscape, each beast pausing for an individual close-up at any moment when the director thought the pace was too hectic. But the most reliable weapon in the armoury of the Australian anti-tourist board has always been the story of the cane toad.

Scarcely believable on the face of it – and the face of it is the face of the cane toad, which is scarcely believable in itself – the story is true in every respect. The first few of the unprepossessing creatures were imported into Queensland in 1935 because it was thought that they would help protect the sugar-cane crop by eating the grey-back cane beetle, a pest. So the cane toads were doing pest control. The thought that the creature imported to do pest control might itself become a pest had not yet occurred to anybody.

1935 was a big year for Australia because *Mutiny on the Bounty*, with Clark Gable and Charles Laughton, was the top box-office movie in the world and therefore the attention of the entire planet was on the South Pacific, a circumstance which always tends to turn the collective head of the Australian media. In such a climate of glory, even a cane toad looked good. Not as good as Clark Gable, perhaps, but at least as good as Charles Laughton.

Alas, it soon became apparent that the cane toad was less inter-ested in eating the grey-back cane beetle than in eating everything else whether living or dead and, most disastrously, in being eaten itself, with stunning results for whatever ate it, because the cane toad was poisonous. Its body is composed largely of poison glands which produce a narcotic that is currently classified officially in Australia as a Class One drug along with heroin and marijuana. Toad licking, we are told, can result in death.

Lucky I was told that soon enough, or I might have tried it as the next step up from the hash cookie. But inevitably, this classification as a drug in Class One induces some people to try it out. The results of ingesting the toxin, however, are seldom good for humans and they can be lethal for almost any other creature, up to and including crocodiles. These facts were found out quite soon after the cane toad was introduced. These facts were found out by the same experts who had thought that the cane toad would be good for pest control. But by the time it was discovered that the cane toad was a lot better at being a pest itself, the cane toad had revealed its other characteristic, a fantastic ability to increase in numbers.

By now, as I speak, there are more than three hundred million of them and their number has increased significantly since the start of this sentence. And as their numbers increase, they travel, because there simply wouldn't be room for all the cane toads if they stayed in one place. They didn't even stay in Queensland for long, and by now they have moved a long way west. You have only to see a close-up of even one of these creatures to know what it would mean for vast tracts of the country to be covered with them even if they were harmless and tasted like hamburger.

A creature with few successful predators ranged against it – and most creatures who want to eat the cane toad die on the spot a few minutes after they try to – usually won't be kept down just because human beings like the taste of it. The first big pest problem introduced into Australia was the rabbit, which, back in the nineteenth century, was brought in to provide country gentlemen with good hunting. In short order there were untold millions of them. Rabbits made good eating but they were eaten only by the poor. When we ate rabbit in our house while I was growing up I was encouraged not to mention it in case we were looked down on. But even if everybody in the country had eaten rabbit three times a day it wouldn't have made a dent in the rabbit population, which went on increasing until a specifically anti-rabbit disease called myxomatosis was let loose.

After an initial reduction in the rabbit population, the long-term effect was the emergence of a super rabbit. Those of us who remember that will be suspicious of plans to introduce a genetic switch in the cane toad that will turn them all into males and therefore extinguish the cane-toad population. The performance of the cane toad so far suggests that even if they all turn into gay males and start collecting

Judy Garland records they will go on taking territory at the rate of fifteen miles a year, which more or less means that there will soon be enough of them in Canberra to demand voting rights.

The news last week was that there are new plans to unleash a predator against them, the meat ant. Confidence in the meat ant is high. Whereas frogs and other kinds of toad will flee at the mere sight of a meat ant, we are told, the cane toad will just sit there cooperatively waiting to be attacked and killed. But there are two things wrong with that story. One thing wrong is that that's exactly what the grey-back cane beetle was supposed to do when the cane toad showed up, and the other is, what if it works and the meat ant becomes the new unstoppable success? Much wiser to concentrate on those voting rights.

If the cane toad can survive so much, then it can evolve, and the signs are that it's already doing so. The evidence was buried in last week's report, but I underlined it and I've got it here in front of me. This is the bit you probably haven't heard yet, but I think it might be crucial. As the advance guard of the cane toad mass moves west, its leading members are developing longer and stronger legs. Have you got that? The cane toads are getting bigger and smarter. Soon they'll be learning to drive. There is a school of thought, not necessarily paranoid, which holds the opinion that cane toads with human skills have already penetrated the Australian media and are even appearing as presenters of reality television shows. That might be a fear too far, but surely it makes sense to start thinking of how the cane toads can be dealt with in another way than warfare.

It's time to negotiate. We need to find out what their demands are. What do they want? One thing they might want is aid. You have to believe me when I say that the same scientists who have measured the longer and stronger legs of the vanguard toads have also diagnosed arthritis. Limping toads, wincing with pain as they advance. Common humanity demands that we should make an antidote available. I say it's time to sit down with their leaders and discuss matters of mutual benefit. If they can evolve that fast, maybe they'll turn into a better version of us. Maybe they already have. Maybe some of them have got on planes to spread the cane-toad message to the world. But no, take it easy. I'm just croaking. I mean I'm just joking. Croak, croak.

Postscript

During this period, in the press, mankind, because of its irresponsible abundance of emissions, was routinely held responsible for threatening the death of ten different species every day, or a hundred a week, or ten thousand a year, or whatever figure sounded impressive after the previous figure had begun to sound unimpressive. It was seldom mentioned that in the natural world most species are threatened continually by several other species: that rendering each other extinct is what species are trying to do all the time. The plundering baleen whale is not telling itself that with its next mouthful it will take just enough krill to ensure the continuance of the species. It just goes whumpf.

Somewhere about this time, the bandicoot was revealed to have become lethal on a scale hitherto unprecedented, but no doubt this was due to Climate Change, because finally mankind had to be the culprit. Nevertheless some species theoretically on the road to extinction were getting there by a circuitous route, especially the polar bears, which continued to increase in numbers. Unfortunately for chiliasts at the IPCC and in the mainstream media, there are responsible government officials paid to count polar bears. The more the polar bears were pronounced doomed, the more polar bears there turned out to be, despite regular appearances in all media of the lone bear standing on the tiny ice floe. The tiny ice floe proved to have been Photoshopped but nothing could threaten the existence of the idea of polar bears running out of ice. The idea went on turning up even in BBC climate-change surveys of supposedly impeccable prestige. Mankind, it was agreed, threatened the lives of all creatures except one. Mankind's bad environmental behaviour could do nothing about the cane toad. Mankind could sit in its Range Rover with the engine running all night and not a single cane toad would even cough. Speaking of which, you will notice that this script ends with a sound effect, in which I imitate a cane toad. In performance, I managed it, but only because I kept it short. The non-comic broadcaster who wishes to be entertaining can't be counselled too strongly against vaudeville.

REPUTATIONAL DAMAGE

Dates of show: 17 and 19 April 2009

A new phrase got into the language this week: 'reputational damage'. People high in the Labour Party have warned the Prime Minister, Mr Gordon Brown, that the next election might be hard to win because the party suffered reputational damage after it was revealed that Damian McBride, a senior aide of Mr Brown, had it in mind to spread misinformation on the Web in order to make life uncomfortable for Tory politicians.

Though called a senior aide, Mr McBride is only thirty-four years old, but in a short career he got plenty of practice at spinning the press against Mr Brown's original enemies, who were all in the Labour Party, before he moved on to greater glory as one who might spin the press against the Conservative Party. At first blush, the inventions he proposed to circulate this time were merely infantile. He was only going to suggest that there were photographs in existence that might embarrass a certain front-bench Tory. He wasn't going to suggest that the same front-bench Tory had begun his career as Osama bin Laden's mistress. But when you think about it, it's the seemingly innocuous vagueness of the suggestion about photographs that makes it dangerous, because it could so easily be true.

I should say at this point that there are photographs of me in existence that would cause me embarrassment if they were published. In the photographs I am semi-naked. There is a rug involved, and a bottle. By the time the photos were published, it would be getting a bit late for me to protest that I was less than a year old at the time they were taken.

What Mr McBride was after was the opportunity to stir things up. We don't have to believe that Mr Brown knew what Mr McBride was up to in order to wonder how he, Mr Brown, could ever, in the past, have had anything to do with such a man. That the incident had caused the Labour Party reputational damage was the least the Labour bigwigs could say. That it was also the most they could say opens up another question which we might get to later, after further examining this government's gift for coining original language.

For now, let's celebrate the fact that the government is yet again the source of a whole new phrase. It has a reputation for giving us new phrases, and if it ceased to do so it might suffer reputational damage. So far there has been no sign that it will cut back on the supply. This government brings us a new phrase almost every month, usually to deal with the consequences of fresh disasters happening at the same rate. The poor become the socially excluded, and a prison riot becomes a challenging incident. After the collapse of the stock market, the government gave us the new phrase 'quantitative easing' as a term meant to cover the complex business of putting money into the economy so as to offset the effects of the economic crisis. There were some who said that quantitative easing was actually a term covering the simple business of printing more money, a process which was bound to exacerbate the effects of the economic crisis.

Perhaps because there were at least two interpretations of what the term might mean, the term quantitative easing has been slow to catch on. 'Reputational damage', however, could have a more solid career, because there is not much doubt about what it means. There is only doubt about whether people who find it necessary to use such language are really very wise. If they ever had a reputation for wisdom, should they be allowed to retain it after they are caught using a phrase like reputational damage? Before getting to that crucial point, we should define the term reputational damage as clearly as possible, by stating forcefully that in order for reputational damage to occur, there must first be a reputation.

From that angle, the case of Assistant Commissioner Quick, a case which hogged the media for several days recently, will not quite do. A/C Quick, you will recall, was to play a leading role in a large-scale police operation meant to foil a suspected Al-Qa'ida threat against this country. A/C Quick, however, inadvertently modified his leading role by getting himself into a position where he could be photographed holding, in plain view, a document listing the key details of the operation. The mere possibility of this information ceasing to be secret was enough to ruin the timetable of the operation and his career along with it.

But we should be careful, here, about saying that reputational damage had occurred. In the eyes of journalists, anyone who does any job at all is always called a mastermind up until the moment when he puts his foot in it. Indeed he usually goes on being called a mastermind even afterwards, and so it was with A/C Quick in the eyes of at least one newspaper. The newspaper was suitably enraged at the size of the pension that the A/C would take with him into the private sector, but the newspaper strangely added the following: 'He will also expect to find lucrative work advising both the private and public sectors on security which could give him an extra six-figure income. His expertise in counter-terror operations will make him a valuable consultant to the organizers of the 2012 London Olympics.' These later statements depended on the assumption that A/C Quick's reputation as a security mastermind – a reputation which he had undoubtedly possessed, or he would not have attained such rank – had somehow survived his achievement in blowing security entirely on the most serious counter-terror operation currently in the works. The assumption seemed very large. Surely the poor man's reputation had not been damaged in a way from which it might recover. It had been destroyed entirely.

If your job is to keep secrets and you are caught conspicuously not keeping them, your reputation is over. The question shifts focus: from you, the individual, to the institution you belong to, which in the case of A/C Quick was the Metropolitan Police Force. Here indeed was a case of reputational damage. The Met suffers damage to its reputation every time the wrong person gets shot, or a man in the vicinity of a demonstration is struck from behind and ends up dead, or even when an innocent person merely gets humiliated, because to that person and those who know him there is no 'mere' about it.

When the police mess up, there are always two main critical views, the reformist and the revolutionary. The reformist view is that everything should be done to make the police perform better, so as to guard society from breakdown. The revolutionary view is that everything should be done to ensure that they perform worse, so as to reveal the true nature of a repressive mechanism without which society would flourish in freedom. Which of those two views you take is really the decisive question about your personal politics.

But if you really deplore police mistakes instead of welcoming them as evidence that your radical views are correct, then you must believe in the concept of an institution's reputation, and in the possibility that it can be damaged. The question then becomes one of how much damage is too much. The different branches of the Christian Church all cultivate a reputation for mercy, in keeping with the charitable personality of the Son of God. At various times in history, less frequently of late, the reputation for mercy has been compromised by a tendency to persecute disbelievers, but one way or another the reputation survives. Almost always the recovery of the reputation involves the repudiation of past excesses on the part of zealots. When it comes to the activities of Mr McBride, the Labour Party is in the position of repudiating a zealot. It won't be enough to say, well, everybody does it, even though almost everybody does.

Among the Watergate conspirators whose activities doomed Richard Nixon's presidency, Donald Segretti was a clever young fellow who had been making mischief since college. He had a reputation for being an especially clever dirty tricks merchant, but his reputation for being especially clever did not survive his getting caught. When President Clinton was in the White House, the Republican National Committee did their best to surround him with a cloud of rumour even more dense than the one he would have generated naturally all by himself. Those involved had learned the lesson taught by Donald Segretti: they didn't expect to retain their reputation for cleverness if their names became known.

What we have here, in the case of Mr McBride, is one whose reputation was for being a clever manipulator. But he was caught at it, so, although his reputation as a manipulator might survive, his reputation for being clever is gone. I saw one newspaper report in which it was confidently asserted that Mr Brown found Mr McBride valuable because of his political astuteness and his gift for economics. We are now free to wonder if Mr Brown's trust in those qualities was ever very well founded, but whatever we wonder, we won't be wondering about Mr McBride's reputation. Only a very small child, after the ice cube melts, wonders if the ice cube is still in existence somewhere else.

But for the government, the question of reputational damage is real. The government might find it easier to get some of its reputation back if it could avoid coining silly new language in the attempt to soften each new setback. The phrase 'reputational damage' is meant to have a scientific air, as if it referred to something that was bound to happen. But there is no such thing as reputational damage. There is only reputation, which can indeed be damaged, and can be restored only if somebody talks straight.

Postscript

Under New Labour the English language suffered from the kind of inflation in which the banks control the Mint. It was a time of phrases fine yet hollow. 'Reputational damage' was only one of them, and unusual in being easily decoded. 'Sustainable growth' was more typical: it meant nothing at all, but seemed to promise a sense of responsibility. A/C Quick's folder marked SECRET was a symbol for the age, as pointlessly self-publicizing as the legendary sign at the golf club that said nothing except 'Do not lean golf bags against this sign.' After a lifetime of trying, and finally forced into extreme compression through lack of space, I achieved, with my brief paragraph about the difference between the reformist view and the revolutionary view, an evocation as neat as I could ever get of the political gulf lying behind Lenin's famous statement: 'The worse, the better.' Lenin was the revolutionary and Kerensky was the reformist. Perhaps partly by nature, I have always been a Kerenskyite, even when I was young, foolish and fulminating about the machinations of the System. Surrounded by clever Leninists, I had to get used to being patronized, but I could already see a basic difference in attitude, and even in personality: whereas Kerenskyites would like to see Leninists locked up, Leninists would like to see Kerenskyites dead.

Apart from its efficacious ruthlessness, one of the chief advantages of the Leninist disposition is that it lasts longer. The Che Guevara beret is never really discarded. Though it might be taken off the head, it continues to be worn internally between the skull and brain, thus to heat the thoughts. In the period under review, the successor to the Che beret was the Hugo Chavez sweatshirt, which heated the heavy breathing. Western mouthpieces of surprising seniority were quick to tell you that Chavez was the saviour of his nation. Even worse, they were slow to stop telling you. My references, in this and other broadcasts, to the depredations of the Republican National Committee will tip off the attentive that I had read and admired *The Clinton Wars*, by Sidney Blumenthal: the kind of book that the Americans do so much better than we do there is no contest.

BRITAIN HAS TALENT

Dates of show: 24 and 26 April 2009

By now every media commentator in Britain on every subject including global warming has delivered his or her opinion about Susan Boyle, the woman of unremarkable appearance who went on *Britain's Got Talent* and proved to have such a remarkable voice that an aria from *Les Misérables* acquired the celestial overtones of a solo passage from a cantata by Bach and even such exalted arbiters of taste as Piers Morgan and Simon Cowell were reduced to helpless protestations of awe. Limping along a week behind the action, I can only hope, as I add my groat's worth of opinion to a mountain range of accumulated wisdom, that I have something to say which might prove useful. All the obvious things have been said. But it is sometimes worth asking whether all the obvious things that have been said are quite true.

Barely had the last ringing note of Susan Boyle's beautiful voice faded in the air before the first media commentators were out of their box to lash Piers Morgan and Simon Cowell for their coarseness in having concurred, with their facial expressions, in the loutish mirth of the studio audience that had greeted Susan Boyle before she began to sing. I looked at the footage carefully and I'm bound to say that I didn't find either Mr Morgan or Mr Cowell looking any more crass than usual. They seemed to me to be striving to be polite while they contemplated her admittedly unshowbizlike appearance, just as she seemed to me to be striving to be polite while she contemplated them: two men whose faces are surely fated to inspire laughter, in the way that faces do when they belong to the kind of man who is deeply, sincerely concerned with the impression he is making.

Mr Morgan, at some stage early in his career, decided that an air of irrepressible shrewdness should be basic to his image, and after many hours of training before the shaving mirror he managed to perfect such a look of penetrating scepticism that if he had been in the front of the crowd when Jesus Christ delivered the Sermon on the Mount he would have put Our Saviour off his stroke.

Mr Cowell, for his own part, has a set of teeth so uncannily perfect that you can see why he has to spend so much time in America, the only country that will admit such a display of radiant gnashers through Customs without X-raying the rest of the body they are attached to, to see if any part of it is made of enriched uranium. Yet Susan, face to face with these two improbably refulgent paragons, was unfazed, and launched without hesitation into her song.

Within four bars she had established herself as a talent. As Seamus Heaney, a great critic of his art as well as a great practitioner, has told us, we recognize a true poet's voice immediately by its inherent strength, its integrity, its coherence and its clarity. We recognize a true singer's voice in the same way. Susan Boyle has got it, and even the more oafish members of the studio audience, who could have come by time travel straight from the Roman Colosseum on a day when children were being fed to the lions, were instantly won over. When Susan finished, there was a fitting tumult.

The next bit, however, was harder to interpret than some of the commentators let on. They assumed that Mr Morgan and Mr Cowell had no advance knowledge that Susan would have a voice. I suppose it's possible, although I must say it seems unlikely to me. I spent twenty long years working in the front line in television studios and I seldom saw circumstances in which a surprise of such magnitude could be kept secret. But really it doesn't matter much whether the two men were choosing their words of praise on the spot, without acting, or whether they had had time to think the words up. What mattered was what they said, and it was very instructive. Mr Morgan was the more blatant in letting the world know that he was stunned. The message from both men was that they had expected Susan's performance to be as nondescript as her appearance was lacking in glamour.

By emphasizing these previous low expectations, they underlined their subsequent large-heartedness in praising her to the skies. Many commentators were able to spot that both men were suffering from an overdeveloped sense of entitlement, in which, while expecting the rest of us to admire them because they were so ready to admit they had been wrong, we would not despise them for having held such low expectations merely because the lady was not a glamour-puss.

With those commentators I was in agreement. The conceit shown by Mr Morgan and Mr Cowell was deeply off-putting and if I had been on a special judging panel to judge the judges I would have told both of them to beware, because a name made from giving opinions in a television studio is a name written in water. There is no more perfect recipe for self-delusion than to suppose that being a television personality is some kind of achievement in itself. The best insurance to stop it happening is to keep a recording of, say, Beethoven's Seventh Symphony nearby in order to remind yourself of what an actual achievement is.

Susan was a lot closer to the world of achievement, as opposed to the world of mere celebrity, than the two men. But right here is the area where the commentators have not yet gone, and ought to. Because the laws of nature had not been repealed, only momentarily jolted, and it remains a law of nature that appearance is a factor even in the world of serious singing.

The judges of *Britain's Got Talent* know quite a lot about the technicalities of putting a song over in a way that Ant and Dec might say wow to, but they don't know much about serious singing, which is a different thing. The facts, alas, say that in every opera house in the world the chorus contains at least half a dozen people with voices as good as Susan's, and most of them won't become stars, so all the hoo-hah about Susan's sudden stardom was at least partly illusory, based on the dangerous notion that overnight prominence on television will always change reality permanently.

In the opera house, music ought to matter more than anything but it remains true that one of the reasons people flock to hear Anna Netrebko and Elīna Garanča singing together is that they look the part almost as well as they sing it. Things shouldn't be that way, but strangely enough they have become more and more that way in the last forty years, during the very period when feminism as a train of thought has done so much to educate us about the restrictive nature of expectations based on pulchritude.

When I first started attending Covent Garden in the early 1960s it was still quite common for the soprano to be an unlikely stimulus for the tenor's cries of passion. Today, most of the sopranos look like film stars. It could be said that the more our primitive male prejudices are broken down, the more we all become free. But one of the consequences of freedom is that ticket-buyers are free to choose, and it is likely to remain a fact that ticket-buyers of both sexes will choose to see the imported dreamboat.

Susan might very well, after this, get a job in the chorus and even sell a lot of records, but if the press expects more than that it could be adding yet another chapter to a long story in which discoveries have been shoved onto the boards to fulfil a role in a fairy story which is fated not to turn out well. So unless all concerned are very careful, there might be a worse injustice on its way for Susan than getting laughed at when she was first exposed to the audience of a show that depends on a regular supply of contestants who are there to be made a fool of. She might be trapped by an even more pitiless expectation: that she will go on being a big star beyond the point where she became a star because she didn't seem as if she could.

Susan's future has undoubtedly been altered but we can only hope it has been altered for the better. At whatever level of musical theatre, there is no automatic equality. It all depends on people having unequal characteristics, and one of those is appearance, in which there is no justice. In view of that fact, a man might try not to bellow with scorn when he sees a woman he regards as a frump. And then, when he evolves into a man a bit better than that, he can try not to look quite so smug when he congratulates himself for admitting that the frump has done something remarkable, and so on.

I was there to see my generation of males being educated by feminism. I was one of the males who most needed education, and I am all too aware that the process is endless, and can have many setbacks. To many women, our purportedly civilized West still looks like a man's world. Perhaps it always will, and one of the things that freedom has confirmed has been a man's freedom to remain prejudiced. But in Afghanistan right now there are women risking their lives to protest against religious laws that could mean they would never be allowed to leave the house without their husband's permission. We might think that nothing could be worse than Mr Morgan generously assuring Susan, and I quote his sensitive words, 'Without a doubt, everyone was laughing at you.' But it's a free country, we were free to judge the judges, and Susan had her moment of triumph, which she carried off with far more grace than she was shown.

Postscript

Strictly according to the label on the tin, *Britain's Got Talent* came through for Simon Cowell and Piers Morgan, who went on to great things, if that was the kind of greatness that you cared for. Simon Cowell was already conquering America, and later on he completed his conquest, gracing red carpets like a less desirable version of Catherine Zeta Jones. Since I have no interest in Simon Cowell's field of expertise – it is concerned mainly with the kind of music I no longer have time to listen to – I can give no details of his later career trajectory, but not to know about the progress of Piers Morgan is impossible, because his every move is tracked by all media, which are largely staffed by people who knew him in his less exalted incarnation and now hope that he will fall under a bus. At one stage a whole year went by when he was going to replace Larry King on CNN, but for some reason the ink never dried on the contract, so speculation went on. Being looked at to replace Larry King must have been a bit like being looked at to replace Methuselah, or perhaps the Mummy from one of those movies where every cave is full of bats.

Anyway, finally the replacement took place, as it were, and the eagerly cherubic features of Piers Morgan appeared on screen to make us forget, if we could, just how drained of life Larry had looked in those last few thousand celebrity interviews. On a smaller scale I have done the same sort of job myself, and it's a good living compared with, say, assembling knock-off designer handbags in an Asian sweat shop; but one hopes that Piers has assembled a few good long thick books for the long nights of waiting for the rush to die down after the mad excitement of interviewing the Rev. Jesse Jackson. A few books, and perhaps a few opera records. My prediction that Susan Boyle would get into trouble proved true, but against my further prediction she soon got out of it. She made more records and I sincerely hope she is happy, although my cruel point about looks in the music world must, I'm afraid, still stand. If it were not true that female pulchritude counted, Puccini would not have composed the way he did. Nor would he have fallen in love with so many sopranos, to the distress of his wife. But if Puccini is a fountain of sensuality, and the totality of Italian opera little short of a waterfall of desire, it all adds up to nothing beside the throbbing libido of Wagner.

Worshippers of his genius try to tell us that *Tristan und Isolde* is about lust transcended, but there is a lot of lust to transcend, and Tristan got that way because Isolde looked good. It helps if the soprano singing the role looks good too. Nowadays she is likely to, which is a bit unfair on any plain girl who can sing the notes. But even if Wagner had been interested in fairness, as an artist he would have been obliged to conclude that Nature wasn't.

LONDON UNDERGROUND

Dates of show: 1 and 3 May 2009

London is not the whole of Britain and sometimes the rest of Britain has reasons to be grateful, because there are things that happen to London that shouldn't have happened to Sodom and Gomorrah. Elsewhere in the country, if you have any money left after recent developments in the world financial market, you might have some hope of building your house higher if you want to, or even adding a bit on to it. In London that's harder, but it's still possible to build downwards. You can put some extra floors under your house instead of on top.

In the past week I was startled to find out not only that this could be done, but that there were people still wealthy enough to do it. They don't want to sell their houses because the property market is so depressed that there is nobody to buy their houses. But they do want to improve their houses, as a sure-fire investment against the day when the international financial market recovers the buoyancy which the rest of us once found such a source of inspiration that we believed the previous Chancellor of the Exchequer when he said London was where it was all happening. Then he was promoted to the position of Prime Minister and it all happened. But just how big a disaster has it been, when so many of the wealthy still have enough cash to improve their houses?

They find it hard, however, to improve their houses by building them higher, or by adding bits on to them. They could do that more easily in, say, Aberdeen. But in London they can improve their houses with least trouble to themselves by adding bits underneath: by, that is, sinking extra levels into the earth, building basements under basements, and extending these subterranean levels sideways under their back garden, if they happen to own one, or under the house next door, if they happen to own that too.

Some of these guys own the whole block, so we are talking about hidden developments on a vast scale, leaving the house itself, lavishly appointed though it may be, a mere pergola on top of an invisible palace. They're not just building swimming pools down there. One character is building a diving pool. How can you build a diving pool underground? Well, how can you build an indoor ski slope in Dubai? You do it with money.

The applications for planning permission to build downwards are a tip-off that not all the rich have suddenly got poor. The latest Sunday newspaper rich-list supplement, an annual pornographic round-up in which men with large amounts of money perform the same emblematic function as women with large breasts, reveals that the steel mogul Lakshmi Mittal has indeed lost almost two-thirds of his money since he stopped going out with Salman Rushdie. My secretarial staff has just passed me a note saying that I have got Lakshmi Mittal mixed up with Padma Lakshmi but my figures are correct.

Mr Lakshmi Mittal has indeed lost more than sixteen billion pounds. But since he has almost eleven billion pounds left, he is only relatively impoverished, and there are other men of untold wealth, such as Mr Mohamed Al-Fayed, who have actually got richer in the past year. All of the Duke of Edinburgh's schemes to render Mr Fayed penniless having failed, Mr Fayed has gained in wealth by seventeen per cent. Strangely enough, he is not yet among those who have applied for permission to build downwards. There has been no application to build extra floors under Harrods, perhaps because the Egyptian tradition is to build upwards, with the building coming to a point, instead of downwards, with a secret chamber below the Food Hall, the secret chamber joined by a tunnel to Buckingham Palace so that ninja-clad operatives of Mr Fayed's elite security staff can place listening devices in order to be apprised in time of the Duke of Edinburgh's plans to release moths in the menswear department.

But not very far away from Harrods there is a startling application for subterranean construction from Mr Jon Hunt, who founded the Foxtons estate agency and made three hundred and seventy million pounds when he sold it in 2007, which, in retrospect, was a good year to sell. Indeed, in retrospect, 1066 would have been a good year to sell, or any other year except late last year, when suddenly there was nobody to sell anything to. But Mr Hunt sold at the right time, which is the whole art of getting rich, and now he wants to improve his property in Kensington Palace Gardens, that exclusive part of London in which members of the British royal family, if they have the right credentials, are allowed to live among people from all over the world who have more money than the entire populations of the countries they come from.

Mr Hunt wants to improve his already very large property by going downwards. Among the many other rooms and galleries he wants to build down there, he wants to build a museum in which he can display his collection of classic sports cars. On his planning application it says that the museum will provide an ideal display space for these treasures, but it doesn't say that the public will be invited in to see them.

I suspect the public will not be invited. The display of classic cars will be for the delectation of Mr Hunt's dinner guests. But on the whole it is wise to avoid invitations from the kind of host who wants to impress his guests with what he owns. I myself, on the few occasions when I am invited as a guest to the dinner party of a rich host, do not find it impressive if – when the easy banter is flowing like the wine on the subject of, say, the later poetry of W. B. Yeats or Joanna Lumley's obvious qualifications to be the next Prime Minister – I do not find it impressive if the host breaks into the conversation to insist that all his guests accompany him three flights downwards towards the centre of the earth so that he can show them his collection of classic sports cars. Especially if, when we all get down there and are looking with feigned interest at a Ferrari Testiculone upholstered in tiger skin for the Shah of Persia, the host suddenly holds up his hand and says, 'Hear that rumble? It's the Bakerloo Line.'

Anyone who examines my own application to further excavate under my office building in London will soon conclude that I won't be trying to impress my dinner guests. I have a larger and more humanitarian aim in mind. I wasn't on the recent rich list because I knew who to pay off so that I could preserve my anonymity, but I feel that I can reveal here, among friends, that on the day before Lehmann Brothers crashed and the world economic crisis got irreversibly under way, I just happened to sell my Costa Terribla mass luxury housing complex in Spain for a train-load of American dollars to a consortium of foreign ministers from sub-Saharan Africa who had diverted the economies of their own countries through a Russian money laundry in the Cayman Islands. A certain amount of capital accrued which I have since been putting to constructive use. On levels minus one to minus four of my underground complex will be an assembly shop for a space vehicle designed to leave the solar system looking like a dot in the distance and travel to a planet beyond the reach of reality television. For a suitable fee, anyone can book a seat on the first flight. Anyone, that is, who shares my belief that civilization might be coming to an end.

The chief evidence for this is that people with enough money are starting to dig. It is always an interesting psychological turning point when people with power develop a bunker mentality. Hitler began tunnelling only a few days after World War II started; during the course of the war he had dug-outs all over Europe; and by the time the war ended he was occupying more floors under the Reich Chancellery in Berlin than there had even been above ground before it was bombed to rubble. He was down there with his Wagner records, the musical equivalent of a sports car collection.

And as with the bad guys, so with the good guys. In the USA, the CIA started to go south as an intelligence-gathering organization when it began digging new levels under its headquarters at Langley, Virginia, and finally there was far more of Langley below ground than above. Can anyone doubt that the world is being manipulated from this international network of underground hideouts? It's no use looking for the men behind the men in power. We should be looking for the men below the men in power.

In my testament, which I'm currently dictating to my secretarial staff, deep beneath the earth, I explain it all. Signals from below the soil have corrupted the world's media to the point where you can't believe anything any more. How can we believe that man-made global warming is going to raise the level of the sea by thirty feet if the people who own the newspapers that say so are digging holes under their houses instead of heading for the hills? It's just been revealed that in a recent advertisement for the province of Alberta in Canada they used a picture of people on a beach in Northumberland in the UK because Alberta doesn't have a coastline. How could anyone have paid for that advertisement or run that advertisement or even looked at that advertisement and still believed that anything in any publication might be true? What can we be sure of except that nothing we read about or even hear about is certain? Except for one thing, and to this belief I cling, and so should you. If anyone is rich enough to build himself a bunker under London, he's got enough money to pay his taxes.

Postscript

Public disgust with the big money was intense, but it was notable that there was scarcely any attempt on the part of left-wing thinkers to denounce capitalism, although you would have thought that here was their moment. Why were they silent? Perhaps one of the reasons was that there were scarcely any left-wing thinkers in the old sense still operating. The left, such as it was, was more concerned with pronouncing the imminent collapse of Western society through Climate Change than through systemic economic failure. Another reason could have been that the economic failure just wasn't spectacular enough. There were no marching jobless as in the 1930s; few strong men pretended to sell matches and apples; and on the whole the crisis didn't photograph very well. Meanwhile the new rich got on with their opulent lives, often making extensions in the basement to give the opulence more room. It was a repellent but effective demonstration of the awkward truth that someone with a hundred million pounds can lose fifty million pounds overnight and still not be obliged to limit his outgoings by fifty per cent, or even one per cent. The rest of us have to cut our clothes according to our cloth, but the rich have cloth to spare. I could go on with the analogies, and they would all be equally trite. The facts of inequality seem so brutally obvious. So why not rise up, expropriate the expropriators, and redistribute their wealth among the poor? Yes, but first we must ensure that nobody is using a light bulb rated higher than sixty watts.

In any belief system, it is a fine study to identify the spots at which doubt starts to creep in. With the belief system of the classic left, the key spot was the apparently solid conviction that a planned economy must be able to produce a more rationally distributed abundance than a free market. While Karl Marx was still alive, Lassalle tried to tell him that the development of capitalism had already disproved that idea. It took another hundred years before the general opinion of

intelligent mankind caught up with Lassalle, but when it did, that was
the point around which the catching up took place. Similarly, in the
belief system that we still call Climate Change, there was a key point
at which doubt entered before it entered at all the other points.
The key point was the belief that sea levels would inexorably rise
to catastrophic levels. The idea of sea levels rising a lot would have
had more force if sea levels had recently risen even a little. But in
the Maldives – a tiny nation which had hopes of supplementing its
income from international concern with the supposedly incontrovert-
ible fact that Climate Change threatened its existence – the level of
the ocean, at the time this script was written, had still not risen
back to the level from which it retreated in the 1970s. On the whole
it was dangerous to joke about Climate Change, and on the BBC is
was virtually impossible to mention it in any context except one of
universal apocalypse, but I got away with making the occasional jest
about sea levels because somehow, on that one point, it was acceptable
to be not wholly solemn. In other words – this was never said –
doubts were creeping in.

SHEER POETRY

Dates of show: 8 and 10 May 2009

Poetry has been in the news lately. As the next Poet Laureate takes up her appointment, there have been headline stories, photographs, interviews. But poetry is never in the news for long. Not even in Elizabethan times was it front-page news for more than a couple of days, even if Christopher Marlowe got stabbed in a pub or William Shakespeare broke all box-office records with his new comedy that had a live dog in it.

Those who deplore the debased language of the modern age are always looking back to a time when poetry was a talking point. But Byron, though he got famous overnight, was already less famous the day after, and Tennyson, though everyone knew his name, was always less interesting to small boys than a new steam train. They wanted to drive that. They didn't want to be him. Compared to the tumult of everyday reality, poetry is small-time stuff. But the great thing about poetry in Britain is that it is always there in the background. It was in the foreground last week only because of the handover from one Laureate to the next. Andrew Motion, seemingly born to be an Establishment figure, had given way to Carol Ann Duffy, on the face of it scarcely an Establishment figure at all.

The transition having been accomplished, poetry will go back to the background. But it won't go away entirely. Britain doesn't officially celebrate Shakespeare's birthday, but it does, continually, celebrate Shakespeare's language, the English language. It's just that the continuous celebration is very quiet, with a toot on a cardboard trumpet, the tweet of a penny whistle, and a tap on a tin drum.

The focus of this non-uproarious party is the Laureateship. The Laureateship is the centre around which almost nothing revolves, and has been since the time of Charles II. It wouldn't even matter if a hack had the job. It's the ritual that counts, and it's part of the ritual that it isn't very elaborate. The Laureate doesn't have to walk backwards out of the monarch's presence, or indeed have to do anything. Admirably performed, the duties of the outgoing Laureate, Andrew Motion, were nearly all self-imposed. The Laureate just has to be a poet and do whatever poets do, with a few bottles of sherry from the monarch to prove that the state respects poetry even though the state has no particular use for it from day to day. The diffidence of the post – just do us a poem whenever you feel like it, old boy, or in this case madam – is part of its stature.

More aesthetically-minded countries do without a poet laureate because they can't bear for art to matter so little. Italy is a far more artistic country than Britain. You will meet Italians of quite humble education who know the difference between Michelangelo and Raphael, and in the gallery at the opera during *La Bohème* you will see a truck-driver mouthing all the words of Rodolfo's first aria along with the tenor, and somewhere in the country there is always somebody, an accountant or a librarian, who can recite the whole of the Divine Comedy.

But poetry isn't part of the state structure. This week, Italy's Prime Minister, Silvio Berlusconi, was served notice for divorce by his wife, who has finally had enough of his belief that a pretty face and a nice figure are good qualifications to stand as a European MP. But there is no Italian poet laureate sweating through the night while wondering how to dodge the duty of writing up this national crisis in a suitable poem. If the Italians had the equivalent of a Poet Laureate-ship occupied by Carol Ann Duffy, she could have tackled the subject. A wonderfully accurate observer, Duffy could have started the poem with the details of the strange event which has been taking place on top of Mr Berlusconi's head for some years now without ever quite turning into a hair transplant.

Duffy has written a deservedly popular series of poems about great men seen from the viewpoint of their wives. She would be good at pretending to speak for Mrs Berlusconi, perhaps evoking the wronged wife's state of mind as it finally snapped under the strain of failing to protest about the discrepancy between her husband's hair arrangement and his evident belief that adolescent females were drawn to him by his physical charm. When Duffy spoke for the wife of King Midas, she proved that she had one of the most precious qualities a poet can have: wit. What would it be like to serve King Midas with his dinner?

> For starters, corn on the cob.
> Within seconds he was spitting out the teeth of the rich.

Isn't that a fabulous little stretch of writing? So much happening in a flash. No wonder schoolteachers love teaching her poems. There's always a phrase to catch the attention even of the little boy with the pyromania problem. When someone speaks so wittily, it's impossible not to appreciate it, especially when you can't do it yourself. And even Carol Ann Duffy might have had to pick some of it up by example. She had a mentor, the poet mysteriously named U. A. Fanthorpe.

A schoolteacher who never published a poem until she was fifty, U. A. Fanthorpe had wit to burn. But being an essentially British poet she was quiet about it, so you had to go and find her. Fanthorpe was still not famous when she died at seventy-nine, on the same day Duffy took the post of Laureate. I myself knew Fanthorpe for only a single poem, about Paolo Uccello's painting of St George. In the poem, St George, the dragon and the king's daughter all get to speak. The king's daughter speaks like this:

> It's hard for a girl to be sure if
> She wants to be rescued. I mean, I quite
> Took to the dragon. It's nice to be
> Liked, if you know what I mean. He was
> So nicely physical, with his claws
> And lovely green skin, and that sexy tail.
> And the way he looked at me,
> He made me feel he was all ready to
> Eat me. And any girl enjoys that.

Partly inspired by Fanthorpe's example, Duffy has never been afraid to make her poems funny. It's lucky that Duffy is a dream to teach, because poetry still has to be taught. For a long time I thought that poetry could be made more popular if it was banned in schools, with possession of poetry regarded as a misdemeanour and dealing in it as a felony. But I had forgotten that I had been taught poetry myself. In the Australian schools after World War II we were made to memorize a poem or we couldn't go home. Looking back on it, I am glad about that method, but it did amount to a prison regime, and others may have suffered. Indeed some of my classmates are probably still there, growing old in their desks, forever trying to remember what comes next after 'I come from haunts of coot and hern.'

There are better ways, and there could be better prizes. The bolder teachers could always remind their more precocious pupils that a memorized love poem is hard to beat as an instrument of seduction. But the best way, surely, is for the teachers to read out one of the phrases that drew them into a particular poem in the first place. Every good poem has at least one of them, the phrase that makes your mind stand on end.

I heard one of these yesterday, on a marvellous website called Poetry Archive, a creation for which Andrew Motion was partly responsible. On Poetry Archive you can hear the famous poets read out what they wrote. One of the poets is Richard Wilbur, the American poet who helped, fifty years ago, to do for me what Fanthorpe did for Duffy – provide an example. The Wilbur phrase that caught me this time, and took me back to when I was first under his spell, came from a little poem about mayflies. He visualizes millions of them rising and sinking in the light, and he calls them 'the tiny pistons of a bright machine'.

I was knocked out, and I couldn't imagine anyone hearing that and not wanting to know more about Richard Wilbur. When they look him up, they will find that he was a soldier throughout the last campaigns of World War II from Cassino onwards, but when he came back from the slaughterhouse he hardly ever wrote about it. He preferred to write about mayflies. It's a reminder that it isn't the poet's job to keep in step with events. It isn't even the Laureate's job.

Her job is to provide part of what Seamus Heaney called the redress of poetry. Poetry is part of the artistic compensation for the fact that the workaday world isn't artistic, and can't be. Sometimes the poet can respond to events only by waiting for the events to go away. In the short term, what happens to us in the world is all there is. In the long term, it's all an illusion, as Shakespeare told us when he gave us that farewell speech by Prospero as the old wizard lost the last of his power over his magic island,

> And like the baseless fabric of this vision,
> The cloud-capped towers, the gorgeous palaces,
> The solemn temples, the great globe itself,

Yea, all which it inherit, shall dissolve,
And, like this insubstantial pageant, faded,
Leave not a wrack behind.

Shakespeare was never asked to be Poet Laureate, a fact which reminds all Laureates that it's just a job. But it's an important job, because its very existence, no matter who holds it, is an acknowledgement by the state that there is something a state can't control, which is the national memory, and that the national memory travels in the language, like an arrow shower, as Philip Larkin said, sent out of sight, somewhere becoming rain.

Postscript

Of the two senior public posts for poetry in Britain, the Laureateship is a cushier number than the Oxford Professorship of Poetry because the latter job involves at least a few things that must be done. The Laureate doesn't really have to do anything except write the occasional poem, and Ted Hughes got close to not even doing that. His 'Rain-Charm for the Duchy' was the only attention-getting poem he wrote in connection with the job, and it was more about rain than about the Duchy. It was supposed to have something to do with the Queen Mother but she received no direct mention. Hughes was in a great tradition of inactivity that stretched back to Dryden, the most gifted poet of his time but not very energetic in the role of Laureate. In recent times, Andrew Motion threatened to spoil everything by inventing duties that had never previously been performed or even mooted. He got out there to preach poetry in the schools, he recruited poets both living and dead for his poetry website. He was a dynamo. He was worse: he was Serpico, the honest cop who threatens to spoil the racket for all the other cops who are on the take.

My joke about encouraging poetry by banning it in the schools was only half unserious. It was a joke I used often, in various contexts, but always to the same purpose: I wanted to raise the possibility that to encourage people to appreciate poetry might do little good, and that to encourage them to write it might do no good at all. Even Seamus Heaney, who in his Harvard post had to read the manuscripts of thousands of creative writers, must have had moments when the nearly good but giftless poem revealed itself as a threat to the art he loved. Yeats said, 'Always I encourage, always.' My own motto would be precisely the opposite if I were not so afraid of seeing tears. On the other hand, and speaking from the more civilized hemisphere of one's brain, it is terrific fun to throw out some blood and guts and watch the water boil. Big-game fishermen call it 'chum'. You throw out a quotation to the class and see whose mouth opens. In this broadcast I got a real thrill out of finding room to mention U. A. Fanthorpe and quote her marvellous stanza. The beautiful fragment from Richard Wilbur I misquoted, having foolishly trusted my memory: the 'tiny pistons' should have been 'fine pistons'. But I still bet there were a few takers. (Young poets, especially, flip when they first read Wilbur, as if they had been taken for a ride in the back seat of a Tomcat.) When talking about poetry on stage, I try to quote as often as possible, on the principle that half a good line from someone else's poem beats any ten minutes of my own prose. There are, alas, speakers about poetry who can't quote it very well. Too many of those bad speakers are poets themselves, confirming your suspicion that the reason their work has a halting voice is because they can't recite.

But the actors are the worst. Nearly all actors should be forbidden to read poems aloud on pain of death. Actors tend to add emotion to a stretch of words that is already packed with it to the limit. When you have heard a famous actor go through a Shakespeare sonnet as if its lines ran straight on each into the next, it is quite permissible to conclude that you have wasted your life. Yet soon, if not straight away, some other voice will remind you that poetry is still your reason for living, and occasionally you will hear someone who recites poetry with the ideal combination of reticence and emphasis. In his series *Civilization*, Kenneth Clarke recited poetry ten times as well as the actor who was brought in to mangle the longer passages, and I once saw a little programme about John Clare in which the poet P. J. Kavanagh recited so effectively that I sat up reading Clare for half the night. And once in a thousand times, even an actor can do it. Listen to John Gielgud being Prospero. (You can get it on YouTube.) Why did so few critics remark on the lilting musicality with which Gwyneth Paltrow spoke the verse in *Shakespeare in Love*? About poetry one could go on for ever – the very thing that a poem, by setting boundaries to itself with its form, tries not to do.

EXPENSIVE MISTAKES

Dates of show: 15 and 17 May 2009

We were never supposed to know about what the MPs were claiming on expenses. If somebody hadn't pushed for disclosure under the Freedom of Information Act, the whole thing would have stayed nicely buttoned up. But then one thing led to another and all the data got onto the kind of secret disk designed to be left in a taxi but this time somebody tried to sell it to a newspaper and only sold half of it but then he sold the rest of it and so on until you don't want to know how it happened, all you know is that it's happening, and filling the news with great waves of hoo-hah by which you are meant to be stunned but somehow aren't.

I speak for myself here, but I am reminded of the immortal words of Gertrude Stein when she said, 'It is remarkable how I am not interested.' And all I can say, as I sit here going through my own expenses – replacement of ball-point pen, fifty pence – is that when I find out that the richest man in the Cabinet, the one who's already got seven properties, has done better than all his colleagues out of juggling his first and second residence is, if that's a revelation, with what revelation will you be astounding me next? That Jordan and Peter Andre are splitting up?

Please. Try to contain your excitement as I just annotate these receipts for expenses relating to my forthcoming book, called *Take It Easy*, on the importance of relaxation to the working writer. Research trip to Acapulco including first-class flights and ten days at Hotel Las Brizas, twenty thousand pounds. Massage by muscle-detensioning operative Fifi La Bonza Ph.D., eighty pounds and thirty-nine pence. Lip balm, two pounds fifty.

The *Daily Telegraph* spilled the stories about the Labour MPs first.

With the conspicuous exceptions of three MPs who didn't claim all they could – a peculiar characteristic which we'll get to later – most of them seem to have been working the system in the direction of the limits allowed. Some of them went near the edge of that and might lose their jobs for it, but at worst they were shuffling the first and second residence system in order to maximize what they could claim. Even the most active of the Labour MPs seemed pretty unambitious when it became the turn of the Tory MPs to have their stories spilled. Your typical Labour expenses claimer claims the expense on an extra radiator to heat his bedroom. Your typical Tory expenses claimer claims the expense on extra pipes to heat his swimming pool. It's a different level of expectation. At either level, upmarket or down-market, the tacit claim, the one that doesn't get written down, is: I need these things to live.

Another way of putting it is a sense of entitlement. With the Tories it's ingrained. These comforts are what used to be delivered automatically if you were a member of the aristocracy. With the Labour MPs it's aspirational. These comforts are what one ought to have if one is a member of the meritocracy. But either way, the deep-down assumption is that a certain standard of living should go with the job.

Well, there's something to it. And I write this as I sit vibrating at my desk while the brick walls of my office are replaced with Portland stone so that I can get this place reclassified as a listed building and have the loft insulated by the National Trust. Though it's sometimes easy for the media to forget it, most MPs really do need two places to live, one in the constituency and the other in the capital city, and it's only simple justice that the London residence should be reasonably civilized.

In the bad old days, MPs from out of town crashed in a cheap hotel or festered in bedsits. Only an unreconstructed Maoist radical would say that they should go back to that. The belief that a politician must live like a student is one that only a student would hold. The trouble is that the whole business of running two homes tends to be more expensive than the salary easily allows, so there is an imperative to make up the difference with claims, and the imperative to make up the difference easily turns into a temptation to make up more than the difference, especially when there is a sense of entitlement.

Entitlement, like empowerment, is one of those words that can send you to sleep the moment it is uttered, and I myself have just had to plunge my face into a sink full of cold water in the bathroom which is currently being re-grouted by a plumber employed by my brother. But although entitlement is a tedious word, a sense of entitlement is a useful phrase, because it sounds like a dangerous thing to have, and indeed it is. The phrase cropped up almost as soon as the danger did, when executives in public service started expecting a large salary, with large perquisites to top it up, because, they claimed, that was what they would be worth on the free market. Claiming that, they started claiming everything, and the mood soon spread.

It spread fast, and spread far, not because most people are anti-social, but because they are too social. If everybody else is doing it, perhaps I should too. At full stretch, the sense of entitlement means that almost everybody takes what they can get. On a low level of ambition, the result is what the Americans call the Serpico scenario, when the honest cop is shunned by the other cops because he won't take the free sandwich from the deli.

On a higher level of ambition we get newspaper proprietors who don't pay taxes here because they can get away with paying less somewhere else. Some of the reporters currently pounding out stories about MPs avoiding thousands in tax are working for proprietors who avoid millions. It's a continuing source of shame to journalists and one of the chief reasons for their bad diet. Lunch claim: two meat pasties and one individual fruit pie, five pounds fifty?

But it isn't corruption, it's just working the system. And the answer to it is to fix the system, by improving the regulations. There is no mystery to this principle, and no heresy: even if you believe that a free market is essential, you can't believe that a free market is sufficient and still be a politician. If you did believe that, you would be a war lord. Regulating the free market is what a government does.

In liberal democratic societies, where the free market is regulated by government, there is a limit to corruption. What we are all asked to be amazed at right now is that there is such a thing as human dishonesty, but really we should be amazed at how it has been kept within bounds. In countries where no bounds are set, and corruption reigns unchecked, hardly anyone can afford to be honest. Yet even then, some are. It's one of the great divisions in mankind, and one of the hardest to explain.

As it happens, I am privileged with the regular company of three honest women who are so socially responsible that they continue to sort the household rubbish into the colour-coded wheelie bins even though, the last I heard, the economic crisis has resulted in the recycling system grinding to a halt somewhere on its way to China. Just a second: to replacement of wheelie bin with broken wheel, fifteen pounds seventy pence.

I don't think I have any special propensity towards larceny. Certainly if I have, it is overcome by fear, and I took great care early on, in my career as a freelance, to acquire an accountant whose whole aim in life is to make sure that the revenue service receives every penny of my taxes on time, with a urine specimen just in case they need it. But I am still struck by how these honest women are prone to what I see as an unrealistic view of mankind. They expect other people to be honest naturally, as they are, and as those three Labour MPs were who neglected to claim for everything they could. It is often the way with the saintly, however, that they have a restricted insight into the cupidity of the rest of us. Most of us, alas, have to be made virtuous. It follows that the most successful system of government frames its laws on the principle that whatever is not nailed down will soon walk.

At the moment the world's most conspicuous and disheartening example is sub-Saharan Africa, where too many government officials export the economies of their countries to European banks because they think everyone else would if they could. But the terrible truth is that the full force of corruption is doing its dreadful work even among us. We, however, have the luxury of being able to call it crime, not politics. There is always a romantic dream of a version of theft that is not theft. But it doesn't exist. The reality of the Mafia, for example, is that it built its international bank by stealing from the poor in Sicily. From the poor, not from the rich. The apparent scam of MP expenses looks bad, but the fact that it looks bad is the very thing that makes it not so bad. The outrage that we are encouraged to feel means that we live in a country where corruption is not the norm. If it were, some people on the front benches would be laughing at us right now, instead of sweating. If you want to order my book, incidentally, remember to get the title right. It's called *Take It Easy*. But it isn't called *Taking It Is Easy*, which is about another subject altogether.

Postscript

I was quite pleased with my muscle-detensioning expert Fifi La Bonza Ph.D. because she embodied, as it were, a recurring theme in the history of parliamentary corruption. There is often a sexual element. MPs, and especially gay MPs, are touchingly apt to assume that the public purse might help them defray the cost of an emotional companion. Many of the politicians concerned, having been made, through fame, attractive for the first time in their lives, are unable to offset their new-found pulling power with the tempered knowledge of how thoroughly desire can warp judgement. I can quite imagine being carried away in a similar direction myself. I can see myself taking on a research assistant to advise me about the Middle East who knows nothing about the Middle East but looks good in a tailored dark suit and high heels – always a dynamite combo, particularly in women. What I can't imagine is being an MP. Nobody would elect me, and if by some miracle I got the job, the grind of detail would quickly finish me off: like most writers, the nearest I ever got to a sense of responsibility was to find an organized way of doing what I liked. But during my brief Westminster career I would undoubtedly recompense myself for my dedication by taking everything that was coming to me.

Some MPs are paragons, but most of them take what's on offer. It follows that what's on offer needs to be strictly specified. After this scandal, which dragged on because it made good copy, both parties promised to clean up the system, so by the time the next election arrived it was no longer much of an issue. New rules ensured that what had been available to steal, which had always been chicken feed by the standards of major fraud, was still further reduced. MPs were obliged to find better ways than embezzlement for scoring a fast buck. As Tony Blair was already proving, the really big money lay in becoming Prime Minister and giving a lot of after-dinner speeches after you left office. In his own mind, the size of his comparatively honest latter-day earnings must have expunged the awkwardness of those earlier questions about flats in Bristol, etc. Honesty is the best policy, as long as the law gives you comfortable latitude on the subject of what honesty actually is. In that respect, it remained true that the newspaper proprietors had the politicians beaten. At the time, and still at the time I am writing this, the average newspaper tycoon earned, through dodged tax, more money in five minutes than any modern MP could fiddle in his entire career. Everybody knew about this scandal and nothing was ever done, because it was still believed – and perhaps it was true – that newspapers helped to decide elections. Tony Blair's visit to Rupert Murdoch on Hayman Island was the beginning of his run for office. It might also have been the beginning of his fierce interest in the big money: a passion which I will believe desirable in a Labour politician on the day that I become a monkey's uncle.

Though Rupert Murdoch had no direct grip on the BBC senior staff – not being elected by popular vote, they didn't need to care about what his editorial writers might say – there was a limit, it was felt, to what could be said on air about him and his empire. Scripts mentioning his name would slow down on their way past the lawyers, especially if there was any suggestion that he might have helped to elect the government. What I have written here was about as far as you could go at the time, when nobody had an inkling that his empire might come crashing down. By now, of course, everybody is saying it was all inevitable. But back then, only a few short months ago, it all looked as evitable as anything could be. Murdoch had so much influence that he influenced the behaviour of honest men and women who, not being in his pay, should never have been in his thrall. But they were, mainly because the cost of fighting him in the courts would not have been worth it. What that said about the structure of British justice would be a separate subject, and one beyond my competence; although I'm bound to say that I liked the idea that Timothy Garton Ash put forward in his *Guardian* article on the day Murdoch's bandwagon definitively shed its wheels. It was 15 July 2011, and Garton Ash said that the thing to do was to have a moratorium on the law for a short, specified period, and use it to rewrite the book on all the laws that touched upon the freedom of the press. With the benefit of his wide and deep knowledge of modern European history, Garton Ash was almost certainly referring to the period after the collapse of Nazi Germany when the Allied Control Commission rewrote the laws of the Western zones of Germany so that the police force – the key to the whole issue under the Weimar Republic – could never be suborned again. The debate about press interference in private lives is an eternal one. But there can be no debate about press interference with the police: if there is, the damage has already been done.

FEMINISM AND DEMOCRACY

Dates of show: 22 and 24 May 2009

In a week when the troubled parliament of Britain continued to swamp the front pages with tales of fiddle, fraud and the incredible disappearing Speaker, there wasn't much room for news about the parliaments of other countries, but there was one story in the middle pages that might have been calculated to remind us of why democracy really matters. The parliament in Kuwait has just acquired its first four women MPs.

Kuwait is by no means a perfectly constituted democracy. As far as I can figure out, there is a ruling family whose Emir chooses the government and calls elections for parliament. But women have now been elected to the parliament, by popular vote. It should hardly need saying that this would have been unlikely to happen if Saddam Hussein had been allowed to continue to rule the country by terror, but let's leave his awful memory aside for a moment, if we can, and dare to put forward a general reflection.

Democracy is the best chance for women. Or if that sounds too naive, too pro-Western perhaps, then let's put it this way. The absence of democracy is seldom good news for women. Or, to get down to bedrock, if women can't vote for women, then they haven't got many weapons to fight with when they seek justice.

My own view, which I'm ready to hear contested, is that this is the main reason why some feminists in the West have been so slow to get behind those women in the world's all too numerous tyrannies who have to risk their lives to say anything. It's just too clear a proof that men have a natural advantage when it comes to the application of violence. When you say that women have little chance against men if it comes to a physical battle, you are conceding that there really might be an intractable difference between the genders after all.

Ideological feminists in the West were for a long time reluctant to concede this, because they preferred to believe that there was no real difference, and that all female handicaps were imposed by social stereotyping that could be reversed by argument. But this belief was really possible only in a society where the powers of argument had a preponderance over the powers of violence. And since many Western feminists are still convinced that the social stereotyping of the West is the product of fundamental flaws within liberal democracy itself, they have a tendency to believe that undemocratic societies are somehow valuable in the opposition they offer to the free countries which the feminists are so keen to characterize as not free enough.

I have to pick my words carefully here, because this is the touchiest theme I have ever tackled in these broadcasts, but I do think it's high time to say that if feminist ideologists find liberal democracy unfriendly, they might consider that the absence of liberal democracy is a lot less friendly still. Helping to give me courage, here, finally, is that quite a lot of women are already saying it. But they tend not to be Western pundits. They tend to be women out there, in the thick of a real battle, not just an argument. Why their bravery doesn't shame more of our feminist pundits I hesitate to say. It certainly shames me.

This importance of democracy, or at any rate of an amelioration of tyranny, should have become clear when, after Saddam Hussein was deposed, the first provisional government in Iraq included women members. But it didn't become clear, because too many of our commentators wanted to call the provisional government a puppet government, under the control of the US. Even as it became steadily more clear that nothing in Iraq was under the control of the US, feminists in the West continued to do a stunning job of ignoring the risks that women in Iraqi public life were running. An Iraqi female MP could get murdered and it was held to be a natural result of US imperialism, almost as if she had been murdered by George W. Bush in person. But she hadn't been. She had been murdered by local men who were making an example of her. They feared what she would bring: the spectre of women claiming an importance equal to that of men.

Last year the excellent Australian feminist journalist Pamela Bone finally died of cancer, but while she was still fighting it she published, in 2005, in response to what she regarded as the thunderous silence that had greeted the stand taken by Ayaan Hirsi Ali, an article called 'Where are the Western feminists?'. What Pamela Bone meant was, that she was amazed why so many of her colleagues couldn't see, or didn't want to see, that democracy was the best hope for women.

Pamela Bone was well aware that there is a necessary quarrel about how democracy can be brought about in countries that don't have it, and I hasten to concede that of the two possible main views about the invasion of Iraq, for example, my own view, in favour, soon became the minority view. But Pamela Bone couldn't see how there could be any doubt that women in the countries without democracy were in a battle that they were bound to lose if the men could prevail by force. Men will always monopolize the means of violence if they can. Women can learn to shoot guns, but there are no all-female armies, and even the Amazons were probably a myth. Women, on the whole, would naturally like to do something else, whereas an army, for too many men, is a home away from home, and often their only home.

It's the only home for the junta in Burma. The junta is in the news again this week because it found a pretext for locking Aung San Suu Kyi into prison, instead of just leaving her helpless under house arrest. The terms of Aung San Suu Kyi's house arrest were that she should receive no visitors, and some poor demented American Vietnam veteran made sure that the terms were violated by swimming to her front door. Like many a head-case he probably just wanted to discuss his theories about how aliens control everything, but the all-male military junta in Burma really does control everything and here was their chance to dump Aung San Suu Kyi into jail until the next election is over.

Aung San Suu Kyi not only has the stature, she has the right, to lead the government of her country. If the public got a chance to say so, she would do so, and bring immeasurable improvement not only to Burma but the whole area. I say all this because in some moment of optimism I allowed my name to get put on the masthead of the organization in this country that campaigns for her release, the Burma Campaign, but I have done nothing else for her before today, mainly because I don't believe that my going to dinner with like-minded humanitarians is likely to help much. What she needs is an invading army, but even if there were one available, armed intervention, since the Iraq incursion, has been out of fashion: no doubt with good reason, but those appalled by the moral cost of toppling a tyrannical regime are still stuck with counting the moral cost incurred by leaving it alone. The regime in Burma will most likely go on being left alone. Aung San Suu Kyi's slow martyrdom makes the cost obvious. The current best plan for getting her sprung is to bring persuasion to bear on India so that India will bring pressure to bear on the junta, and so on until she grows old and grey.

Being who she is, she grows old slowly, and at the age of sixty-three she looks like her own daughter, but time is still against her. If time is all you've got going for you, it isn't much. What justice needs, when it is ranged against naked force, is a contrary force, and the fact that there isn't one is enough to reduce the onlooker to despair.

Despair can coarsen one's judgement. I knew enough about what Saddam Hussein and his talented son Uday were doing to women to want that regime toppled. The price of doing so might have seemed too high, but at least now, six years later, it is no longer official policy to rape a woman in front of her family. There may be unofficial forces still on the loose in Iraq who would like to do that, but the government no longer does it. Fighting the Taliban in Afghanistan still seems worth it when you have read about what the Taliban want to do with any woman who seeks an education, but it's easy to despair when you think of how hard it is to stop them.

Sometimes despair overwhelms us when we read of just a single so-called honour crime in which the men of a family have ruined the life of a daughter for what seems no reason at all, and the men walk free because that's the culture, and the culture runs the government. I felt despair when Aung San Suu Kyi got taken off to jail, and for her I thought I had no despair left.

But heartbreak feels out of place when we see this news story about the four women MPs in Kuwait, and there's a photo of one of them, rejoicing with her friends. I'm looking at the photo right now. Her name is Aseel al-Awadhi. She has a merry face and an exultantly elevated thumb. It will be a better world for all of us if women like her are free to do well, and if she could hear us it would be our simple duty to say good luck to you. And another duty, alas, to say: mind how you go.

Postscript

Somebody who had listened to the first two paragraphs of my broadcast, but apparently not to the rest, wrote in to point out that Saddam Hussein had been ruler of Iraq, not Kuwait. But Saddam Hussein had indeed been ruler of Kuwait, until he was driven out. Though it seemed fair to assume that people should have known this, I made a mistake in not spelling it out, just in case they had never noticed, or, more likely, had noticed but forgotten. When it comes to politics, you should almost always spell things out, even at the risk of being tedious. Later on, in September of the same year, I wrote, for *Standpoint* magazine, a whole essay in celebration of Pamela Bone. In that essay (which can be found now on my website) I further deplored the silence of Western feminists on the subject of so-called honour crimes, and tried to analyse the insidious mechanism by which a nominally liberal ideology, namely feminism, can find itself allied with extremism. I thought it needed spelling out at the level of nuts and bolts, or let us say knives and guns.

There is a theoretical point to be made but you have to look at the practical points first. When a sufficient number of women all over the world get cut up or buried alive or have their faces burned off with acid, finally even the Western feminists notice. (Even then, the breakthrough series of articles in 2010, a long, multi-part report for the *Independent* about honour crimes all over the world, was signed by a man, Robert Fisk: not normally a reporter for whose political opinions I have any great regard, but he covered himself with glory on that occasion.) The practical point is that feminists, who are nowadays multiculturalists almost to a man, or woman, find it inconvenient to countenance the possibility that any other culture might have deplorable aspects when compared to the West. The practical point having been spelled out, one is ready to promulgate the theoretical point, which is that all ideologies are in alliance with extremism, because any ideology depends on a refusal to consider the dissenting voice. The so-called Green movement, for example, wishes, in almost all its manifestations, to reduce the population of what it calls the Planet. But mouthpieces for the Greens are slow to specify how this reduction is to be brought about. How else except through coercion?

Alert listeners and readers no doubt detected that I found the brave and beautiful Aung San Suu Kyi impossible not to love. Much good that did her. Our helplessness to aid her case was just one more demonstration of a political truth that will always need spelling out even more than all the others. The wiser course might often be to do nothing, but it will seldom be without moral cost.

NEWSFLASH FROM THE FAR EAST

Dates of show: 29 and 31 May 2009

This is the last broadcast in my current stint and I would like to thank little Kim Jong-Il of North Korea for handing me, at the eleventh hour, a useful peg around which to do a wrap-up. Throughout the series I've been trying to stress the advantages of liberal democracy over less representative forms of government.

I didn't pretend that liberal democracy can infallibly deliver justice to everyone in all walks of life, or always deliver a sensible foreign policy, or even deliver a disk full of secret personal information without leaving it in a taxi. But I did try to point out that liberal democracy is more likely to guarantee a life lived under the rule of law than any system that rules according to the desires of an oligarchy or a despot. Sometimes the despot has been democratically elected but that doesn't make his regime a liberal democracy. So let's just call liberal democracy 'democracy' for short, and save a word.

The minimal definition of democracy that was devised in New Zealand by the exiled philosopher Karl Popper during World War II still holds. It's a democracy if the government can be changed at the people's whim. The French writer Albert Camus added a valuable nuance when he said that democracy was the form of society devised and maintained by those who know they don't know everything.

One way or another, those two descriptions are at the heart of the case for favouring a mechanism by which no group can consolidate itself in power, or any individual rule alone unchallenged. Democracy gives justice its best chance to realize itself as a principle. This fact is obvious, and in fact every commentator in the West accepts it even when he earns his living by railing against its deficiencies as if they were built in. He still calls the police if his house gets robbed, and sometimes the police even turn up. If they don't, he can write to his MP.

Aha, you might say, our MPs are currently in disrepute. They've all had their hands in the bag, we scream, even though it's remarkable how many of them haven't, despite a temptation that amounted to a standing order. I've already pointed out in a previous broadcast that the expenses scandal could have been far worse. At least we were shocked. In a truly corrupt non-democracy we might not have been shocked: we might have thought it normal. Here it seems abnormal enough to crowd the headlines.

But I've already made that point, and even though the headlines continue to be crowded week after week, it would have been a feeble wrap-up to make the same point again, except to say that it's high time to remember just how hard and long, including during the holidays, most MPs work, for what really is a tight salary. Those who bumped the salary up by claiming their expenses were doing what was allowed, and those who made too good a thing of it will either walk the plank now or lose their seats next time, so really our form of government is still democratic, or else the rogue MPs would have staged a coup by now, roped in the army and shot us down in the streets.

But I can hear you nodding off already. Again, it's obvious. Damaged doesn't mean destroyed, and repairs can be made. Indeed the party that shows it knows how to make them will probably win the next election, which might even have a high turn-out, as people remember what their vote is for: changing the government at the people's whim.

That was the sublime cunning of Karl Popper's minimal definition. He said the people's 'whim'. He didn't say that the people had to be fully informed, or wise. He said that all it took was for enough of them to want a change, and it could be made to happen. In a despotism you can want all you want, and there will be no change, except that, if you do any of your wanting aloud, the police really will turn up on time, and set about demonstrating to you and your family exactly why Saddam Hussein, of fond memory, won every election by 100 per cent of the vote.

If you are fighting sleep as I grind out these truisms, get set to be propelled even more deeply into the arms of Morpheus when I launch into a short version of the other wrap-up I thought I might be stuck with, namely the Oxford Poetry Professorship imbroglio. Yes, poetry, normally a tight little world, got itself into the headlines for the second time in three weeks when, after Carol Ann Duffy was appointed to the Laureateship, Derek Walcott not only pulled out of the election for the Oxford Poetry Professorship, but the winner, Ruth Padel, resigned from the post.

Never before in the history of English literature had poetry been a news story twice in quick succession: it was as if the murder of Christopher Marlowe had been succeeded within a fortnight by the revelation that the boy genius Thomas Chatterton was a forger. Yet the dust-up over the Poetry Professorship wasn't really the fault of the participants, it was a fault of the system. Carol Ann Duffy was appointed to the Laureateship, whereas Walcott and Padel both hoped to be elected to the Professorship. Election proved to be a bad way of choosing a poetry professor, because the press got into the act, not just to report the issue, which was its right and duty, but to help decide it, which wasn't. The great sixteenth-century French poet Ronsard is only the first of the poets I can think of whose candidature for election to the Oxford post would have been sunk by press coverage of his attitude towards personable young women.

Ronsard was of advanced years when he repeatedly struggled up the stairs of the old Tuileries palace, before it burned down, and made advances to a young lady of the court called Hélène, to whom he undoubtedly used inappropriate language. After she gave him the freeze, Ronsard took revenge, warning her in a sonnet that when she was old and grey she would regretfully remember that Ronsard had sung of her when she was young. '*Ronsard me célébrait du temps quand j'étais belle.*' It was a wonderful sonnet and he would have been able to deliver a wonderful set of lectures on how to write sonnets, but the press would have screwed his chances of winning an election.

If Byron had run, he would probably have been jailed for what the press uncovered about him. Sodomy, incest, forget about it. Nice draft lecture about how you wrote *Don Juan*, my lord, but sorry, no chance. Goethe was more than eighty years old when he proposed marriage to the beautiful teenager Ulrike von Levetzow and the whole of Europe burst out laughing after she turned the old goat down. He consoled himself by writing the Marienbad Elegy, one of the triumphs of German literature, but there goes the Oxford Poetry Professorship, lost in the blaze of a *Sun* headline: Kraut Bard's Last Grope. Ulrike says, 'What part of the word Nein don't you understand?'

In our own era, the ageing W. B. Yeats, sustained by monkey-gland injections, wrote some of his greatest late poetry while not only pursuing young ladies, but catching up with them. And Philip Larkin, the supreme poet in English of the late twentieth century, customarily kept half a dozen women on a string at once, while avoiding marriage with the dexterity of a dodgem. After his death it all got into the papers, and it would have got into them before his death if he had ever run for the Oxford Poetry Professorship. A gifted critic as well as a mighty poet, he would have been ideal for the job, but he would have had to be appointed, not elected.

How, you might say, if I am so much in favour of elections to government, can I not be in favour of elections to a professorship? Because Camus was right: the whole democratic system depends on the realization that we don't know everything. The people know enough to know when the government needs to be changed in order to preserve democracy, but a fully developed democracy contains, within it, all kinds of areas where specialized knowledge really counts, and popular opinion, especially when it is whipped up by the press, is largely irrelevant.

We don't have popular elections to a medical board. We ought to have government oversight of a medical board through the people's representatives, but a popular election in every field would be government by plebiscite, and would produce more injustice than it avoided. Within a properly constituted democracy, there is room for all kinds of alternatives as long as they are enlightened. Theatre, for example, is always an enlightened despotism. And a poetry professorship falls within that realm of alternatives. The professor shouldn't be elected by the whole of the people, or even, as in Oxford, by a bunch of graduates. The professor should be appointed by a panel of properly qualified literary figures who are fully aware that good poets are often frail people, and people who are not frail are seldom good poets.

It's an essential part of democracy that it can shape and employ the idea of authority, so that authority can stave off the effects of populism run rampant. As for authority running rampant, well, in a democracy it can't, or at any rate shouldn't: a consideration which makes democracy superior to any system where power is concentrated perpetually in a few, or sometimes only two, hands.

But so obvious a point would have been a pretty down-beat wrap-up if a sudden flash of light on the other side of the world had not suddenly made the point so terribly clear. The all-knowing Kim, a bouffant hairstyle joined to a pair of elevator shoes by a psychotic personality, has got his own atomic bomb. And he can drop it whenever he likes. I hope I'll be speaking to you again one day.

Postscript

Oxford kept its electoral system for the Poetry Professorship and got lucky on the next try. Geoffrey Hill won the race, a result which pleased everybody who cared about poetry, although too many people who didn't care at all had been among his competitors. In the field of politics, elections still looked to have the edge on dictatorship. In his role as unchallenged Dear Leader, Kim Jong-Il proved to be even better comic material than his father. Kim Il-sung had been hilarious for his conviction that there was something profound about his Thought, which with the aid of a staff of scribes he expounded in many volumes of text uniformly unreadable in any language. Promoted by full-page advertisements in the world's major newspapers, his Thought was North Korea's major export for years on end. But his poisonous offshoot Kim Jong-Il not only showed his father's gift for comporting himself as if to maintain an entirely arid totalitarian state were something to be proud of, he had a hairstyle to match. He was begging to be parodied. (Actually he was begging to be assassinated, but we'll get to that in a minute.) The best portrayal was done by the inspired bunch of wits who put the movie *Team America* together. In my house people eventually had to be forbidden from singing 'Lonely' in the Kim manner.

The success on screen of the Kim Jong-Il puppet did something to offset the sad fact that in real life being funny about him was all we could do about him. In view of the sufferings of his people it would have been a blessing if outside forces could have invaded his country and shot him. But it wasn't on. It hardly ever is, because of the cost. As Iraqis continued to murder Iraqis while their liberators took the blame, those of us who thought that Saddam Hussein's regime had been too horrible to put up with were obliged to consider that the cost of toppling him was great, even if we were reluctant to align ourselves with those who said that his regime had not been so horrible after all. Such retroactive wishful thinking, indeed, seemed part of the cost. But perhaps it would have been better to leave him alone until he died of shame after seeing himself caricatured so wittily in *Hot Shots Part Deux*.

Such sarcasm is rarely a spur to action; instead, it is a solace for the embarrassment of being able to do nothing. Chaplin's magnificent spoof of Hitler in *The Great Dictator* exactly caught his homicidal megalomania but did little to mobilize the world against him. Many of those in the audience who laughed until they cried would have remained inactive if they could, even citing Chaplin's achievement as a blow against war. It wasn't meant to be; it was meant to be a blow against Hitler; but until they were forced to choose, most people thought that you could be against both. Finally it took half the world to put Hitler out of business: a fighting effort in which humour was useful only for purposes of morale. When humour is the only weapon there is, it lacerates. And anyway, it is often directed at the wrong target, or at any rate against the easier one. George W. Bush was always a more potent generator of cheap laughs than Osama bin Laden. Some of the Bush jokes were mine, but I tried to remember that bin Laden was still out there somewhere, with or without his beard. The monster with few characteristics is safe from satire. Pol Pot, who had no characteristics whatever, was never reached by a joke. In the course of too much time, the North Vietnamese deposed him, but not before he had reduced his country to a charnel house. For that event, wits in the West came up with exactly one gag – HANDS OFF DEMOCRATIC KAMPUCHEA – and it was unintentional.

2009 – SERIES TWO

THE GOLF-BALL POTATO CRISP

Dates of show: 23 and 25 October 2009

What do I *know*? Montaigne asked himself, and in answering that question during the course of several volumes of great essays he touched on many subjects. But he never touched on the subject of the golf-ball potato crisp. As far as I know, this essay I am writing now is the first ever devoted to the subject of Montaigne's relationship to the golf-ball potato crisp, and my essay starts from my certain knowledge that he never ate one. Or anyway my almost certain knowledge. There's a difference, which I shall try to bring out.

But more of the golf-ball potato crisp in a moment. Let's get back to Montaigne, and his attitude to knowledge. He was a sceptic. He didn't want to take things just on trust. As it happened, there were lots of things he did take on trust. If he liked the sound of an ancient legend, he would refer to it as if it must have been true. He thought astrology had something to it, and his position on the religious quarrels of his own time was that all this Lutheranism could undermine the Church and lead to atheism, substance abuse and the contemporary equivalent of reality television.

From our viewpoint, he often doesn't seem very sceptical at all. But at the time, he seemed sceptical enough to excite a whole generation of readers with the idea that some falsehoods might masquerade as facts, and that an enquiring, critical attitude was the one to have. Shakespeare was only one of his many readers who caught fire at that idea. Shakespeare knew Montaigne's writings inside out. They helped set the standard for the way our greatest playwright separated what he knew from what he didn't know. But not even Shakespeare had an opinion about the golf-ball potato crisp, because it had not yet arrived in the world.

Or it had probably not yet arrived in the world. There may well have been, at the time, some form of sliced and roasted potato, specially prepared for the king, that you could have called a crisp. And there was possibly some primitive form of French golf already in existence, in which a ball of some kind was hit with some kind of stick towards some kind of hole, while Peter Alliss, then in his first days as a commentator, said something like, 'Typically delicate stroke there from the Duke of Guise. Finely judged. Taking full advantage of the new oblong ball, and it does roll much straighter than the old square one.' But the chances against the existence of an actual golf-ball potato crisp were overwhelming, because it needed a particular conjunction of circumstances.

The golf-ball potato crisp had to wait until our own time before it could come into being. What you must have is a golf course, and, nearby to the golf course, a potato field in which potatoes suitable for making crisps are mechanically harvested, and part of the mechanism must be an enormous machine that sorts through the plucked-up potatoes and removes any stones or other roughly potato-shaped objects that are not wanted. Apparently this machine, though highly sensitive to the presence of foreign objects, is not yet sensitive enough to detect a golf ball that has flown in from the adjacent golf course and settled among the potatoes.

The mistakenly harvested golf ball goes to the crisp-making factory along with the correctly harvested potatoes, and in the factory it encounters another machine which, also unable to tell a potato from a golf ball, slices the golf ball as if it were a potato. Apparently a golf ball yields precisely eighteen slices. All eighteen slices of the golf ball, along with the thousands of slices of potato, go into the cooking process and emerge at the other end as something hard to distinguish, visually, from crisps. Indeed statistics indicate that some people, when they chance across a golf-ball crisp in a packet of potato crisps, eat it, thinking, well, that one was a particularly crunchy crisp. Why don't you try one, darling? They're the ones with the dimpled edges. Really, really chewy.

I am not certain whether I myself have never done this. Famous in my family for eating anything, I usually think something is all right if I can actually swallow it. But some people have complained, with the result that the more responsible crisp manufacturers are now faced with the task of further developing the initial potato-sorting machine, the one out in the field, so that it can detect a golf ball.

The machine might need visual sensors, so it can read. If the object bears the brand name Tiger Woods Ultraflite Thunderball Mk 56, plus a short paragraph explaining how it was designed to be simultaneously long off the tee and responsive on the green, the machine will toss it back onto the golf course.

Such a development is not only possible, it is likely, in line with the standard progression by which the unforeseen deleterious effects of technology, once they are detected and protested against, are cured by further technology, just as it was the cleaning up of industry, and not the abandonment of industry, that brought fish back to the Thames. If anyone said the infestation of packets of genuine crisps by golf-ball crisps was unstoppable, I would be sceptical, just as I would have been sceptical about the existence of a golf-ball crisp until I was presented with solid evidence.

Indeed, as I have suggested, I would probably have remained sceptical even after I ate one, thinking it to be the kind I like best, with a bit of tough skin in it for extra texture. But once I heard the facts – from my son-in-law, who has important contacts within the potato-crisp industry – I altered my opinion. What remained constant was my scepticism, which is surely, as a human attitude, more valuable than gullibility. In fact, in everyday life, everyone is sceptical. Even if they believe that the supreme being is watching over them personally, they still want to read the fine print before they sign their house away.

In Montaigne's day you could get into terminal trouble for taking scepticism too far, which is probably one of the reasons why not even he pushed it on the subject of religion. Since then, a sceptical attitude has been less likely to get you burned at the stake, but it's notable how the issue of man-made global warming has lately been giving rise to a use of language hard to distinguish from heresy-hunting in the fine old style by which the cost of voicing a doubt was to fry in your own fat. Whether or not you believe that the earth might have been getting warmer lately, if you are sceptical about whether mankind is the cause of it, the scepticism can be enough to get you called a denialist.

It's a nasty word to be called, denialist, because it conjures up the spectacle of a fanatic denying the Holocaust. In my homeland, Australia, there are some prominent intellectuals who are quite ready to say that any sceptic about man-made global warming is doing even worse than denying the Holocaust, because this time the whole of the human race stands to be obliterated. Really they should know better, because the two events are not remotely comparable. The Holocaust actually happened. The destruction of the earth by man-made global warming hasn't happened yet, and there are plenty of highly qualified scientists ready to say that the whole idea is a case of too many of their colleagues relying on models provided by the same computers that can't even predict what will happen to the weather next week.

In fact the number of scientists who voice scepticism has lately been increasing. But there were always some, and that's the only thing I know about the subject. I know next to nothing about climate science. All I know is that many of the commentators in newspapers who are busy predicting catastrophe don't know much about it either, because they keep saying that the science is settled, and it isn't.

There is no scientific consensus. There are those for, and those against. Either side might well be right, but what should be clear is that if you have a division on that scale, you can't have a consensus. Nobody can meaningfully say that 'the science is in', yet this has been said constantly by many commentators in the press until very lately, and now that there are a few fewer saying it there is a tendency, on the part of those who do say it, to raise their voices even higher, and harden their language against any sceptic, as if they were protecting their faith.

Sceptics, say the believers, don't care about the future of the human race. But being sceptical has always been one of the best ways of caring about the future of the human race. For example, it was from scepticism that modern medicine emerged, questioning the common belief that diseases were caused by magic, or could be cured by it. A conjecture can be dressed up as a dead certainty with enough rhetoric, and protected against dissent with enough threatening language, but finally it has to meet the only test of science, which is that any theory must fit the facts, and the facts can't be altered to suit the theory.

The golf-ball crisp might look like a crisp, and in a moment of delusion it might taste like a crisp, and you might even swallow it, rather proud of the strength it took to chew. But if there is a weird aftertaste, it might be time to ask yourself if you have not put too much value on your own opinion. The other way of saying 'What do I *know*?' is 'What do *I* know?' That shade of different meaning wasn't there in Montaigne's original language, but it is in ours.

Postscript

If you'll allow a metaphor so horridly mixed, the golf-ball potato crisp was a red herring. By such means, I hoped, I would be able to sneak up on the forbidden topic of Catastrophic Anthropogenic Global Warming, sometimes referred to as CAGW by writers who supposed their readers were insufficiently bored already. Because my brand of scepticism about the claims of the alarmists was still widely regarded as criminal indifference to the future of the Planet, it seemed wise to avoid tipping off the audience at the top of the show. Lull them first and needle them later. But it was a mistake, I discovered, to say that one knew next to nothing about climate science, because people who knew less than nothing, but who nevertheless had intuitive powers to predict the coming catastrophe, took one's confession not as a sign of modesty, but as proof of the malevolence behind any attempt one might make to express an opinion differing from the opinion they supposed to be prevalent in the scientific world.

In actual fact, the scientific world had been divided on the subject from the beginning, and the division had by this time become apparent to anyone with a wider source of information than that provided by the mainstream media. For reasons of its own, however, the BBC, although it didn't have to, had decided to copy some of the more upmarket outlets of printed news and opinion – in Britain, these were most conspicuously the *Guardian* and the *Independent* – in handing over the whole field of science to a science correspondent. If it was editorial humility that led to such delegation of responsibility, the result was orthodoxy in each case, and nowhere was the orthodoxy more rigidly imposed than at the BBC. This tiny broadcast was the very first case of the BBC letting someone on the air alone to put a differing view, and it was certainly not the prelude to a flood. Until the so-called (dumbly called) Climategate scandal broke at the University of East Anglia in November, cases of heresy expressed unfettered on the airwaves remained very rare, and after Climategate they became only slightly less rare, because the BBC, though forced, like the mainstream media as a whole, to report a news event, was slow to admit the implications.

Slowness was understandable, since one of the implications was that in their coverage of Climate Change (to give a poltergeist the dignity of capitalized initials) they had been wasting their time, and

everybody else's, for years on end. Nevertheless, even though the
script for this broadcast aroused consternation when I submitted it,
I was allowed on the air. In this instance as in so many others, Mark
Damazer, controller of Radio 4, was prepared to back the contributor against the full weight of the building he was sitting in. But
the message did come filtering down the stairs that I might do better
to back off for a while, and talk of other matters. Meanwhile, in
the outside world, things were starting to boil. I was only one of the
tiniest bubbles, but the reaction of the *Guardian*'s Climate Change
pundit George Monbiot was indicative. He said that the only reason I
could hold such opinions was that I was an old man who didn't care
what happened to the Planet. Well, he was right about the first part
of the description, but the day will come when he himself realizes that
the second part proved he had little insight into how an old man feels
about the world when the time draws near that he must leave it.

There was no point, though, in fighting back on the level of
personality, because one could only be cooperating in a conspiracy to
bore the public. Quite early on, the climatologists had made their
eventually decisive mistake: they had turned the supposed difference
of views – or difference of supposed views – into a plebiscite. This
counting of heads was a competition they were bound, in the long
run, to lose, because the matter would eventually turn on the exercise
of critical reason; their opponents, under no obligation to prove a
negative, had only to go on asking for proof.

The sceptics made just as big a mistake in supposing that when
the position of the alarmists collapsed, everyone would suddenly turn
sane; that the newspapers and television channels would automatically
resume their erstwhile positions as arenas for debate; and that
governments would stop spending the public's money on hopelessly
expensive and inefficient alternatives to the cheap power we already
had. Eventually that became the next debate, and once again it was
almost impossible to hear it happen. But just because it was so
dauntingly clear that people living near a wind-farm in the making
would soon be reduced to re-inventing smoke signals and the talking
drum was no reason to think that common reason would soon
prevail. There was just too much money in building the wrong thing.
The money amounted to a tax on the poor; a fact which should have
put the left on the alert; but the left, no longer worthy of its name,
had long ago fallen silent.

ON STRIKE

Dates of show: 30 October and 1 November 2009

Nowadays a strike is usually called industrial action but I've never much liked the term, because any proposed industrial action aims to produce industrial inaction, and usually it's better to have a word for something that evokes the something instead of its opposite. Besides, the word 'strike' is short if not sweet, and it sounds like a blow, which is what it is meant to be.

At the time I write this script, the postal strike, after a brief lull, has once again hurtled into action, or inaction, and the chance is getting low that your Christmas cards will make it through to your maiden aunt in that little town where the train has been replaced by a bus, the local shops by a supermarket she can't walk to, her hip by a stainless-steel gadget, and that nice man Nicholas Parsons's smiling face on the telly by Russell Brand's petulant snarl.

In fact she, you and I might already be hoping that somebody will reinvent the pony express. A few days ago I got a letter from someone I sent a letter to months ago. She said she had only just received my letter. But her letter was dated from weeks ago. For at least part of the total period, the Royal Mail was theoretically not on strike.

All too often, the Royal Mail feels to me as if it is on strike even when it isn't. Whose fault is this? All I can suggest is that in matters of industrial relations, often a way of saying lack of industrial relations, we should be slow to point the finger. Not necessarily as slow as it takes a letter to get there, of course, but still slow. Maybe the fault goes deeper and further back than we think.

Last Sunday I happened to be on Andrew Marr's television show when the chief executive of the Royal Mail, Adam Crozier, was one of the guests. For a man in his position, he seemed refreshingly normal.

Some of his predecessors in the post, however, might as well have been wearing flying helmets and flippers. You might remember that the Royal Mail's top management once took the inspired decision to change the name of the Post Office to Consignia. They might not have realized – or, even worse, they might have realized – that their new word Consignia, meant to be equally unintelligible but universally awe-inspiring to people of all nationalities, sounded very like the Spanish word *consigna*, meaning 'left luggage'.

But they certainly realized soon afterwards that the British public disliked the new appellation, so they thought hard and changed it again, at huge expense. They didn't change it back to Post Office, they changed it to Royal Mail plc. To do this, they had to ask the Queen. Kindly she said yes, instead of saying that on the whole, when organizations whose names were prefaced by the word 'Royal' were concerned, she would prefer it if the management could restrain itself from faffing about, because she had her own brand name to consider.

I might say here that Mr Crozier struck me as someone who might be rather better than some of his predecessors at listening to other voices. But the damage may already have been done, over the course of years. When industrial relations go sour, they tend not to be fixed without a blow being struck, and what you think about that tends to determine your politics.

My own politics, in this matter, remain where they always were, on the old-style left. I think it's up to management, and always has been. If the managers can't manage to sort it out, preferably in advance, then they ought not to be managing. But quite often they haven't been. They've just been sitting there, failing to notice that the workers have begun to arrive at work facing backwards, ready to walk out.

When there is dignity in labour, workers usually want to work, even if the task is a drudge. They should beware of any outrage expressed on their behalf by false friends on the playtime left who have never done a hand's turn. While it is a fine thing to be an artist, it is an even finer thing to be a doctor or a nurse, and can be just as fine a thing to stack shelves or clean lavatories. One of the few virtues of the old Soviet Union was that it respected the dignity of the workers. It also slaughtered them by the million, but that was an effect of totalitarian rule, not a sign of any innate conflict between management and labour. To the extent that there is such an innate conflict, modern history has consisted largely of the long process of resolving it.

Back in the nineteenth century, the future prosperity of my homeland, Australia, was ensured partly by the energies of people who had been transported to the colony because they were machine-breakers. Those victims of progress were some of our first trade unionists, having discovered the hard way that a free market, though necessary, will never produce justice by itself. In the twentieth century, it wasn't just the Soviet Union that responded with force to any signs of independence from labour. In America in the 1930s, Detroit auto workers were beaten up for going on strike, and some of them were shot. Unions in the free countries had to battle every inch of the way for workers' rights.

Admittedly it was very easy for unions, once they had consolidated their power, to become corrupted. Jimmy Hoffa of the Teamsters union was unusual only in being such a silk-suited hoodlum. Less spectacularly dressed, in Britain after World War II, there were honest union leaders who led their members into a Luddite cul-de-sac and the country into stagnation. In the time of Harold Wilson, trade union leaders like Jack Jones and Hugh Scanlon were practically in residence in Downing Street, and later on the grief was by no means universal when Mrs Thatcher broke the power of Arthur Scargill.

She could never have done it if the nation had been behind him, but in truth he never even had all the miners behind him. The idea was ripe by then that there had to be a balance. If the managers couldn't manage, there was even less hope in the unions doing the managing instead. I myself can well remember when the print unions ruled Fleet Street through what were called Spanish practices, and phantom workers drew real salaries. Strikes were endemic. Too often writing a column on Friday for a paper that failed to come out on Sunday, I found myself in the uncomfortable position of being grateful to Rupert Murdoch, when he broke the grip of the union bosses.

Not that he or any other boss is an attractive prospect if his workers have no choice but to obey him. There has to be a concord of management and labour, and the lesson was taught most sharply by what happened when the Nazis brought Germany to ruin. As the great German historian Golo Mann pointed out, the division between management and labour was the crack through which Hitler had got

in. And when the war was over, those few labour leaders who survived the concentration camps emerged convinced that for industrial
harmony the workers needed more than their rights and conditions,
they needed a seat on the board.

The workers must feel that they are in on the planning for how
the job is done. When Japan was being rebuilt after that same war,
the workers on the production lines were rewarded for their ideas
about efficiency. The idea that they should be rewarded came from
American advisers who took the chance to transplant the hopes of the
New Deal, free from the inflexible old capitalist orthodoxies that had
hampered them at home.

A labour–management concord was the solution in Germany and
Japan and one way or another it will be the solution here: it's just
slow to come. Making the slowness slower, alas, is the still lingering
twin effect – weaker now but not dead yet – of a conservatism that
thinks the workers are out to wreck the nation and a radicalism that
would like to see the nation wrecked, as if some kind of purity could
ensue if people no longer had to work for a living.

But everyone has to work for a living, except those who contrive
to get paid for preaching otherwise. The trick is to support the true
and essential human feeling that work, any work, if well done and
properly managed, has dignity. And if it doesn't feel like that, then
the managers should be fired first, before the workers are. When new
technology comes in, some workers are bound to lose their jobs, but
if they have no new job to go to, then the highest managerial layer of
all, which is the government, is at fault.

In the liberal democracies, and precisely because they are so
productive, this conflict in the centre, about how to manage work as
the nature of the work changes faster and faster because of its own
success, is the main theme of all the domestic politics that matters.
And like it or not, at the centre of it all, at the centre of the centre,
is the worker's right to stop work if the work has been dehumanized
to the point where it is not worth doing: the right to strike.

Ideally it shouldn't need to be exercised, and there must always be
some people, of course, who are never free to do so. One of those is
the Queen, but she must sometimes wish she were. You can imagine
her getting a phone call from the managers of Hellosailor.com, wanting to change their name back to the Royal Navy. 'Couldn't you have

put all that in a letter?' she says. 'Well, no, come to think of it, one supposes not.'

Postscript

Two hundred years after the industrial revolution began to transform the world, the relationship between management and labour remains one of the permanent points of dispute in a developed society. In fact if it doesn't have that point of dispute, it probably isn't developed. (In undeveloped societies, it isn't a dispute, it's a one-sided battle.) As someone born into the industrial proletariat, I have never forsaken my solidarity with the workers, and still count myself as left wing in politics, however conservative I might be in matters of culture. But the solidarity is mainly notional, because although I work quite hard when it suits me, I have no capacity at all for working when it doesn't suit me, which is practically the first requirement in the ability to hold down a job.

People who enjoy their work, and will therefore work night and day unless somebody stops them, have a bad tendency to look down on those who don't enjoy their work. But on the part of those who fancy themselves to be imaginative, it's a failure of imagination not to realize that only a few people are blessed with an all-consuming purpose that they would pursue even if they were not paid. Most people have to clock on in the morning, and live with the knowledge that their time is being used up. To make them feel that their efforts are worthwhile is the whole art of management. In the years running up to World War II, management in Britain had not been very brilliant. Strikes were frequent, and when the war started the strikes did not stop. Even in the vital aircraft factories, the workers would down tools for more pay. Churchill was outraged when he heard about it, but it was a bad failure of imagination on his part. He thought that assembling the structure of a Wellington bomber's left aileron ought to be as satisfactory for those doing it as reading vital documents half the night was for him. But they were two different kinds of activity.

British resistance to Hitler saved the world from barbarism, but after the war it turned out that the nations who lost had learned their lessons better. The Japanese car industry, in particular, achieved an industrial-relations revolution by encouraging its assembly-line workers to participate in quality control, and rewarding them for their contribution. The result was an irresistible export drive. By the time the British car industry caught on, it had been almost wiped out. The American car industry suffered a similar humiliation, spiced by the knowledge that many of the quality-control precepts used by the Japanese had been developed by American engineers and introduced into Japan after a lost war had reduced that country to a *tabula rasa* on which some of the dreams of the New Deal could be made actual. The key man, W. Edwards Deming, is revered in Japan to this day. There is a statue to him, but perhaps his lasting memorial is one that not even he foresaw: the principles of quality control – be precise, keep it clean, be consistent, involve the workers – so vital to the pressed-metal industries, were even more fundamental to Japan's initial dominance in what we now know as the electronics revolution. That's to give the word 'revolution' a lot of prominence; but in the context of industry, rather than of politics, the word seems appropriate, because an industrial revolution really does change people's lives for the better in the long run, even if, in the short run, the fate of a wage-slave might not seem sufficiently distant from that of a victim of the guillotine.

HIGH ROAD TO XANADU

Dates of show: 6 and 8 November 2009

'Weave a circle round him thrice,' raves Coleridge in the last few lines of his poem *Kubla Khan*, 'And close your eyes with holy dread / For he on honey-dew hath fed / And drunk the milk of paradise.' Coleridge is talking about himself. This, he is saying, is the impression he would make on anyone who saw him while he was all fired up by the excitements of Kubla Khan's pleasure dome in Xanadu, where there were gardens bright with sinuous rills, and the earth breathed in fast thick pants. Even to modern ears, however, the fast thick pants are the only discord in the poem, which is indeed as fabulous as it was meant to be, a ride on a rocket sled into the lyrical sublime.

Coleridge, by his own account, was high on opium when he wrote it. He was in the early stages of an oil-burning habit which would rule him for the rest of his life. Opium, in the liquid form of laudanum, was legally available at the time, but it's a miracle that anybody else got any, because Coleridge was drinking it at the rate of two quarts a week. Since, in his last years, he managed to write *Biographia Literaria*, which T. S. Eliot later hailed as the work of the greatest literary critic in the English language, the question of whether drugs ruined Coleridge, or else helped him to express his genius, is not easily answered.

But one thing we can say for sure. Even more than his contemporary Thomas De Quincey, who wrote *Confessions of an English Opium-Eater*, Coleridge was the one who established the romantic connection between getting wasted on drugs and yet being granted the entrée to a deeper reality than the rest of us get to see. Later on, in France, Baudelaire and Rimbaud followed Coleridge down the same road, but even if they thought they were opening up a French autoroute, they were in fact only extending a British motorway, the road to Xanadu. Here in the twenty-first century, we tend to think that the drug problem started in the twentieth century, forgetting that it acquired its most insidious element in the nineteenth century, with the notion that the world of drugs might be more exciting than the real world. That notion has bedevilled the whole discussion ever since. What do you do if people actually *want* this stuff?

The discussion never ends and probably never will, but it's been especially hot news in the last week or so after the Home Secretary, Alan Johnson, fired the chairman of the government's Advisory Council on the Misuse of Drugs, Professor David Nutt, for talking out of turn. I won't go into details, because the newspapers have been going into nothing else for day after day, but broadly we can say that this particular brouhaha would never have arisen if the government had not put itself into a position of asking for advice that it might not want to take.

If the government is still there after the next election, it might eventually want to take the advice which Professor Nutt was apparently all set to offer, which is that cannabis is not so bad after all. The government might even eventually want to legalize cannabis, or at least follow the example of California, where you can buy it for medical purposes. But suppose one or more of the panel offered the advice that a much more powerful drug, namely heroin, would be less destructive to society if it were made legal?

It's not impossible to imagine that advice being given, and given by an expert, because there was a time within living memory when heroin, in Britain, *was* legal. Heroin wasn't criminalized until 1968, and when I arrived in London in the early sixties you could still see the famous midnight queue at Boots in Piccadilly, where the addicts gathered to get tomorrow's allowance of their prescribed heroin pills. The point was that there weren't many addicts. There weren't many in the whole country.

After the drug was banned, however, it became more popular. The gangsters got in on the act, and the whole thing escalated until now you not only have thousands of adults shooting up with needles, you have children shooting each other with guns. The reasons for this disaster have been analysed to shreds, but one factor hard to rule out is that it makes a story. Drugs aren't humdrum. There is danger, special kit, a racy vocabulary, a ritual. That was already true for

Sherlock Holmes, whose creator, the physician Arthur Conan Doyle, for some reason equipped the world's greatest detective not just with a super brain but with a taste for the needle.

Way back before World War I, there was an element of the young upper crust that fooled with morphine. It was legal and available, but the fact that older people frowned upon it made it look glamorous to the bright young things. If you read the diaries of Duff Cooper, you find Lady Diana Manners and her glittering friends getting off on the stuff all the time. Nowadays, however, when the stuff is banned, even the less privileged look glamorous if they are sticking needles in themselves. Nobody would make a movie like *Trainspotting* if the characters were just holding down jobs and going to the supermarket. With exotic powders in the picture, the drug world can so easily be made to seem more intense than the real world.

In America cocaine was banned in 1914 and heroin in 1925. Traffic in the banned drugs quickly became a major theme for crime fiction. In some of the pre-war crime movies, and in almost all of the post-war ones, drugs are fuel for the action. It's been said of modern Hollywood that it's a factory where people high on cocaine make movies about people high on heroin, but somebody must have his head screwed on because people want to see the movie even when it makes drugs looks awful.

Back in 1955 *The Man with the Golden Arm* should have finished off heroin's career as a desirable product: Frank Sinatra got so strung out he could barely react to Kim Novak. Fast forward to the 1983 version of *Scarface*, and you can see Al Pacino destroy his criminal career with a nose-dive into a pile of cocaine bigger than his head. But no amount of didactic condemnation from the big screen has ever slowed the trade down, and on the small screen it's doubtful if even that magnificent series *The Wire* has done much to persuade the corner boys that they would be better off trying to improve their grades.

The Wire is a test case. If you haven't seen it, it's about how the whole black inner city of Baltimore is turned into a war-zone by drugs. It's a tremendous piece of work, *The Wire*. It's got everything, including a precision of language that you have to call poetic. And it's got an unpalatable message: the war on drugs can't be won.

To coincide with the last episode, the creators of *The Wire* published an article in *Time* magazine which recommended that nobody should be jailed for a drug crime unless violence was involved. If the work of art they had created was true, and it seemed terribly true, then this advice was in conformity to the facts. To the minds behind *The Wire*, legalization is the only answer.

But in addition to that article they have also published a couple of books, and one of the books, called *The Corner*, has a couple of pages that don't quite fit with the rest. Almost every character in the book is sucked into the system. But there is one character who volunteers for it. He makes only a fleeting appearance, but I can't get him out of my mind. His name is Gary McCullough and he has brains, energy and a gift for organization. He assembles all the necessary equipment for busting out of the free-fire zone he was born into. But he tries a taste of the stuff and he is lost. His previous life was exciting, but not as exciting as this.

Here, I'm afraid, is a way through to a further fact that we might still be faced with even if the whole vast mess of drug crime could be made to go away. Decriminalize all the drugs, put things back the way they were before the roof fell in, and you might still be stuck with people for whom real life simply isn't thrilling enough, even when they are otherwise quite good at it. I think they're wrong, but it isn't easy to make a case. Western civilization is up against it in that respect. Now that religious faith is so weak a force, how do you convince people that ordinary life is worth the effort?

It's not just a matter of persuading the young in America's black inner cities that it's worth going to school even if it leads only to some boring everyday job such as the Presidency of the United States. It's a matter of persuading young people in all the liberal democracies that the real world has a glamour of its own. Charlie Parker, the wonderful saxophonist who ruined himself with drugs, tried to tell his fellow musicians that they were fooling themselves if they thought they could play better when they were high.

Few musicians listened to what he said, so why would anyone listen to Nancy Reagan saying 'Just Say No'? She sounded so square. Even when all the drugs in the world are freely available at a special booth in every block, to advocate the opposite of self-destruction will always sound square, unless we can summon the language to persuade the candidates for a waking sleep that real life, with all its complications, is the only worthwhile mystery, and drugs are an escape to simplicity, which is no mystery at all. But finally it would be up to them. Would fewer choose oblivion if all were free to do so, at the booth marked Xanadu?

Postscript

Like industrial relations, drugs constitute an abiding dilemma for liberal democracy. It is hard to see how a free society can eliminate drugs and in fact no free society any longer tries: the most common plan is for a soft drug to be tolerated as a means of staving off traffic in the hard drugs, and there would probably be no returning to a state in which alcohol was permitted only so that all drugs could be banned. Certainly there will be no returning, in any free society, to a state in which alcohol was banned as well: the American experiment put the lid on that. Nobody wants to hand power to Al Capone. But the question remains of how to keep hard drugs in check. The obvious answer is to legalize them, but the obvious answer has the drawback of being purely rational; and purely rational answers to genuine dilemmas are almost always to be avoided, because dilemmas arise in the first place out of irrational needs that demand to be satisfied. Eugenics, for example, had a purely rational answer to the problem posed by handicapped children. In pursuit of that policy, Nazi Germany, by passing laws to suit itself and obeying them to the letter, had already revealed itself as an irredeemably criminal regime even before it got started on the mass murder of the Jews.

A free society is no such danger, but creates dangers of its own. One of them is the elevated position given to the arts. This narrow conception of creativity generates many casualties, because there are young people who think they have failed if they do not gain fame by expressing themselves. Intelligent and decent parents of a young addict go mad with grief and worry because they can see that there is a point to life, whereas their errant child can't. Probably the best thing to do is let the child go to hell in its own way, but this is only a rational answer. To fight back effectively, you would have to convince young addicts that their ambitions are too high. Not everyone can be a star, and there are real, and possibly more essential, contributions to be made in ordinary life. But it's a hard sell, because ordinary life visibly includes them, and all their pills, powders and needles. And often, like terrorists, they have gone to war not against a free society's vices, but against its virtues. One of the chief virtues is that all are free to express what is in them. But what if there is nothing? A question to put the mind in torment, and make its owner long for sleep: the drugged sleep which is very closely allied to the totalitarian dream, in which no more thought is necessary. It's another dubious blessing of the West: our home-grown, native-born suicide bombers spread no carnage in the streets, but detonate their explosive devices only within themselves, lacerating nobody except their parents, brothers and sisters, who pay them the generous compliment of being broken-hearted instead of relieved.

THE MAN ON THE FOURTH PLINTH

Dates of show: 13 and 15 November 2009

A temporary plastic statue of the Battle of Britain commander Sir Keith Park has been temporarily installed on the fourth plinth in Trafalgar Square, the fourth plinth having been temporarily empty of any permanent statue since, as far as I can make out, the year 1841. The plinth was designed as the base of some heroic permanent statue but the permanent statue never arrived, and in recent years the plinth has housed a temporary statue of one kind or another more or less permanently.

I promise to make as much sense as I can of this account as soon as possible, but we should record that some of the temporary exhibits on the plinth in recent times have aroused controversy, and sometimes seem to have been meant to, especially during the period when Ken Livingstone was mayor. It often seemed that Ken Livingstone had taken office in order to be controversial. Such was the level of controversy he continuously maintained that when he was replaced by Boris Johnson the new mayor's personality, which on any objective scale is like a hunt ball held in a cricket pavilion, has been experienced as a centre of calm.

Even in the Ken era, the controversy aroused by whatever statue was on the fourth plinth was not always pointless. At one stage the plinth held a statue of a deformed woman and I'm bound to say that I, for one, was probably better off for being reminded that Fate can play cruel tricks on human beings, which some of them may heroically defy. There was a dignity to that statue that made me think.

At a later stage, however, indeed quite recently, and under the reign of the theoretically less controversial Boris, the plinth has held a work of art by Antony Gormley. Under Mr Gormley's supervision, a different ordinary person, chosen by ballot, occupied the plinth for an hour, every hour of every twenty-four hours for one hundred days, thereby proving that there were 2,401 people in Britain with nothing else to do. 2,400 of the people were the aforesaid ordinary persons and the 2,401st was Mr Gormley.

I tried to be enlightened by that but couldn't manage it, and was rather glad when the temporary statue of Sir Keith Park was temporarily installed, even though the temporariness of the statue seemed only emphasized by the fact that it was made of plastic and was taller than a camel. Usually a plastic replica of a war hero is only a few inches high, like an Action Man figurine, but apparently this one was a kind of rehearsal for the real statue of Sir Keith Park, which will be made of bronze and will probably be installed in Waterloo Place.

It will be smaller than the plastic one but still a lot taller than the actual Sir Keith Park used to be, which again seems strange, but with a strangeness we will have to get to later. There is something even stranger that we should deal with first. Because if there is nothing especially inspired about the plastic statue except its size and plasticity, it has certainly inspired a great moment in journalism, a moment which, I think, is at the centre of the question about whether liberal democracy might not be losing its memory, and, along with its memory, its mind.

I won't name the journalist concerned, except to say that she has a column in one of the serious newspapers, and in this column she unblushingly announced: 'I'd never heard of Keith Park GCB KBE MC before the campaign to plinth him began, and I still can't figure out what all the fuss is about.' That was her talking. This is me talking again, saying that I won't name the serious newspaper either, except to say that I hope its editor, when he returned from holiday later that day, called her into his office and explained that if she really thought ignorance was a more honest form of knowledge then she should go and work for the kind of newspaper where she could interview Katie Price's previous chest.

But there is always the chance, alas, that he is pretty young too, and didn't know who Sir Keith Park was either. Or maybe they both did, and were just feigning ignorance because that was a fun way of filling space, and after all, what does it matter?

And right there, of course, is the catch in freedom. If you're born free, you're free to think that freedom is a natural state, and free to think that your own freedom owes nothing to some gung-ho old dead guy with a stack of initials after his name. But if Keith Park had never done what he did, our journalist might have had to compose her column in German, and you can bet that if she was writing about a statue of a Luftwaffe hero to go on the fourth plinth, her tone would have been a lot more reverent. Luckily for her and for all of us, things worked out differently; but it didn't seem like luck at the time. A lot of things had to go right, and one of the things was that the right man was in the right spot.

Keith Park was born in New Zealand, and had to take a long road to his date with destiny in 1940. In the First World War he started off with the Anzac army at the Dardanelles, he was in the Battle of the Somme, and after he transferred to the Royal Flying Corps he laid the groundwork for his future career by shooting down German aeroplanes. That was when he won the MC, twice. It was an equivocal war and nobody knew that better than he did, but when the Second War loomed he knew there was nothing equivocal about it. As the Germans prepared to invade Britain, the man in charge of the air defences was Hugh Dowding. Dowding's strategy for fighting the battle was controversial: really controversial, not just controversial as in 'what on earth is that thing on the plinth supposed to mean?'

Dowding's strategy was to assign 11 Group, commanded by Keith Park, to fight the incoming German formations while 12 Group was held back to guard 11 Group's airfields. The commanders of 12 Group resented this and brought a lot of political pressure on Dowding, so that he had to resist them as well as the Germans. But he was convinced that unless a reserve of trained pilots was maintained, the battle would be lost.

Meanwhile, Park was in charge of the first line of defence, flying around in his personal Hurricane from airfield to airfield, inspiring the defenders as they grew weary, the ideal battlefield commander. He wasn't British but quite a lot of the pilots in the Battle of Britain came from somewhere else, and not just from the Dominions but from Ireland, America, Czechoslovakia and Poland. The Poles and Czechs knew exactly what they stood to lose. They had already lost once. It wasn't just an Empire fighting for its life.

The whole force took a lot of coordinating but Park was the man to do it. He never wavered from Dowding's principle that there had to be trained pilots in reserve, and it was hard for him to see pilots getting killed who had scarcely been trained at all. In the control rooms, the young women recorded the numbers as the young men died. But the RAF, just, could live with its losses. The Germans couldn't, and eventually they switched to night bombing. Flying over burning London in the morning after the first big night raid, Park knew that the battle, if it had not been won, at least had not been lost.

Though historians argue still over the details, there is no serious argument about the result. Hitler, denied command of the air, could not invade, and he turned away. Even before he did so, another battle had started in Britain. This time it was a political battle. Those who had thought Dowding to be wrong in not committing his whole force were better at catching Churchill's ear. Dowding couldn't do PR and neither could Park. Park went off to defend Malta but really he had been written off. In the official history of the battle he was not even mentioned. Unlike Dowding, who spent his last years further developing a life-long interest in spiritualism and ended up believing in fairies, Park kept his head, and back in New Zealand, where he went home to die, there is a memorial garden, with a statue. But there is still no statue here.

Park and Dowding are both much honoured in the movie about the Battle of Britain – it's called *The Battle of Britain*, if our journalist can marshal her intellectual resources and search out the DVD – but by now even the movie is going back into the past. And Dowding, played in the movie by Laurence Olivier as an act of homage, has a statue. Life-sized instead of super-sized, it stands on a little plinth outside St Clement Dane's in the Strand – the right place, because inside that church is the beautifully handwritten book with the names of all our young people who were killed in the battle.

Personally I hope that the bronze permanent statue of Park (played in the movie by Trevor Howard, who looked just like him) can be scaled down to human size, because really for a man like that there is no scale bigger. The statue could be placed on that plinth beside Dowding, to commemorate how they worked together to save not just Britain, but the whole of civilization. Those were the stakes, and only a fool could doubt it. Only a fool, or someone young and careless.

Park's statue, if it stood there, would be looking up into the battlefield that shows no trace now of where the young men fought, because the condensation trails were only water crystals and they faded in a few hours – the battlefield where he led his pilots to a victory that cost so much, and you could say cost too much, except that defeat would have cost everything.

Postscript

The deliberate repetitions in the first paragraph of this script are examples of what can sound quite clever in a broadcast or a stage routine, but might be less advisable in an essay for the page, because the reader can take the necessary time to spot the workings. Thus we see that almost all rhetorical devices began as aids to speaking, not to writing. Personally I love treating the readers as if they were listeners, but it's an urge more easily overindulged than kept in bounds. The writer for the page has a tempting amount of room, whereas the writer for the studio and the stage is always short of time. There wasn't time to mention that the official history Keith Park was left out of was the one published just after the battle, whereas in the official history published later on he was duly acknowledged. I wish I had had the time to mention Josef František, the top-scoring pilot of the battle. As a Czech flying with the Poles, he was enough all by himself to scotch the notion that the pilots were mainly from public schools. Actually only about thirty per cent of them were. Most of them were NCOs, sergeant pilots from an ordinary background, a fact acknowledged by Churchill in the historic conversation with Halifax (see Martin Gilbert's *Finest Hour*) during which Churchill observed that 'the boys from the State schools' had done well in the battle and would deserve their chance to rule when the time came. In 2010 a prominent wit drew some well-deserved opprobrium when, wearing his serious hat, he revealed himself as being under the impression that all of the Battle of Britain pilots had been public-school boys. Astonishment at his ignorance was compounded with disquiet at his possible influence, since he himself was in the process of opening a school. What would it teach?

Meanwhile 'our journalist' went on with her career, and got noticeably better in the aftermath of her debacle. It's often the way. Exuberance frequently leads to excess in the early stages, whereas those who begin judiciously aren't always interesting later on. I myself, when making my start in Fleet Street, had some unfortunate moments. There was a crack about the Archbishop of Canterbury that drew dark mutterings of admonishment from upstairs. But the people upstairs, of course, had all been through the war, and knew the difference between news and opinion. The problem for any young journalist now is that the executives to whom he answers tend to share his illusion that the facts are elastic.

BLOG DE JOUR

Dates of show: 20 and 22 November 2009

For several years, the true identity of Belle de Jour, author of a blog called *Diary of a London Call Girl*, had been a mystery. Journalists, always excited by mysteries, strove to find out who she really was. Was she really a woman at all? Experienced male journalists who could do sentences with three clauses in them speculated that she might be a male journalist because of her unusual literary skills. Some of them suggested that Belle de Jour might be Toby Young, a wag about town who is not on the face of it a figure to arouse agonies of sexual desire among males, but who knew?

When Belle de Jour's daintily scurrilous blog was collected into a hit book, several critics noted that she had a command of language comparable to that of Martin Amis. Perhaps Belle de Jour was really Salman Rushdie. Surely no mere female could concoct a diary so exactly fulfilling male fantasies. When the book was turned into a television series, Billie Piper was up there on screen like Catherine Deneuve in the art-house movie from which our blogger, knowledge-able about art-house movies, had lifted her, or his, name.

The Catherine Deneuve movie was the story of a refined woman answering her imaginative needs by spending her afternoons in a bordello, taking on all-comers, but never chipping her nail polish. In the blog of our latter-day Belle de Jour, that was the soignée image that the author strove to project. In the TV series, as Billie Piper delicately primped, it sounded, and looked, very like a male's imaginative needs being fulfilled. But finally, last weekend, Belle de Jour stood revealed as a female after all.

And what a female. The voice behind the most celebrated of all soft-porn blogs had turned out to belong to a woman of outstanding beauty and brilliance called Dr Brooke Magnanti, student of informatics, epidemiology and forensic science. She must also have been a student of military strategy. When it became clear to her that one of the tabloid newspapers was about to blow her secret, she reacted like Rommel. Attacking out of defence, she stepped in ahead of time and spilled all to one of the weekend broadsheets, thus positioning herself invulnerably upmarket, where she will undoubtedly stay, the glossiest British-based femme fatale since Lady Bienvenida Buck, and much less likely to be forgotten.

Judging from her qualifications, Dr Magnanti's sudden appearance at the top of the media heap was only fitting. She would have been wasted down there in the land of tabloid fantasy, where the mind is not regarded as an erogenous zone to be expanded, though every other erogenous zone is expanded to the limit. Dr Magnanti is a different kind of sex goddess altogether, with the emphasis on the goddess. She is the thinking man's dream girl, and as such she is a nightmare for all those who occupy themselves with the condition of what we now know as the sex-worker. Common sense tells us that sex-work ranges from outright slavery at the bottom end, where kidnapped foreign girls are kept drugged by ruthless pimps, to a delusional miasma at the top end, where supposedly high-toned escorts delude themselves that they are doing the using instead of being used.

Above all this Dr Magnanti floats like a lily on a bog, but she makes a good show of having turned the work into an art form, first with a book deal, then with a TV series, now with an all-media fame that is already looking highly exploitable. Just think of the merchandizing possibilities. Belle de Jour Informatic foam bath crystals. Belle de Jour Forensic Science foot-massage cream. The only question is whether all those other females with doctorates in informatics are going to feel inadequate if they have never been courtesans. Not for the first time in history, a courtesan has made honest women look a bit pedestrian.

Proving that sex-work, even at its most elevated, has the same relation to work as bad breath has to breath, our Belle de Jour is in a modern tradition of the higher hooking that reached its first peak in nineteenth-century Paris, where fashionable society was briefly dazzled by the short career of Marie Duplessis, who presaged Dr Magnanti in every aspect except the blog.

The blog, and an early death. Marie Duplessis, born merely Rose Plessis, lived only twenty-three years, but in that brief span she emerged out of nowhere to become one of the most socially accomplished women of her day. She enslaved men, and they gave her things in return for her favours. When she transferred her favours to other men, the original men still gave her things. One of the men was the writer Alexandre Dumas the younger, who was her lover for a year. When she transferred her affections upwards beyond mere writers, he took no revenge but wrote the book that made her immortal, *The Lady of the Camellias*. Eventually Verdi turned the book into one of his greatest operas, *Traviata*, and Garbo starred in *Camille*, the most beautiful of her movies after *Ninotchka*.

The richness of Marie Duplessis's life after death should not distract, however, from the richness of her life while she lived. She reached a high state of mental cultivation and could converse delightfully on many subjects, although it is not certain whether informatics was among them. She loved music and musicians loved her. One of them was Liszt, who wanted to move in with her.

The brilliance of her mind, along with her startling sexual attraction, made her salons the focus for all the fashionable men of her time. These eventually included the nobility, and when she succumbed to tuberculosis the French count she had married was in attendance, while, even more remarkably, the Swedish count that she hadn't was there too. She died broke but hundreds of men came to her funeral. She was a poetic young lady and they were all proud that she had spent their money, but there can be no romantic view of how she had earned it.

The myth of the happy hooker dies hard, mainly because it isn't always a myth. Another nineteenth-century courtesan, Lola Montez, slept her way so close to the very top that Ludwig I of Bavaria was shaken on his throne. Liszt was on her list, too. She had a ball all the way. It isn't easy to think of a woman like that slogging away at an honest job. But that's where the catch comes in: just at that point where men get sentimental on a woman's behalf. When Dr Magnanti tells us that she could never have financed her degree course unless she had yielded to the hard fact that what she would have earned from a boring week behind the cake-stall was comfortably exceeded by what she could earn in half an hour on her back, she isn't saying that she found a better kind of work. She's saying that she found something better *than* work. And it might even feel like that, but it still leaves the idea of work sounding like something that only stupid people believe in.

As long as men are romantic, there will be women realistic enough to cash in. Or anyway they fancy themselves as realists, although I notice that most of them, however they proclaim the legitimacy of their trade, get out early if they can. But let's forget about the women's realism for the moment, and concentrate on the men's romanticism, which is surely the nub of the matter. Far from looking for a relationship uncomplicated by feeling, a romantic man, when he tries to solve his problems with his wallet, is looking for a feeling uncomplicated by a relationship. As far as I know I've never met a sex-worker, but to the extent that I can intuit what goes on, she offers the illusion of a contact that consists of nothing but emotion. It can't be had in real life, so men pay up to enter the dream world where they can find it.

After Dr Magnanti got in early and gave her story to the broadsheet, the tabloid that had tracked her down was left stuck with the revelations of some of her acquaintances. My favourite among these – you understand I read this only for purposes of research – was an ex-boyfriend who still pines for the lyricism of what they had together. Apparently they plighted their troth with two rings, buried the rings in the beach, walked along the beach hand in hand, leaned back against haystacks and gazed up at the stars. He is still convinced that her love for him was true. And so it might have been, but it was also perfectly suited to his dreams. With Dr Magnanti we are dealing with a master, or let it be a mistress, of public relations.

One of her female acquaintances fears for Dr Magnanti's future. 'I wonder, though,' wonders the female acquaintance, 'if she is ready for the inevitable media blitz.' I would be surprised if she is not ready for it like Robbie Williams. She has been getting ready for it all her life. My own guess is that she will marry a future crowned head of Europe, but if she settles for mere showbusiness she will probably be the first person to win *Celebrity Come Dancing* and *The X Factor* in the same year. There can be no doubt that she dances like Ginger Rogers and sings like Anna Netrebko.

There is nothing this woman can't do, and you can tell by the history of her blogging. She has been blogging since blogging was invented. Fresh out of school, she blogged about restaurants. After that, by a sequence of events that will no doubt be explained to us in due course, she blogged about autopsies. She wrote short stories for her blog. She was Ernest Hemingway. She knows everything. She even knows what informatics is. I looked it up, and basically it means information theory. Someone interested in that was never going to keep a secret. She was only ever going to decide when she would sell it.

Postscript

There is no getting out of it: pulsing beneath the veneer of my moralistic sermon is the eternal male response to the allure of the adventuress. Given space, no commentator should ever dodge the question of why Ludwig I, with all the beauties of Bavaria to choose from – their mug-shot portraits sill decorate the Nymphenburg Palace – risked his throne for Lola. Surely it must have been the soft light of the half world, the flattering shadows that it casts not only on the adored one, but on the helpless males who adore. It makes them feel like pirates, even when they are already kings. Verdi, whose love affair with Giuseppina Strepponi was as powerful as it was decent – doubly decent because it remained a love affair even after he married her – had nothing frivolous in him on the subject of passion. But *Traviata* proves that there was nothing frivolous either about the passions that the doomed young courtesan aroused.

As a type, the Lady of the Camellias is most at home in Paris, which is probably why she wreaks her greatest devastation in London, where theoretically she is not at home in the least. My mention of Lady Bienvenida Buck was, as the academics say, no accident. Except for a sufficiency of funds, Bienvenida had everything, including the foreign extraction. She had a particularly *fatale* appeal to men placed high in the Defence department and the armed services. She was like Beachcomber's beautiful spy Dingi Poos: she had only to stand there in a peignoir and generals would hand her the plans. Before I get carried away by romanticism, however, it would be honest to record that the brilliant career of Britain's very own Belle de Jour was happening at a time when the traffic in East European slave girls in London became too blatant for the police to ignore. The traffic was, and alas remains, entirely horrible, and it seems a fair inference that all organized prostitution is horrible enough. But for the women out on their own, running their own lives and thriving on the adventure, sympathy sounds patronizing. Gladstone took prostitutes home with him in order to save them. He was probably sincere, and they probably needed saving. But what about the woman who doesn't need saving, and who has the gift of convincing you, the customer, that you are the one leading a restricted life? And what is to be done about her argument that she would earn so much less in an ordinary job that she would never be able to complete her degree in particle physics? It's yet another of liberal democracy's dilemmas. East of the Elbe, in the good old days of the Warsaw Pact, women like that all worked for the security services, and their contribution to society was beyond cavil.

SPIRIT OF THE GAME

Dates of show: 27 and 29 November 2009

I haven't followed round-ball football seriously since the 'professional foul' first got its name back in the 1980s. What was the point of trying to stay interested in a sport where breaking the rules was a recognized tactic? But round-ball football, let's call it soccer, is so big that it will come and get you even when you try to ignore it. I lost count of the number of news programmes and annual sports round-ups and documentaries about Argentina when I had to watch the ball make contact with Maradona's hand before it continued its journey, went into the goal, and put England out of the 1986 World Cup. Even today, Maradona will turn up on a cooking programme to show you the hand that handled the ball. He calls it the hand of God.

Well, I suppose he wouldn't call it the hand that brought a whole sport into disrepute. So Maradona stirs the gazpacho with a wooden spoon held by the hand of God while the producer cues the footage that once again shows the tarnished angel cheating. Any footballer's hand can get hit by the ball accidentally, of course, but in a real sport, if the result was unfairly advantageous to his side, he would tell the referee. Not in soccer. Because soccer is too important?

No, because soccer is a pain in the neck. Now a whole new cycle of football cheating footage has begun with Thierry Henry's success in handling the ball in such a manner that Ireland went out while France went up, or went somewhere. I couldn't care less, except that I know I'm going to have to see that footage again a hundred times, especially when I'm trying not to. I'll be watching an historical programme about Louis XIV and there it will be.

Everyone in the world saw Thierry Henry handle the ball except the referee. The obvious question is why, if we can see such a thing happening live on television, the referee can't see it shortly after-wards, even if he couldn't see it at the time? In American football, America being America, a tribunal the size of the Senate on a busy day examines the replay and sends down its ruling to the referee. Employing this method, the American football world avoids the anomaly by which the soccer world puts the referee in the position of not being able to visit Ireland for the rest of his life.

America, of course, as any soccer fan will tell you, pays the penalty of having a pointy-ball football code ludicrous beyond belief. But I actually prefer watching American football when I can. The level of aggression is nuclear but everyone can see what's going on. There is a lot of palaver, and an hour of play, what with all the interruptions, lasts longer than *Lohengrin*, but at least the rules rule. That's probably the main reason why there is so little violence off the field, among the fans. All the violence is on the field, and none of the fans feels robbed by a bad ruling, because there won't be one. Hence the fans do not attack each other, or lay waste the surrounding district.

Soccer fans frequently feel robbed and react accordingly, but almost always they are attacking the wrong people. Their real enemies are the people who wrote the rules, long ago. The off-side rule, for example, was written by a Druid that the other Druids couldn't understand. After the first grand final at Stonehenge stadium, the referee was evenly distributed around the pitch. The philosopher Wittgenstein once said that a game consists of the rules by which it is played. Though rumours persist that he played inside left for Cambridge United under a pseudonym, Wittgenstein in fact knew next to nothing about football; it would have presented him with a game that consists of rules impossible to interpret. But perhaps he knew that and was talking about something else. Lawn bowls. Chinese chequers. Mud wrestling.

Football fans know all about the bad rules but they love the game anyway. It could be that I just don't love any variety of football enough to put up with the drawbacks. I was the worst scrum half that the Sydney Technical High School third grade rugby union side ever had and you don't get over that much early evidence that you lack talent. I was similarly untalented in athletics, and later on, though I strove to get interested, I lost interest quickly when drugs turned out to be involved.

They began in the East. It was East Germany that started turning some of its women sprinters into men. They even did it to the swimmers. Not long before the Sydney Olympics I hosted a black-tie fundraiser for the Australian Olympic team and I met some of my Aussie women swimming heroes, who spoiled my night by telling me that they had never got over the revelation that the best years of their lives had been wasted competing against robots built in East German laboratories.

Eventually the drugs spread West and ruined the Olympics completely. When the beautiful American sprinter Marion Jones got busted I strove to tell myself I had no reason to care, because I could never run very fast anyway, so why should it bother me that those who could were faced with the choice of cheating or coming second? But I could never drive a car either and yet I loved Formula One motor racing. I even went on loving it right through the period of Team Orders, when the team decided which of their two drivers was going to finish first, or at any rate ahead of their other driver. I strove to stay fascinated even as it became clearer all the time that technical advances were making the sport boring, because the cars couldn't get past each other. A whole Grand Prix season would be one procession after another like a funeral on fast-forward, but you would still find me talking learnedly about how it was really all right for Senna to punt Prost off the road because it was within the rules.

With so much money at stake, everybody bent the rules to the limit but at least nobody cheated. A sport for gentlemen, right? When Lewis Hamilton got the world championship it was a bigger thing for me than Barack Obama getting the presidency. Jensen Button was the next champion and I liked that too. But then Nelson Piquet Jr. of the Renault team said that his team leader had instructed him to crash so that the team's other driver, Fernando Alonso, could win a race. The team leader, Flavio Briatore, was unfairly endowed with wealth, silver hair, Naomi Campbell and Heidi Klum, but I had always tried to like him. After that, I liked him less, and I liked the sport less too. Now I can sometimes miss watching a whole race without much caring. I can never do that with the snooker. I watch every frame.

Snooker is still a game that consists of the rules by which it is played. I knew the producer who picked snooker out as the ideal game for television when BBC2 went to air in colour. His name was

Phil Lewis and he asked himself the question: 'What's the game that *needs* colour?' I was clamped to the screen from the first season. I just loved the way the players respected the rules, and they still do. Despite every attempt by the producers to camp up the tournament with interviews, documentaries, chirpy introductions and dire humour, the game is still essentially two young men in black tie who would rather die than cheat. The black tie, since those first days, has been augmented by enough logos on the waistcoat to rival Shinjuku by night, but the attitude is the same. You won't catch Ronnie O'Sullivan apologizing for being ambidextrous, but he does apologize if he scores a fluke. They all do. And any of them, if he accidentally brushes the wrong ball with his sleeve, will instantly yield the table to his opponent, even if neither his opponent nor the referee saw it happen. They want to win fair and square.

Golfers want that too. Privileged by retirement, I can watch every big match through all four days and I keep watching even if nothing is happening except Tiger Woods looking for a lost ball. He did that several times before missing the cut in the last British Open, the one that Tom Watson almost won even though he is practically my age. What a performance, and especially when he over-hit his approach shot to the last green and must have known straight away that he had blown it. If ever there was a time to break a club over his caddy's head, that was it. But he just pursed his lips.

I thought tennis might be lost to me in the age of McEnroe, because it was quite clear that the All England Club were incapable of dealing with his tantrums, and could even convince themselves that he was within the spirit of the game. But Borg was there to reassure me that the spirit of the game was still safe. I admired McEnroe's brilliance both on and off the court but Borg was my guy. Until Sampras was. And now it's Federer. One well-behaved champion after another. Maybe we've just been lucky, and a top-ten tennis player will soon turn up who tries to poison his opponent. And maybe some aspiring snooker champion will invent the radio-controlled cue-ball. But until then, I've still got two places to hide from Thierry Henry. Wait a second. I can see a TV screen in the production booth. Aagh.

Postscript

The following year, Thierry Henry's unpunished turpitude was richly avenged when France lost in the first round of the World Cup. How we laughed, we who were not French. The England side (how we laughed, we who were not English) was put out of the Cup by Germany, with one of the German goals patently failing to cross the goal line. It was patent to everyone except the referee. Billions of people all over the world saw the ball come bouncing out in action replay, but this unarguable information was not made available to the referee even in written form. Similar lapses in refereeing had done for the chances of Australia, in my view the finest team in the competition. Clearly the day was rapidly approaching when the referee of an important international match would be given the opportunity to see what everyone else saw, but that day had not yet quite arrived. Having already been wondering why I had gone on listening to a hundred thousand vuvuzelas all droning the same note, I resolved to stop watching championship football from then on, and so far I have not felt the loss.

I would hate to stop watching snooker, though. The press, for reasons hard to fathom, would like everyone to stop watching snooker, perhaps because the snooker stars, on the whole, are poised, well behaved and aspirational, with nobody since Alex Higgins even turning up drunk. Snooker scandals, being so few, are highly prized by the tabloids. The supposed scandal of John Higgins, normally a model of comportment, listening to a proposal that he might throw a match was given a lot of coverage. Apart from cubic acres of journalistic hot air, there was not much in it, but Higgins learned the hard way that he shouldn't even have listened. The following year, it turned out that a large contingent of the Pakistan cricket team were in business with the bookies, and in Formula One the Ferrari team flaunted the most glaring case yet of enforcing team orders on their drivers: it was all on the pit-to-car radio, and broadcast to the world. ('Sorry, Felipe.' Sorry about what?) Luckily nobody has yet found a way of corrupting golf. The newspapers, with no angles about golfers cheating at the game to work on, have to confine themselves to the subject of golfers cheating at their private lives. Everyone was agreed that nothing like that would ever happen to Tiger Woods.

IMPACT

Dates of show: 4 and 6 December 2009

In my share of these broadcasts I've placed a lot of emphasis on democracy, and on how it can never be a perfect system, but by the mere fact that no tyrant or oligarchy can ever count on remaining in power unchallenged, democracy can hope to avoid some of the abuses that even less perfect systems are guaranteed to generate.

As somebody once said – I think it was Winston Churchill, but it could have been my uncle Harold – democracy is the worst political system you can imagine, except for all the others. If it was my uncle Harold, it was generous of him to say this, because during the Great Depression he spent a lot of time out of work. Some of the competing political systems sounded quite persuasive in that period, but Uncle Harold didn't like the sound of a lot of people all shouting at once. He himself was a man of few words. When I was very small the longest speech I ever heard from him was, 'Go away.' After he came back from the war he sat down on the back veranda and spent thirty years reading the papers. He only ever got up to go and vote, and if voting hadn't been compulsory in Australia he wouldn't even have done that.

He was the living refutation of the fond idea that democracy should be participatory. The first duty of a government, in his view, was to leave people alone. More than half a century later I feel the same way myself. My last sparks of fiery radicalism have long been quenched. Privately I define democracy as that political system which leaves me free not to care about it. About that, I care passionately.

The first trouble with my view of democracy is that it tends to sound complacent. When the dizzy level of greed which is free to operate in the democratic countries leads to something as ridiculous as a so-called bonus culture in which bankers are rewarded for gambling with your money, and then the banks are bailed out with more of your money so that they can re-establish the very same bonus culture while they gamble with your money all over again, it does sound complacent to say: yes, it looks bad, but it would be even worse if there were no democratically elected government to intervene. The government did intervene, and look what happened.

But think what might have happened if it hadn't intervened at all. Last week, Dubai went bust, largely because it was one vast playground for the dimwit rich that had no other asset except the virtual slave labour of the workers who built it. Will there be any government agency in Dubai to get those workers home to the countries they left in the doomed hope that Dubai would make them less poor? Probably not. A democracy would feel obliged to at least make noises about doing something to ease the suffering, and almost certainly it would never have allowed a situation in the first place by which slaves in all but name would have toiled all day with fifteen minutes for lunch. There would have been questions in parliament, and the lunch break would have been extended to thirty minutes.

At almost the same moment in history as Dubai was going broke, the American film star Nicholas Cage went broke too. He went broke because he had bought too many castles, too many yachts, too many cars, too many everything. He was a one-man Dubai, but that was the point: he was just one man. In a liberal democracy he was free to go mad with his cheque book but he couldn't turn himself into a whole city and hire builders to slave all day trying to earn their passports back. Even in the supposedly unchecked Darwinian struggle of American capitalism, there are mechanisms in place, as the modern saying goes, to ensure that the collapse of Nicholas Cage injures only those people who were left holding his IOUs. There won't be a shanty town of indentured labourers who worked for nearly nothing and now have nothing at all. Nobody will be left desperate by the career of Nicholas Cage except those who have been unfortunate enough to see his movies, in all of which he pops his eyes with his wet mouth half open, looking exactly like a man who wants to buy Windsor Castle and employ the tenants as ground staff.

A Western liberal democracy has institutions that limit damage. But just by saying that, I edge into a second stage of complacency that I have to watch out for, and we all have to watch out for. They have to be the right institutions. Many of them grow automatically, by the operation of the free market, but some of the most vital of them have to be imposed. In fact that's what a democratic government does: it intervenes in the free market for the benefit of all. The intervention, however, sometimes defeats its object. As the apocryphal Hollywood producer once said, 'There'll be a meeting Monday to delete the improvements.' There is a new, or revised, institution on the way which already has many good people in our universities worried about how it might turn out.

The present system of allocating university funds to support research has been known, for the last twenty years, as the RAE, standing for Research Assessment Exercises: more than one exercise because there have been several systems, all of which have been troublesome enough, because they have all laid great stress on the number of publications per member of staff, which led to the possibility that staff members might be thought of as not performing if they weren't publishing.

If that system had been operating in the time of the Cambridge mathematician Alan Turing, for example, he might have been thought of as a drag on the funding of his department because he had produced only one paper. His work eventually led to the code-breaking triumph at Bletchley Park and the development of the computer, but not even he knew that at the time, and if he had had to spend much time explaining to the assessment board what he was on about he might never have got his work done.

The cumbersome system is now to be streamlined but there is a question of whether the improvements might not lead to paralysis, especially in the humanities. The new system will be called the REF, standing for Research Excellence Framework. Excellence is always a bad word in such a context because it presupposes the result at which it aims, but there are stronger reasons than that for being suspicious. Under the new system, a quarter of the rating scores which will affect the funding will be awarded for 'impact', meaning a verifiable effect of the research in the outside world. Traditionally the humanities have defined themselves as those learned activities which are pursued for their own sake, but pursing them for impact is plainly something else.

As Stefan Collini outlines in a recent issue of the *Times Literary Supplement*, impact could be achieved when you write a scholarly work about a secondary Scottish poet and someone decides to make a TV programme about him. But you score for impact only if you yourself, or a representative of your department, makes the contact with the television producer. It isn't enough to wait for the outside world to find you. You have to market your work in what the new guidelines (another bad word) call the wider economy and society (five more bad words).

The philosopher Wittgenstein often turns up in these broadcasts because when I was an undergraduate at Cambridge he was my ideal example of what a thinker should be. When he was teaching at Cambridge he made zero impact in this new sense. Even under the outgoing Research Assessment system he would have been a liability to his department, because he published only one philosophical book in his lifetime. The book was the *Tractatus Logico-Philosophicus* and it had a huge influence in the long run, but it might not have scored many funding points after he told the assessment board they were a bunch of dummies. He wasn't just incapable of diplomacy, he disapproved of it.

If he were teaching now under the incoming Research Excellence system he would be a disaster for his department. You couldn't imagine him making contact with a television producer and saying, 'Look, I've got this terrific idea for a programme about a man obsessed with language and it's perfect for Daniel Day-Lewis.' He would have been hopeless. But that was just what I liked about him. It was what I liked about all the dons, even the crazy ones. There was one guy who was given a fellowship in about 1923 and spent the rest of his life walking around town with a bundle of newspapers under his arm. But that was the price a great university was willing to pay for extending to its scholars the freedom to pursue an interest for its own sake.

In the years I spent pretending to study for a Ph.D., I would sit in the Copper Kettle cafe opposite King's College and read Wittgenstein's *Philosophical Investigations.* Occasionally I would look up to make a philosophical investigation of a passing undergraduette. Then I looked down again to puzzle at another brilliantly compressed paragraph. Wittgenstein was having his impact, and it was an impact that couldn't be measured. A university is, or should be, a place where you can't yet tell what will be useful to the outside world, because it deals with the inside world, the most inside of all worlds, the mind.

For all I know, that was what my uncle Harold was doing. He had done his time in the outside world, fighting for democracy against Japanese soldiers on the Kokoda trail, and now he was gazing within.

Postscript

At the family house in Cambridge I lead the life of a civilian on an army base. I live surrounded by so many academics that if I spent too much time listening I would be stifled with feelings of inadequacy and unable to write a line. Sometimes, though, it pays to tune in. I was alerted to the Impact boondoggle by a raft-load of dedicated young scholars who had taken one look at the new rules and realized that not only the subjects would be under threat, but that the whole of the humanities would inevitably suffer if these mad plans were carried out. Whichever committee decided that the world of the humanities didn't need to know about, say, the early trans-Baltic Normans would soon decide that it didn't need to know about the ancient Greeks either.

I like to think that I would quite soon have been alerted to the topic on my own account, if only by the manic intensity with which its proponents abused the English language. For the academy, anyone talking managerial jargon should count as an invader. Wherever there is an invasion, however, there will be collaborators, and one of the marks of the new barbarism in academic life has always been the number of begowned figures who magically pop up and start cooperating. In Cambridge, at a time when almost every ancient college was sprouting a new building or two, invariably the ugliest new buildings were approved by committees of dons. With their appreciation of the most pretentious and brutalist strains in modern architecture, the dons were merely laying the foundations for their subsequent accommodation to managerial double-talk. And as with any other cast of experts, they were deadlier in committee than when alone. Nigel Balchin, in his fine novel *The Small Back Room*, wrote a pioneering study of how supervisory committees are bad at attaining a desirable goal. E. V. Jones, in his essential memoir *Most Secret War*, put the study on what should have been a permanent basis when he demonstrated that a scientific committee could defeat its own ends simply by being too big, or by having even one self-serving member.

(According to Jones, any committee containing Sir Robert Watson-Watt, nominal inventor of radar, would have been useless even if radar had been its subject.) It's a condition of academic freedom that the universities should organize their own affairs, but the freedom can be fatal when exercised in furtherance of a governmental *diktat* conceived in the name of efficiency, equality, diversity or any other measure except high standards of knowledge.

That being said, several fans of Nicholas Cage told me I had been unfair to him. They were probably right. I had been made angry by how, in *Leaving Las Vegas*, he kept getting between me and Elisabeth Shue. Male film stars obsess me because they are crucial to my fantasy projects. One of those is a script about Wittgenstein, but in my nightmares the studio wants Brad Pitt for the lead. What a wonderful subject, though. It would be ideal for Daniel Day-Lewis, but Rupert Everett might be even better. You will judge correctly that I am whistling to keep my spirits up. It never occurred to me that the universities, in my time, would become the entry portals for the space invaders. Like most goof-offs I was counting on the continued stability of the institutions I goofed off from.

HERMIE'S GHOST

Dates of show: 11 and 13 December 2009

About forty years ago now, the world used to hear a lot from a futurologist called Herman Kahn. Of ample girth and unquenchable volubility, Herman Kahn, who died in 1983, was always making confident pronouncements about what would happen in the future. So and so, he would say, would happen ten, twenny, twennyfive years from now. It wouldn't happen tomorrow, so that you could check up on it straight away, but it would happen ten, twenny, twennyfive years from now. Some of us realized that he had invented a new unit of time, and we gave it a name. As an echo of the Fermi, which is a measure for the size of an electron, we called his new unit of time the Hermie.

The merit of the Hermie, as a unit of measurement, was that, while being vague, it sounded impressive. The prediction itself might or might not have been right. Herman Kahn predicted that within one Hermie everyone in the West would fly his own helicopter and have access to free-fall sex. That didn't happen within one Hermie, but it still might happen in the next Hermie. All we can be sure of is that Herman Kahn's language exemplified an impressive way of talking about the future, a way of sounding impressive that sounded less impressive only when you realized that sounding impressive was its main motive. Big things would happen. It was big talk. And it paid the penalty of all big talk. As you got used to it, you got tired of it.

Over the last ten years we have heard a lot about how civilization would be in trouble if it didn't soon do something drastic about global warming. But this impressive message tended to sound less impressive as time went on. It wasn't just that the globe uncooperatively declined to get warmer during the last ten years. It was that the language of alarm wore out its welcome as it became ever more assertive about what had not yet happened.

The world, when it resumed warming again – this brief, unarguably still hot period when it had somehow refused to grow any hotter was soon explained, although it seemed strange that it had not been predicted – the once-again warming world would heat up by so many degrees, or so many more degrees than that, and within ten, twenny, twennyfive years – within a single Hermie – there would be the corpses of fried polar bears floating past your penthouse window.

According to the media, scientists were agreed, the science was settled, science *said*, that all this would happen. The media promoted this settled science, and the politicians went along with the media. The whole deal had the United Nations seal of approval. The coming catastrophe that had to be averted wasn't exactly like knowing when the asteroid would arrive so you could send Bruce Willis, but unless we did *something*, irreversible damage, if not certain doom, was only a Hermie or two away.

Today, after recent events at the University of East Anglia's Climate Research Unit, that supposedly settled science is still the story, but the story is in question. The top guy at the UN's Intergovernmental Panel for Climate Change has called for an investigation into at least part of the science that was supposed to have been settled. Suddenly there are voices to pronounce that the reputation of science will lie in ruins for the next fifty years. For two Hermies at least, nobody will trust a single thing that a scientist says.

Well, even to a non-scientist like myself, that last prediction sounds suspiciously like the others. My own view is that true science, the spirit of critical enquiry that unites all scientists, or is supposed to, is reasserting itself after being out-shouted by at least half a Hermie of uninterrupted public relations. But I hasten to admit that my view is not only not the view of a scientist, it is the view of somebody who can still remember the first day he was exposed to calculus and realized that he had no more chance of understanding it than of rising into the air like a helicopter carrying its pilot in search of free-fall sex.

As I said in one of these broadcasts earlier in the season, before the events at the Climate Research Unit, my only position on the matter of man-made global warming was that from my own layman's background reading I thought the reported scientific unanimity that global warming is man-made, and likely to be catastrophic, was always a more active area of scientific debate than you would have guessed from the way the media told the story.

Just saying that much was enough to get me condemned by one of the broadsheet environmentalist gurus. He said I was an old man resistant to the facts because I didn't care what happened to the world after I was gone. As I bounced my granddaughter on my knee, rather hoping that in the course of the next Hermie she would not be obliged to star in a remake of *Waterworld* as the sea rose thirty feet above her house, I bit back a rude word. But the guru still had a point when he said that my scepticism about the settled science was a wilful defiance of established fact. Unfortunately the fact had been established largely by the media, who had been telling only one story. If you said the story might have two sides, that sounded like scepticism.

People in my position had to get used to being called sceptics, as if scepticism were a bad thing. We even have had to get used to being called denialists, although clearly it was an unscrupulous word. We were also called, are still called, flat-earthers by people like Gordon Brown and Ed Miliband, but that kind of abuse is comparatively easy to take, because everybody knows that neither man would be capable of proving mathematically that the earth is not a cube.

So what happened at the Climate Research Unit? Well, basically nothing new. A bunch of e-mails got hacked, or perhaps leaked. Some of the phrases that supposedly reveal skulduggery reveal a lot less when you put them in the context of locker-room enthusiasm. In the correspondence columns of the scientific websites – where the level of discussion has consistently been miles above anything the mainstream media has provided for the last decade – there are already wise voices to warn that the sceptics should not make the same mistake as the believers by treating any slip they can find in the arguments of their opponents as evidence of the biggest fraud since Bernie Madoff made off with the money.

That would be Hermie talk, and self-defeating, because the more absolutist man-made global warming case has always looked sufficiently vulnerable just by the way it has been reluctant to listen to opposing voices no matter how well qualified. There has never been any point, and there is no point now, in calling the alarmists a bunch of devious conspirators against the truth. All you ever had to do was notice how their more strident representatives didn't want to hear any other opinions, even when the opinions came from within their own ranks.

Far from there having been unanimity among scientists on the subject of catastrophic man-made global warming, there has scarcely been unanimity among climate scientists. It only takes one dissenting voice to punch a hole in the idea of unanimity, if that voice has a chance of being right. There was a time when almost every scientist except Einstein thought that Newton had buttoned up the subject of celestial mechanics. And this time, on the subject of global warming, there was always, right from the beginning, a number of climate scientists who didn't endorse the alarmist picture.

You could say that the number was small, and a few of them were vengeful because they had been side-lined for not being sufficiently doom-laden in their claims. But a few of them were older men who just wouldn't go along with the prevailing emphasis. One of these few was Professor Lindzen of MIT. I never could convince myself that the Professor of Meteorology at the Massachusetts Institute of Technology knew less about the earth's climate than I did, so I started to watch him. Hopeless on the media, Lindzen is the sort of pundit with a four-figure IQ who can somehow never figure out that you are supposed to talk *into* the microphone. His fellow anti-alarmist Professor Fred Singer was even worse. Singer not only formed a thought too slowly for radio, he was too slow for smoke signals.

But gradually, as I watched the side roads, it seemed to me that these few dissenting scientists with zero PR skills increased in number. The number of scientists who endorsed the orthodox view increased also, but the number of those who didn't went up instead of down. I couldn't do the calculus, but I could count heads. There were scores of eminent scientists who signed the 2007 open letter to the Secretary-General of the United Nations, and then later on there were hundreds quoted in the US Senate minority reports. It could be said that few of them had expertise in climate science, but that argument looked less decisive when you considered that climate science itself was exactly what they were bringing into question.

So science was not speaking with one voice on the matter. It only seemed to be, because the media, on the whole, was giving no other story. Then this Climate Research Unit thing happened, and it was the end of the monologue. The dialogue has begun again. The scientists are arguing on the matter, which is the proper thing for science to do, because in science the science is never settled. Some say that the argument about how all this happened will go on for another two Hermies at least. We can hear, from deep underground, the contented purr of Herman Kahn. It's all turning out exactly as he predicted.

Postscript

This one I had to fight for, and I give Mark Damazer credit that he let me win. As I have said, the BBC, mistakenly in my view, had copied other major outlets of the worldwide mainstream media – the *New York Times* was a powerful example – in taking up a position on Catastrophic Anthropogenic Global Warming which condemned anyone who expressed doubts about it to the status of an eccentric. Theoretically the Web is proof against the print media's urge to conform, but in practice Wikipedia sets the tone – as well as being the port of entry for every print journalist in search of quick background – and Wikipedia was resolutely pro-catastrophe throughout this period, all the way until October 2010, when it finally summoned up the resolve to dismiss the single zealot who had been laundering the stories as they came in. But there was never any excuse for the BBC – under no real commercial pressure except from those administrators of its pension fund who liked the idea of alternative energy futures – to embrace the doom scenario just because everybody else had. Yet a rigid orthodoxy was maintained by the Corporation even as the term Global Warming modulated into the term Climate Change, thus to gloss over the awkward fact that the globe had not warmed significantly in fifteen years. This embarrassing datum was actually admitted by the UEA-CRU's leading light Professor Phil Jones in his temporary panic after the e-mails scandal broke, but he, like his colleagues, soon discovered that all they had to do was sit tight, because it would be in the interests of their university, if it investigated the matter, to make sure they were absolved. It caused me no pleasure to see that happen: as the holder of an Honorary Doctorate from the UEA, I was in the position of having been shown respect by an institution which now seemed intent on losing all the respect it could.

Luckily the UEA's excellent record as a patron of modern writing will always ensure that it stays high in the esteem of any modern writer.

In the following year the UEA-CRU crew were duly found to have indulged in nothing much more reprehensible than schoolboy pranks. A foretaste of that absurd clemency can be found in my script, at the point where, yielding to heavy pressure, I said that there was not much in their unprepossessing behaviour beyond the standard manoeuvrings of ordinary group dynamics. This was humbug on my part and I knew it was at the time, but I was ready to soft-pedal a particular point in order to get my general message on the air. In fact, the CRU team had constructed a neo-Swiftian machine for rewriting the past in order to lend weight to their fantasies about the future, and had taken steps to make certain, by managing the 'peer review' in which they claimed to set such store, that it would not be challenged in the learned journals. They had behaved, that is, almost exactly as the Wegman committee of 2006 had said they had already behaved, and would go on behaving unless they submitted their conjectures to proper statistical discipline. Not to do so, after Wegman caught them out, was their fatal mistake. The same applied to Michael Mann's outfit at Penn State, and to the rest of the surprisingly small cluster of ad-hoc research centres (the one in New Zealand was the first to fold) which had looked like guaranteeing their members a secure career in predicting planetary disaster until the moment when the grown-up scientists arrived at the door of the nursery to find out why the kids inside were making such a row.

Easily surviving one tap on the wrist after another, they all got away with it in the narrow sense, but in the wider sense they were finished, and the thing began to come apart. At the time of writing it is still coming apart. The disintegration happens very gradually because the mainstream media outlets are even slower than governments to let go of the standard story. When the Obama administration, late in 2010, appointed a chief climate adviser – as a career alarmist, he had once been an advocate of Global Cooling – who announced that the proper name for Climate Change was Climate Disruption, the story was over as far as governments were concerned, even if the useless wind farms continued to be erected. The concept of Global Warming had just about survived the declension to Climate Change, but the further declension to Climate Disruption could mean anything. It was widely realized, although rarely mentioned, that something that could mean anything meant nothing. The prospect of coordinated global action by developed nations was as dead as the Kyoto protocol. But in the media the story continued, because too many of the major outlets had no way of switching it off: they had handed the responsibility for geophysical prediction to science correspondents who had correctly assessed that tales of oncoming disaster would play best to the gallery, and unless the science correspondents got fired, the outlets they worked for would continue to propagate a world vision indistinguishable from that of Steven Seagal. How the media got themselves into such a mess has by now become the true subject, thereby falling, if I may say so, within my only area of expertise, which is the language of communication, and what happens when it is duped into communicating poppycock. As my illustrious compatriot the late Murray Sayle used to say, what matters most isn't the story: it's the story of the story.

OPTION SWAMP

Dates of show: 18 and 21 December 2009

I have been registered for Value Added Tax since 1973. Great stories are often introduced by a sentence similarly factual, bald, terse. Gaul is divided into three parts. In the beginning, God created the heavens and the earth. I have been registered for VAT since 1973.

This story I have to tell is not a great story, but the first sentence is pertinent. Annually, during the whole of this period of being registered for VAT, I have had dealings with a certain broadcasting organization which must remain nameless, except to say that it girdles the earth and is much loved by peoples of many nations, not just this one. It is also much loved by me. Proud to be a contributor, I admire every part of this organization, including the accounts department. Or at least I admired the accounts department until about seven years ago, when there was a change in its behaviour. And even then it might be only one small part of the accounts department which bothers me. That small part might even be a single machine, or a small part of a machine.

In which possibility lies my theme. Every year, at tax time, the accounts department of this beloved organization gets in touch with my accounts department, namely my wife, and pronounces itself ready to send the documents required for my accounts department to fulfil the demands of the revenue service. But before it sends the documents, it sends a requirement of its own. It requires a copy of my VAT registration certificate. When told that it has already been supplied with a copy of my VAT registration certificate, indeed has been supplied with a copy of my VAT registration certificate every year for seven years, it replies by saying that it requires a copy of my VAT registration certificate.

The reason I guess that it must be a machine doing this is that no human being could be so mechanical. Beyond annoying, however, and getting into the realm of the truly disturbing, is that there seems no way to communicate with a human being in order to point out that the machine needs to be fixed. This year my accounts department had to go through the same time-wasting farce all over again and once again I found my accounts department, normally quite cool under pressure, leaning its forehead against a wall and beating the wall slowly with its fist.

To have any hope of getting the machine fixed, you have to be able to make contact with the human being behind it. But maybe there isn't one there. It's been a couple of decades now since one of America's most famous magazines, let's call it *Famous American Magazine*, automated its subscription service. Such was the level of efficiency attained that every subscriber's weekly issue of *Famous American Magazine* arrived a day early, anywhere in the world. But one subscriber, living at number 312 Somewhere or Other Street, Something, New Jersey – the name of the street or district doesn't matter, but the number does – started receiving 312 copies of the magazine every week. Each copy was wrapped separately. His house was already half submerged in a drift of magazines before he managed to get in touch by phone with the head office of *Famous American Magazine*, after which weeks went by while they got in touch with whoever had designed the new system, so the glitch could be fixed. By that time the subscriber's house was invisible and they promised to send him a truck to take the magazines away. The punchline of the story, in which 312 trucks arrive, is probably an embellishment, but all the rest of the story is true.

That story contains the core, or kernel, or festering seed, of another problem: how to get in touch by phone. Getting in touch with any large organization by phone has got harder and harder as the system for getting in touch has purportedly been made more efficient by the provision of options.

Options is nearly always a bad word where the telephone is concerned. On a computer screen, you can see the options and scan them. But on a telephone you have to wait while you listen. If your call is about how you can help in the latest appeal for flood relief, press 1. If your call is about how to secure a flood-relief poster for your front window, press 2. If your call is about advice on how flood relief could relate to your sex life, press 3. And finally, after you have pressed all the buttons as far as 8: if your call is about how we can help you if your house is underwater, press 9.

Finally, if you're lucky, you get to it, but only after a lot of listening. Combine the telephone with the postal service and the result can be a deadly cocktail. At my office, I frequently get a white card through the door telling me that there was an attempt to deliver a parcel but it would not fit through the letterbox. The correct wording of the card should be, 'Would not fit through the letterbox under the large hand-printed sign saying: please leave parcel outside door if too big for letterbox.' But at least they tried, and presumably it was an actual human being trying.

On the card, however, the machines have begun to take over. There is an instruction saying that if I want the parcel to be redelivered, I can phone this number. Making the huge mistake of phoning the number, I run fill tilt into option swamp, a version of terra firma that could be called quicksand if only the word 'quick' were not so obviously wrong. Because the number doesn't get me to the relevant department, it just gets me to the post office. If your enquiry is about difficulties in sending letters overseas now that your local branch has been turned into a kebab house, press 7. If your enquiry is about your desire to meet Kristin Scott Thomas in private circumstances, press 8. And finally, if your enquiry is about the redelivery of a parcel, press 9.

So I press 9 and get an actual human being. His voice is remarkably firm for someone who might have played a post office official in an Ealing comedy in the 1950s. After we have established that the parcel can be delivered only in hours when I am out, he advises me to come and get the parcel myself, at the depot. Only at this point do I realize that his voice has the dulcet undertones of a woman in Bangalore.

I have been the route to the depot before, but nevertheless when I have a spare day I gladly go that route again. Only a few miles away, the depot is just off Mandela Road, a thoroughfare marked by the guardian presence of a Russian T-34 tank painted pink, as a memorial to the politics of the council that built the area. They could have done worse. Most of the houses are fit for human habitation and beside the back door of the depot, which is the entrance to the parcel-redelivery area, there is a pot of geraniums. Here I find out that the parcel is the manuscript of a novel written by an old friend who thinks it might have a better chance of publication if I rewrote it for him and put my name on it as co-author. It's flattering, it's even heart-warming, but it's time-wasting. And time, at my age, is what I'm running out of, so it can be frustrating when the devices meant to save time actually fritter away more of it.

There ought to be a rule, oughtn't there, that if the new machine, along with all the wonderful new things it can do, can't do what humans used to do, then we should be able to opt out of using it. I wonder if a sad realization of that fact might not lie behind last week's announcement – a very quiet, oblique, shuffling announcement – that the great computerized central information system for the entire NHS, so very long in the works, has finally been, well, sort of postponed: not exactly abandoned but deliberately left incomplete. With untold millions spent on it to date, it's now not to be, or not immediately, pushed through to an all-encompassing conclusion. Areas will be left open for local systems to contribute. Those local systems sound as if they might have human beings in them, sitting at desks.

My scientist daughter tells me that there are huge and vital advantages to a centralized system of information about the nation's health, but somebody else might have concluded that the thing just wasn't going to work. I myself am not qualified to have an opinion. How computers work is beyond me. I use my computer to run my website and do my e-mails and I feel pretty high tech as my fingers fly around the keys, but sometimes I hit the wrong key, or squeeze the mouse at the wrong angle, and a whole new universe opens up on the screen that I didn't even know about. Clearly the machine can do practically anything. But it can't really imitate a human being. The man who wrote the original scientific paper that led to the computer, Alan Turing, proposed a machine that you would think human if you fed it lines of dialogue through a screen and it fed all the right lines of dialogue back. How could you tell the difference?

Ah, but there is a difference. The machine doesn't care. The accounts department of a great broadcasting organization doesn't get angry. My accounts department does. If you thought this broadcast was relevant to you, press 1. If you thought this broadcast did not have enough jokes about Tiger Woods, press 2. If you would prefer to revert to a pre-industrial society and so regain the purity of authentic human relations, build a fire and send a smoke signal.

Postscript

I was behind the times. A few days later, a young man who had listened to this broadcast came up to me in the street and told me that when the voice at the other end of the telephone gives you a list of options, your best chance of talking to an actual human being is to choose the option that has something to do with taking your money. Since then I have employed this method with some success. The awkward truth, for any curmudgeon who prides himself on his awareness that things are getting worse, is that they generally get better, but faster and more completely than he can cope with. If your computer catches fire, a telephone call will most likely bring you an engineer, and it will seldom occur to you that he might have arrived more slowly if the telephone call had not gone via Bangalore. The late Bernard Levin used to make part of his large salary by continually retelling the story of the old lady for whom the gas man either never turned up or else turned up with the wrong tools. Nowadays Levin would find it harder to tell the story, and the old lady would find things a lot easier, although probably more expensive. The equation, or rather the non-equation, can be simply stated: though our expectations go up geometrically to match the capacity of available services, our anger increases only arithmetically when they don't work. On the flight to Australia, if my aircraft gets held up for an extra hour at Dubai, I get merely twice as annoyed as Captain Cook did when it took him a week to get out of harbour and start his voyage. Only twice the anger, whereas the voyage is a thousand times as fast.

Rather than say the modern world doesn't work, it would make more sense to say that our expectations of it are absurd. The performance of which mankind is capable has accelerated out of reach of the imagination. On the other hand, the moral framework in which Western man must live remains largely as it was. In *Samson Agonistes*, Milton says that Dalila must be of feeble understanding because she is only a woman. It is a misogynist statement now and it already was when Milton made it, because Shakespeare had already shown that a man could think of women as being the equals of men, and that there was an injustice in thinking otherwise. (At the end of *The Taming of the Shrew*, we know that she will educate him, and that his real life has only just begun.) Today, in this respect at least, we have caught up with Shakespeare and left Milton behind. Nevertheless, for all the progress that has been made, women are still more likely to find themselves exploited by men than vice versa. It's a natural result of women being defined by men, instead of being defined by their jobs. To be defined by his job is a man's privilege, and frequently his salvation. When the story broke about Tiger Woods and his various concubines, the press was full of stories about how he might never win at golf again. But he was a golfer, not a clergyman.

TALKING ABOUT THEIR GENERATION

Dates of show: 25 and 27 December 2009

Another year is coming to an end and once again my granddaughter and her gang of friends and cousins are invading the house, the whole bunch of them with an average age of about four but with the energy of a pod of dolphins and the noise level of a hailstorm on a tin roof. Owing to my highly trained powers of perception I am able to detect that they are a bit bigger than last year. My granddaughter herself will soon be as tall as our Advent rag doll, code-named Tommasina, who once again is in service to provide mystery chocolates. Actually the mystery of the chocolates is the worst-kept secret in the world, because every gang member knows that Tommasina of the many pockets has always got a chocolate on her somewhere. I have already been caught checking her pockets myself, and warned off.

There is a rearrangement this year by which one of the big dinners is at our house but one of the big lunches is at my elder daughter's house or perhaps the other way around. Either way, all the presents must apparently be carried from one house to the other except for the presents that have to be carried in the other direction, and I will be a key factor in the carrying. Everyone knows that my mind went long ago but that I can still lift weights and carry them about. Actually if they knew how my arthritic ankles ached they would probably take that job away from me too, but I don't tell them. The most tragic line in all of Shakespeare is: 'Othello's occupation's gone.'

The Shakespeare of Russia was, or was going to be, Alexander Pushkin, a divinely gifted poet who died young, and mainly from his own folly. But he was one of those foolish young men who have wisdom as a gift to squander, and he said a marvellous thing about children. 'They crowd us from the world.' If he had lived long enough, eventually they would have done that to him. It's why children are here: to replace us. If we're lucky, we've grown old enough to need replacement. I like to think that I've got a few more years left in me yet. I like to think that I've got a few more decades left in me yet, but on a more objective scale of assessment I've already started to remind myself of the knife that had four blades and three handles before somebody lost it.

And yet when the kids are scooting around the house I can't help rejoicing that they can bounce on their heads upside down on the furniture just the way I once did but now can't. I mean I not only rejoice that they can, I rejoice that I can't. What could be worse than eternal youth if it meant denying the next generation room to live? Only a fool or a churl would not be glad that life will continue when he is gone. If it did not do that, what would be the point of having lived at all? Chesterton once said that a madman is someone who has lost everything except his capacity for reason. But there is a more subtle version of a madman, and much more insidious; the man who sincerely believes that the party is over when he leaves it.

Gabriel García Márquez, not one of my favourite writers but a terrific coiner of titles, has a phrase for the twilight of a man's life: the autumn of the patriarch. There should be pride in it, that you behaved no worse. There should be gratitude, that you were allowed to get this far. And above all there should be no bitterness. The opposite, in fact. The future is no less sweet because you won't be there. The children will be there, taking their turn on earth. In consideration of them, we should refrain from pessimism, no matter how well founded that grim feeling might seem.

When I was the age my granddaughter and her friends are now, the modern world was at its worst. Children my age, their age, were being murdered for no reason at all. At the hands of the Nazis, one and a half million children perished horribly. And that figure was just a fraction of all the innocent people who died pointlessly for the fulfilment of idle political dreams, in the period between my birth and adolescence. By the time I was a strong young man, and could read, I knew all about it. If I was ever going to despair for the human race, that would have been the time. But I wasn't only reading about all that had been destroyed, I was reading about all that had been achieved.

It was one of my countrymen, Howard Florey, who did the crucial work in developing penicillin, and penicillin saved my life when I was ill. So right there I had an example of what human creativity could do to overcome the pitiless workings of nature. Modern ideological maniacs could only kill people. But creative spirits, working in freedom, could make life better, and after World War II you could see it happening in the West even as China and all the lands of the Soviet bloc continued to suffer from compulsory madness.

The industrial revolution continued. It had long ago got past the stage when it ruined the lives of factory workers. It had reached the stage when you had to be a die-hard anti-capitalist to believe that modern technology was not improving lives. My mother, cruelly deprived of her husband by the war, would have had every reason to warn me that I should place no trust in the human future. But the human future had already arrived, in the form of labour-saving devices. First the refrigerator came to our house, and then the vacuum cleaner, and then the washing machine. Her everyday life was transformed, along with the lives of all the women in Australia, and throughout the West.

You can still meet theorists today who rail against the alienating effects of industrial society, but it was industrial society that furthered the liberation of women. A lot of bad stuff came along with the abundance: crummy advertising, crass materialism, pollution. But none of that was as bad as the slavery that had been rendered obsolete. Our mothers knew all that, and even as they voted Labor they were careful to warn us against any voices who preached against prosperity. Prosperity didn't guarantee freedom but there could be no widespread freedom without it. Knowledge like that was handed down, from the generation that had once suffered to the next generation which would not.

Today, several generations along into the continued prosperity of the West – so abundant that it holds together even when the banks collapse – that knowledge becomes even more important, because the question arises of how it can be passed on when those in the next generation have no memory of anything else. On television they *see* something else: they see the sufferings of the deprived and oppressed all over the world, and they hear voices saying that all the deprivation and oppression are the fault of the society they themselves live in. The best of the young will always tend to believe this, because compassion is a powerful motive among the good. And anyway, in the harshest days of colonialism it was true, and partly it is still true now. But the larger truth is that the poor countries can make little use of our wealth, even when they are handed it for free, if they have not embraced liberal democracy first.

The importance of liberal democracy has been the only real idea I have felt qualified to pass on in these broadcasts. Qualified because I was born and raised at a time when liberal democracy was under threat, and have lived into a time when it has become obvious that liberal democracy is the first and essential requirement for all the nations of the world. Whether there is a painless way of learning that lesson, without having to learn it from experience, is a real question, to which I don't yet have the answer. I want to write a book on the subject, which is why this will be not only the last broadcast in my share of the series, but my last for some time.

A few years back I published a book about culture and politics in the twentieth century, and this new book will deal with the further subject of how historical lessons can still be learned if the prospect of political tragedy is eliminated. But even more misleading than pessimism is optimism, and it's probably optimistic to think that things will ever get that good. There will always be a salutary disaster somewhere, even if it's not happening to us. At the moment, very slowly and quietly, just such a disaster is happening to Aung San Suu Kyi of Burma. I want to end my stint by paying tribute to her, for her personal bravery, and for what her life under house arrest symbolically represents.

I am very conscious, when I think of her, that I am an armchair warrior and she is a warrior. She was a child when her father was assassinated, but she must have learned a lot from his example. Spending his short life in the quest for Burma's independence, he rebelled against British imperial rule and backed the Japanese version of the same thing, until he realized that it was even worse. After the war, having learned his lesson, he led his country towards democracy, and paid the price for getting too close. And now his daughter is still paying the price, for her own people, and for us. And for all the small people in my house except Tommasina, who will never grow up, never have doubts, never know disappointment, but only because she will never live. She doesn't know what she's missing.

Postscript

And so I bowed out, playing to the gallery even as the curtain fell. Through three years of broadcasting I had made capital out of the mileage I had on the clock, with many a philosophical remark meant to convey my equanimity at the thought of approaching death. But that was just autumn talking, and in truth I had relished the opportunity to sum up: reflecting on experience is, after all, the one thing that an older guy can do more of. I walked away congratulating myself that I had played the fogey role to some effect. Hubris had its due reward. A few days later, over the New Year weekend, my waterworks packed up and I almost bought the farm. After they saved my life in Addenbrooke's Hospital I found myself being a lot less philosophical about death, and equanimity was in short supply. From the radio studio I had been trying to convey that the prosperous Western world, with its democratic institutions, was a decisive improvement on nature; and here, in the collective technical miracle of the clinics and the wards, was the proof. Technology saved my neck, and the machines needed bags of cheap electricity. From my angle at least, those unarguable facts put paid to any idea of 'de-developing' industrial society: a potentially lethal fantasy which I had already poured cold water on several times in my broadcasts.

But I like to think that I would have gone on promoting the same conclusion even if my health had stayed sound: on behalf of the next two generations in my family, I had always been suspicious of doom-sayers who claimed that anyone holding my opinions must be harbouring a callous indifference to the fate of 'our children and grandchildren'. Anyone who wants to make the lives of children in Africa dependent on windmills and solar panels doesn't really care if they live or die, and we only have his word for it that he cares more than we do about the children here at home. Frequently, at the lunch table, I had been watching one of my children attempting to bring the blue plastic-handled spoon of my grandchild under control, and although it was true that the generation after next could be a terrific pest, I couldn't help wishing that, in the life she would lead after her grandfather's departure, the world would continue in its modern tradition of being a more benevolent place than the cave or the savannah.

Really, indifference is the last thing I felt, and even as death's door loomed I cursed all those propagandists who wanted the West to expiate its blame for the world's poverty by making itself as poor as possible. The wish was not only callous, it was historically illiterate. In the twentieth century many millions of lives had been wasted in a hideous practical demonstration that the growth of an economy could not be fully planned by governments. In the glaring light of that fact, the assumption that the shrinkage of an economy – a Great Leap Backward – could be fully planned by governments seemed worse than Quixotic, it seemed wilfully murderous. But that was only one of the issues that had marked the period without being thoroughly discussed, and at least the heavy curtain of silence had now been at least partly lifted. Though most of the mainstream media outlets went on peddling their standard line about imminent destruction, its credibility had been steadily eroded by the obviously limitless flexibility as to just how imminent the imminent was, and a true discussion now seemed possible.

The same was not true for an issue that had always been more important. The savage ill-treatment of women by backward cultures and religions was another salient issue that had barely been debated, least of all by Western feminists, who had surely missed an opportunity while shirking their duty. In the following year, while I lay in hospital, Aung San Suu Kyi sent the world a message that she was in despair. Here was the time to spring from my bed, change into my Superman costume, and fly to her aid. Oh, and on the way back I could descend from the sky in Iran and take care of that little matter about the woman scheduled for death by stoning. I could pick up a couple of the designated stoners and bang their heads together until they saw the point. But I wasn't strong enough to make the leap, and wouldn't have been even if I had been well. Eventually, later in that same year, Aung San Suu Kyi was allowed out, but probably on the understanding that if she got too active in the cause of freedom she would be locked up again. As usual, the men with the guns called the shots.

We have no super powers. If my three seasons of broadcasting were united by a single theme, that was the one: for most of us, our only magic weapon against fate is our power of speech, and all it can do is state the case reasonably. Truth, justice, equal rights, fair play: if radio is the modern pulpit, then a broadcast stating such elementary principles is the modern sermon. Preaching it, one should not scant the duty to be entertaining – even in a mere ten minutes, people will go to sleep in their pews if you aren't – but nor is it wise to underestimate the forces of confusion against which one fights. As Eve found to her cost, the Devil is his own best advocate: that forked tongue of his drips a smooth liquid. Nobody who shapes a speech should ever forget that he is following in the sinuous trail of an expert. The difference between you and the Devil, though, is that one of you can trust the intelligent public to tell good plain water from snake oil – always provided, of course, that you know the difference yourself.

About the intelligent public, there is a book to be written. Where do they come from, these marvellous people? They must have been there before the BBC was created, but undoubtedly the BBC helped to create another generation of them, and has gone on doing so. The interplay between civilized institutions and the people they serve is a complex subject, but there is one conspicuous and unsettling thing that we know about it for certain. Though ideally it should be scarcely visible and operate with a light hand, a strong and confident democratic state is crucial. Without that, to rely on the continuance and efficacy of an intelligent public is the merest sentimentality. For proof, we need only think of those millions of cultivated German citizens in 1933 who suddenly found that their good will was of no effect, and put them in danger.

Conclusion

Three years, a long time in an individual life, is no time at all in the eye of history: scarcely time for a fashion to have its reign. Afterwards, the period of its supremacy is remembered as a mere moment, if it is remembered at all. Then it melts as mysteriously as it took shape. Even when it shakes the world for decades on end, the incontestable belief will fade away without having to be contested, as if the capacity to be forgotten had been part of what made it memorable in the first place. Sometimes the belief will leave millions of corpses behind it when it retreats. It won't go without putting up a fight. But almost always it goes without putting up an argument. When Nazi Germany collapsed in 1945, the occupying Allies couldn't find any Nazis. It turned out that there had never been any. Apart from the few prominent fanatics who committed suicide or stubbornly continued to proclaim the dominance of the master race even as they sat without belts and shoelaces in their jail cells, nobody had ever really believed all that stuff. Reasonable people had worn Party buttons in their lapels only so that they would be allowed to conduct orchestras, like Herbert von Karajan. A pity about the Jews, but really they had died by accident.

Throughout 2010, the year after my brief career as a radio preacher, the mainstream media in the English-speaking countries continued to leave the Catastrophic Anthropogenic Global Warming thesis unquestioned. (Though the best of the German commentariat had already got out of the whole business after a key article in *Der Spiegel*, and the Chinese and the Indians had never got into it, the Anglosphere can still be depressingly provincial in its tendency to think of itself as the whole world.) But journalists who had built their careers on the theory had begun to intercalate their articles about the approaching disaster with other articles about how not enough people were listening to them, and this second category of articles had the

merit of being demonstrably true. The assurance was ebbing from
the belief, and it became possible to suggest that some of those who
had been most noisily assured had never believed at all. Al Gore fell
silent, or as close to silent as he ever gets. For my generation he had
never been a very persuasive figure. After World War II we were
brought up to question the wisdom of buying anything being sold
from the back of a truck by a large, loud American called Al. But
those less blessed with wisdom, or at any rate less crippled with
arthritis, had found Al more plausible on the subject than his slim
scientific credentials might normally have permitted. Now, finally, he
had ceased to proclaim the crack of doom, and it became necessary
to ask whether he had ever believed it. Why had he had so large a
carbon footprint, flown so often by jet, bought a house at sea level
when 'sea level rise' was one of the factors ensuring, according to the
United Nations University, that there would be 'fifty million environmental refugees' by 2010? The nominated year having been and gone,
it was time for the newspapers to notice that the number of environmental refugees was zero.

They didn't, of course; or if they did they said nothing. But the
silence was stentorian. For the media, indeed, the silence was the
message. This was equally true for politics. In Australia, when Prime
Minister Kevin Rudd was removed from office by his own party, it
soon became fashionable for the reporters to say that his polling
figures had sunk because he had gone silent on his own cherished
Emissions Trading Scheme, and was therefore being punished by
voters of a Green persuasion. But there weren't that many people of a
Green persuasion and it seemed much more likely that he was being
punished by potential voters of every stamp, simply because his
sudden silence on the subject of 'the greatest moral, economic and
social challenge of our time' was an indicator that he had never really
believed in its existence. Admittedly, for having said that time was
running out and then later deciding that there was plenty of time
after all, Rudd was unusual in being called to account. Before the
make-or-break, do-or-die climate crisis international get-together in
Copenhagen, Gordon Brown of Britain had said, with the aid of the
Independent newspaper and other megaphones, that there were only
fifty days left to save the world. When, after fifty days, it transpired
that the day of decision could be put off indefinitely, he was not
called upon to explain why he had ever promoted such a load of

millenarian flapdoodle. He lost an election, but for other reasons. Nor has Prince Charles yet been punished for having said, in March 2009, that there were only a hundred months left to save the world. It was more time than Brown had allowed, but it was still a measurably short span, and after it expires, people might well say something.

They have said nothing yet. Personally, as someone who feels that Prince Charles will make a good king, I hope that he will get rid of any among his environmental advisers who encourage him in the belief that, should he ever decide to run his Aston-Martin on biofuel, he can do so without damaging the rainforest. But he should start by firing the writers who sent him in front of the television cameras with a speech contending that there were only so many months left to decide against the green planet's certain death. This contention, which started off sounding inflated and is bound, well before the stated number of months runs out, to end sounding hollow, could have no business except to rouse a rabble: not, normally, the proper concern of a monarch in waiting. The business of the future king is to be a pillar of reason, not a focus for panic. Prince Charles, ever the thoughtful student of the heritage in which he operates, might care to look at the passage in Clarendon where London catches fire and the desperate population, thinking that there must be a malicious cause, pick on all the resident French, Dutch and Catholics. Many members of these target groups were assaulted or locked up even as the flames leapt from street to street. Properly more disturbed by the persecutions than by the fire, the King sent his men to all parts of the city, telling the people that there was no blame to be placed.

In the three years I was broadcasting, there was a similarly widespread belief that anyone who did not think the climate was in crisis must be in the pay of an oil company. Being sceptical about the alarmist version of global warming was not only held to be the product of a general scepticism against science itself, it was thought to be explicable only as the result of a devious initiative by big business. Even quite late into 2010, Judith Curry, the climate scientist who has done the best job of reminding her erstwhile colleagues that they were supposed to be pursuing critical enquiry and not propaganda, held to the notion that any questioning of the theory earlier on – i.e. before she herself finally realized that too many of her fellow researchers had gone into showbusiness – had been made possible only by the surreptitious support of Big Oil. If only: I, for one, could have used the money. BBC radio pays peanuts, which have some oil in them, but not a lot.

During this period it was no fun watching, even from a distance, my first homeland turn itself into a burlesque house. Luckily the rest of the world wasn't paying attention – which is the real fear of the Australian intelligentsia whatever the subject – but if you were Australian yourself it was embarrassing to log on and be deafened by the clatter of slap-sticks and the yelp of clowns with their loose tights on fire. The joke was intensified by the lingering inability of Australia's literate classes to realize that they were being led by a character out of Molière. Enunciated with unblinking urgency during the course of three long and shameful years, Kevin Rudd's brain fever on the subject of the oncoming climatic menace should have been readily detectable from how he always left out the crucial fact that Australia produced somewhere between 1.4 per cent and 1.5 per cent of the world's emissions. That was the only number anyone needed to know. Knowing that number, you knew that Australia's part in resolving the putative crisis could only be symbolic.

But symbolism mattered, to the point where it infected the facts. In whatever field – not just climate but in any area of the human story, so long as the focus lay in the future – it was as if no fact could any longer exist without the context of a belief. In Oxford a new academic boondoggle got started which called itself post-normal science, an expansive non-discipline which held, if it held anything, that a projection could be a correct 'narrative' whether the ascertainable facts fitted it or not. Post-normality made great play with rubber figures, a device by which any figure cited in favour of your own argument could be infinitely flexible, whereas any figure cited in favour of the opposite argument could be ignored. When cooking up a figure, it was always useful to talk in millions if you could, but for the sake of plausibility it helped to add an increment which made it sound as if a careful audit had been taken. Whether talking about square miles of melting ice or the number of African children per day currently dying because of excessive Western consumption of carbohydrates, one and a quarter million will sound even better than two million, because it will sound a bit less as if you made it up. Swift, the first man to study the mind-set of the Projectors, was also the first to spot the utility of the precise-sounding increment to the purveyor of rubber figures. Thus, in Laputa, the celestial students engaged in plotting the course of the comet whose perihelion could destroy the earth have established that it carries 'a blazing tail ten hundred thousand and fourteen miles long'.

Ten hundred thousand and fourteen: it not only sounds a lot, it sounds precise. In *sounding* precise lies the whole art of post-normal science, to whose fruits Oxford is welcome. One says so in the hope that Cambridge keeps itself free of such developments. I myself got part of my education in Cambridge, and I still live there. Though I never fully understood what had gone on in the Cavendish Laboratory, I always had a pretty clear picture of the likelihood that it had had to do with real atoms, and not narratives. But for all I know, post-normal science might be the way ahead. To the layman, it could scarcely be more incomprehensible than string theory, although we should never lose sight of the fact that there is a difference between the difficult and the vacuous. Quantum mechanics, for example, is not a field that most of us can understand, but we had better understand that by now there is a connection between quantum mechanics and almost every machine in the house more complicated than a kettle. Whichever way science goes, however, it would clearly be fatal for journalism if it continued to allow itself the dubious liberties of treating the merely conjectural as beyond objection. It would clearly be fatal because it has nearly been fatal already.

Some of the most famous newspapers in the English-speaking world are convinced that their circulations are threatened by the Web. But their circulations are also threatened by their declining authority, the vestiges of which, in this period, further declined until you could barely see them. In journalism, authority depends on the power of analysis. To parrot a fashion won't do the trick. There was a day when the best journalists could puncture a fashion early in its career because they were sensitive to bogus language. But from the 1960s onwards, pseudo-science got such a grip that it infected every field. (The climate change craze is an example of pseudo-science finally invading science itself.) The largely nonsensical procedures of literary theory and cultural studies should have been rumbled at the start, simply from the double-talk in which they were expressed. Significantly, they were swallowed whole and faithfully revered, ruining the education of countless innocent students until a couple of academics wrote a spoof. The spoof having become news, the matter was finally up for discussion. It shouldn't have taken the spoof to do it. Similarly, it shouldn't have taken the Wikileaks revelations of late 2010 to demonstrate that the figure for war-related deaths in Iraq was more like 175,000 people than the 655,000 (note that precise-sounding extra five thousand) previously promoted by the *Lancet* and faithfully adhered to in the Western mainstream media for years on end. The first figure was still a lot of people, but the second figure had not only been made up out of 'models' (projections), it had been wolfed down by the very people who should have been first to question it: journalists.

The deep story of this period was that journalists had become the last people to question anything. One can only hope that they will return to their traditional role of critical enquiry – i.e. scepticism – while printed newspapers still exist to be written for. I did my time in Fleet Street and I loved my craft, but it could just be that its time is up. Time will tell, and probably sooner rather than later. Meanwhile, in whatever medium, the best way to sound human when writing is to cleave as closely as possible to the spoken voice. When Aung San Suu Kyi was allowed out, the first thing the common people wanted to do was just to look at her. After that, they wanted to hear her. And I was all wrong in my projections about the future career of Susan Boyle. People wanted to hear her too. Against all the odds, Subo flourished, rather like the human race.